The Business of Metaverse

*How organizations can optimize the
opportunities of Web3 and AI*

David Palmer

KoganPage

First published in Great Britain and the United States in 2024 by Kogan Page Limited

2nd Floor, 45 Gee Street
London
EC1V 3RS
United Kingdom

8 W 38th Street, Suite 902
New York, NY 10018
USA

www.koganpage.com

Kogan Page books are printed on paper from sustainable forests.

ISBNs

Hardback   978 1 3986 1308 9
Paperback   978 1 3986 1306 5
Ebook   978 1 3986 1307 2

British Library Cataloguing-in-Publication Data
A CIP record for this book is available from the British Library.

Library of Congress Cataloging-in-Publication Data
A CIP record for this book is available from the Library of Congress.

Typeset by Integra Software Services, Pondicherry
Print production managed by Jellyfish
Printed and bound by CPI Group (UK) Ltd, Croydon, CR0 4YY

CONTENTS

PREFACE

I have had the privilege of developing some global platforms over the past decade, including a new global platform that I co-founded at Vodafone called Pairpoint. This platform combines cellular technologies with Web3 and AI to power new automated machine to machine payments in the emerging Economy of Things. What was important in our approach to the creation of Pairpoint was the convergence of key technologies like IoT, Web3 and AI that were combined to provide the connected, automated trust and intelligent enablers required to support autonomous payments, as well as focus on the business case, business models and opportunities. In my exploration of *The Business of Metaverse* I highlight similarities with the development of the metaverse, where the convergence of VR, MR, Web2, Web3, fintech and AI technologies present a generational opportunity to fundamentally change the business and consumer landscapes, and also help to redefine the boundaries of opportunity for consumers, businesses and nation states.

The forecast for the size of the metaverse opportunity is significant in terms of global Gross Domestic Product (GDP), and the journey to realize this opportunity comes at a time when digital adoption is at its highest levels, but also at a time when the emergence of generative AI is forecast to drive this to new levels. In this book, we explore the role of the metaverse as the new web browser and interaction point between businesses on the one hand and content and data on the other, with specific focus on the relationships between the metaverse and AI. Will the metaverse become the digital environment where people and businesses will interact with AI? Will AI become a significant part of the metaverse workforce and content creation? Will AI help accelerate technical development of the metaverse?

Perhaps one of the most exciting aspects of the metaverse we explore are the opportunities that it presents to reset the boundaries of opportunities for people and businesses across the globe, such as geography and the need to travel, access to financial services, the cost of setting up businesses, while on the other hand access to the internet and metaverse access devices will become critical if these new opportunities are to be realized, leading to the need for clear government policy.

We look at the business and economic layers of the metaverse and the potential for the creation of new economic and business models which extend the role of digital communities, and incorporate Web3 tokenization, DAOs (decentralized autonomous organizations), DeFi. Will the token economy become the currency of the metaverse economy? Will the smart contracts implement legal agreements in metaverse? Will AI apply the law and adjudicate legal disputes?

There has been much discussion about the readiness and maturity of the metaverse to determine if the metaverse is already here or coming in the next five to ten years. In this book we explore the current position of the metaverse embedded in existing platforms in the context of the consumer, industrial and shared metaverses, with focus on the role of the shared metaverse to augment the Web2 platforms and enhance the creator, producer and overall content economies.

What will this new world with embedded immersive experiences look like? Which platforms and ecosystems will be the first to adopt? Where are the immediate opportunities? How should businesses position? How closely linked are metaverse adoption and AI adoption? What is required from technology? What is required from governments, regulation and legislature? What are the key milestones and timelines for metaverse success, and how can we tell if we are on track?

The book explores the business of the metaverse and the key technical capabilities, milestones and critical success factors including Web3 automation, decentralized digital identity, tokenization and NFTs (non-fungible tokens) and their potential role in digital ownership across metaverse platforms. On the business side we consider the use of these capabilities to power DAOs and new virtual business entities, with wallets, smart contracts, agents, and AI providing solution gateways beyond business so that they can include new metaverse financial services and marketplaces in their overall value propositions.

For businesses, it can be argued that there have never been so many innovative technologies emerging at the same time, but what is also clear is that to realize these metaverse opportunities, businesses must become technology and innovation companies, and be flexible enough to evolve to become metaverse businesses where market forces demand. The book explores the importance of the metaverse as the emerging interaction point between consumers, businesses and services, and the potential role of the metaverse as a new digital operating system to bring together AI and other technologies to support. How these technologies are put together in the context of the metaverse could be the keys to future business success and competitive advantage. We look at the extent to which all businesses will become metaverse companies in the future.

I hope this book becomes an essential read for students, professionals, businesses and government leaders who want to understand AI, Web3 and metaverse, and explore the associated opportunities, building blocks for success, and how to position as the transition to this new digital world evolves.

01

What is the metaverse?

History of the concept

Many associate the first introduction of the metaverse concept with the Neal Stevenson novel *Snow Crash* in 1992. Set in the context of a Los Angeles which had split from the wider US and was now in post-economic collapse in the 21st century, *Snow Crash* portrayed the metaverse as a virtual reality universe, and explored the transition between physical and digital boundaries, virtual economies, and the potential roles of the virtual world for liberation but also for control and manipulation.

The 1999 film *The Matrix*, the *Second Life* platform which was formed in 2003 by Linden Lab and the science-fiction novel *Ready Player One* in 2011 were all key steps in bringing awareness to the concept of the virtual world and the metaverse.

More recently Matthew Ball's book *The Metaverse* published in 2022 contributed valuable insights on the metaverse concept, highlighting its transformative potential and outlining a vision of a connected, immersive, persistent digital world.

In terms of adoption, gaming has been key, with centralized Web2 gaming platforms like *Epic Games* and *Fortnite* boasting over 400 million registered users in 2022 and *Roblox* boasting over 219 million monthly active users so far in 2024. In contrast the Web3 metaverse platforms have relatively low adoption with *Axie Infinity* boasting just over 350,000 monthly active users, and metaverse land platforms like *Sandbox* only 200,000 and *Decentraland* 8,000 respectively.

The above suggests that the power to drive adoption historically initially lies with centralized Web2 platforms, but the technology fit for the metaverse may be more aligned to Web3. These are both themes we will explore later in the book.

History of AR and VR

In parallel, VR (virtual reality) emerged in the 1990s with the first consumer headsets like the Sega VR which was used to explore the cave automatic virtual environment. Oculus, which was founded in 2012, raised $2.4m with a Kickstarter campaign and introduced the concept and the first test series for the Oculus Rift and Oculus Touch controllers. Oculus was then bought by Facebook in 2014 for $2 billion, and the first consumer VR headset, the Oculus Rift, was launched in 2016.

Further products including the HTC Vive also launched in April 2016, as well as Pokémon Go which popularized AR (augmented reality) on mobile devices, and which took a different approach to VR goggles by instead focusing on mobile phones as the access point to the virtual world by overlaying digital content on the real world. When playing the game, users would see a combination of the real world around them and AR-generated digital characters from the virtual world like Pokémon superimposed on the real world through their smartphone camera.

The introduction of stand-alone VR headsets in 2018 further increased accessibility and usability and a significant step was taken in 2020 when Facebook released the Oculus Quest 2, which combined a low price point with improvements and advances in computer vision, graphics, the performance of the hardware and improved realism and user comfort, as well as higher-quality VR experiences. These technological and product advances have served to bring VR and MR technologies closer to mainstream adoption at the same time as interest in the metaverse saw exponential growth when Facebook announced its entry into the metaverse by changing its name to Meta in 2021.

History is still writing itself

Despite the relatively speedy evolution of the metaverse concept, global awareness and the underlying VR and MR technologies, some of the questions as to what the metaverse is and how it should be built and accessed are still open.

Although we have seen rapid growth in investment, the acceleration of AR and VR and the emergence of platforms with significant users, what we have not seen is a fully considered strategy. The launch of the Apple Vision Pro spatial computing and mixed reality (MR) headset in 2023 introduced the most advanced headset features to date, with access to Apple store content and ecosystem. This included interoperability across Apple devices, collaboration with other Apple users, 3D games and video content from Apple TV and Disney+ – which was a big step in introducing the potential of AR and VR to over a billion Apple customers globally, but was this introducing these customers to the metaverse as we know it?

What was clear from the introduction of the Apple Vision Pro headset is that, as with other products, it was designed to work with Apple hardware, software and applications within the Apple ecosystem, leading many to describe this as the Apple Metaverse. However, to realize the full potential of the metaverse it needs to be universally available to all, at a price that is not a barrier to adoption – with an entry price of over $3,000 there is a danger that a luxury metaverse for the wealthy few will emerge that will leave behind many.

Web3, incorporated into a standard, universal metaverse operating system has the potential to provide interoperability and ensure that users can move freely across Apple, Meta, Android, *Decentraland*, *Fortnite*, *Roblox*, *Sandbox* and other metaverses with portability and exchange of value in line with the wider metaverse vision.

What is the metaverse now?

The metaverse is emerging as a new digital operating system, incorporating many technologies and capabilities for immersive, global, interoperable applications, but as it is expected to incorporate many technologies it may be best to explore the current metaverse in the context of the wider technological landscape.

The metaverse is emerging at a time when there are over 8 billion people and 90 per cent penetration of mobile phones, 17 billion IoT devices and 4 billion digital wallets, with the number of devices that have AI-powered assistants set to reach over 8 billion by 2024.

In contrast, there are only just over 300 million cryptocurrency wallets and 400 million users of metaverse applications expected during 2024, and so for the metaverse to gain adoption it is logical that it will need to be accessible through mobile phones and be integrated with digital wallets to ensure an AI standard can be incorporated (see Figure 1.1).

The metaverse has the potential to be the new web browser and touch point for how we interact with content and people online. The combination of VR, MR and AI has the potential to significantly upgrade current experiences, but with Web3 there is the possibility to introduce new opportunities with interoperability, digital identity, trust for collaboration and new automated digital asset ownership, portability and medium of exchange, bringing a new economic and monetization dimension to the metaverse browser.

FIGURE 1.1   Predicted growth across key drivers between 2024 and 2040

	2024	2030	
Population	8.1 billion	8.5 billion	• The AI market will be worth 100 billion by 2030
Mobile phones	7.4 billion	8.0 billion	• Over 90 per cent of the world population will have a mobile phone by 2030
IoT devices	17 billion	30 billion	• 65 per cent of the world population will have a digital wallet by 2030
Digital wallets	4.0 billion	5.6 billion	• Blockchain and crypto still have low adoption and the adoption by 2030 will depend on how easily the technology can be accessed and the value added
Blockchain users	320 million	?	• The current forecast for the size of the metaverse opportunity does not match the active user forecast. Realizing the opportunity depends on adoption
Metaverse users	400 million	700 million?	Could integration with mobile, IoT, and digital wallets be key to blockchain and metaverse adoption?

There has been much discussion on the development of AI prompts and how these could eventually replace text search with voice initiated natural language translation, and even extend to prompting AI with our thoughts. This would represent a significant shift from the current way we interact with the internet and content, but we are not there yet.

There will also be proactive search in the future where we move forward from prompt and search associated with the Web2 platforms of today to one where AI suggests what you should search for, what job you should take and which forums you should socialize in. The evolution of the web browser to a digital assistant in the metaverse is very real, and the scale of what you can do and search for will expand given there is more that can be done, and a more effective way when you combine immersion, collaboration capabilities and new business models.

Given the current levels of technology penetration, the metaverse role as an operating system for new immersive applications will be dependent on the ability of the metaverse to incorporate other key technologies, and adopt the right business models to realize the size of the metaverse opportunity (as outlined in Chapter 3) with a firm dependency on the speed of technology integration within this new operating system.

Figure 1.2 outlines the current metaverse and the roles of AI, Web2, Web3 and fintech to power the first phase of metaverse applications.

1 The metaverse replaces the internet browser and is the new customer touchpoint, gateway and access point for consumers and businesses to generate, access and interact with content and services.

2 AI is the intelligence layer, providing consumers and businesses with the tools to generate intelligence from data and provide automated information-based tasks. AI can now read PDFs and videos for information – and large language models (LLMs) become new intelligent data assistants to users in the metaverse.

3 Web 3.0 and fintech provide interoperability, security and gateways to finance and commerce through secure digital wallets. At this

FIGURE 1.2 The metaverse phase 1 big picture

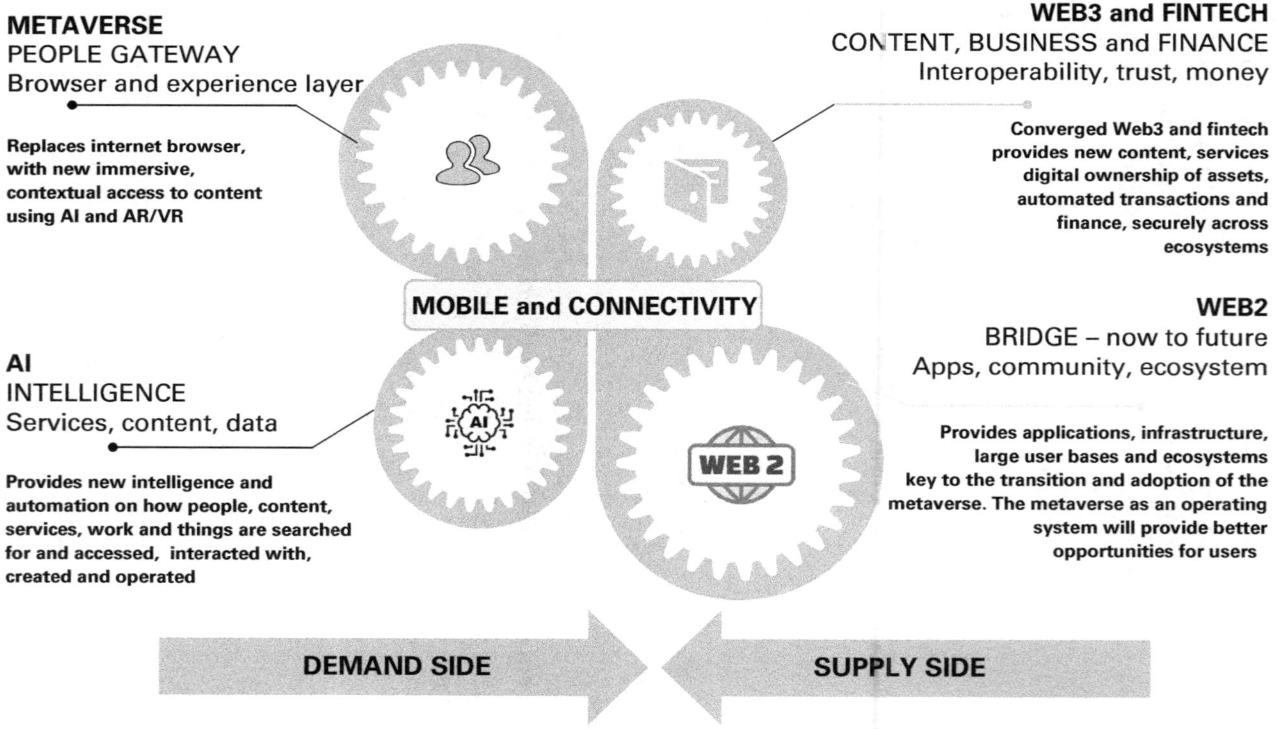

METAVERSE
PEOPLE GATEWAY
Browser and experience layer

Replaces internet browser, with new immersive, contextual access to content using AI and AR/VR

AI
INTELLIGENCE
Services, content, data

Provides new intelligence and automation on how people, content, services, work and things are searched for and accessed, interacted with, created and operated

MOBILE and CONNECTIVITY

WEB3 and FINTECH
CONTENT, BUSINESS and FINANCE
Interoperability, trust, money

Converged Web3 and fintech provides new content, services digital ownership of assets, automated transactions and finance, securely across ecosystems

WEB2
BRIDGE – now to future
Apps, community, ecosystem

Provides applications, infrastructure, large user bases and ecosystems key to the transition and adoption of the metaverse. The metaverse as an operating system will provide better opportunities for users

SUPPLY SIDE

DEMAND SIDE

stage blockchains provide trust, asset tokenization capabilities, integrated cryptography, decentralized digital identity and verifiable credentials to automate and bring new liquidity and payment capabilities to support the experience.

4 Web 2.0 accounts for a significant number of existing users and by incorporating metaverse spatial computing and VR, MR capabilities this introduces the technology to many users and communities, ecosystems and applications, which enable access to the metaverse. These Web2.0 platforms, like Google and Meta, as companies with large customer bases like Apple will be key to metaverse adoption.

Fast, low-latency connectivity available on premises via fixed lines and on mobile networks will be critical to the metaverse infrastructure demands for increased bandwidth, processing and the associated mobile coverage at a greater scale. There is also a social side to this as being able to connect to the metaverse at high speeds from different geographies across socio-economic groups will become a universal right and critical to work and business. For this to materialize the link to the mobile phone is key; although now the high price of VR and MR headsets remains a barrier to equality, as does the equality of access to fast connectivity (see Chapter 4).

The current metaverse started to receive significant investment in 2022, and Meta and its Reality Labs unit alone is expected to continue to invest around $20 billion in the metaverse annually. Given the role of the metaverse to act as the virtual environment for people to interact with AI, and with Apple and other big companies now entering the metaverse market, annual investment is set to increase.

How did the metaverse evolve?

Since the introduction of industrialization and economies of scale, some exciting and disruptive technologies have emerged, with significant developments in particular over the past 40 years. Some key milestones on this journey include the microcomputer, internet, mobile phones, e-commerce, cloud, IoT, fintech, open banking, Web2,

FIGURE 1.3 The technical evolution to the metaverse

Evolution to the metaverse

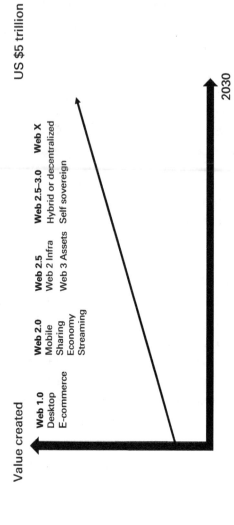

'New world being created'   'New opportunities'   'New social experiences'   'New business'   'New economy'

'Redefine geography'   'Redefine possibilities'   'Redefine social and work'   'Redefine business models'   'Redefine economic policy'

'Redraw travel'   'New ownership models'   'Social, Gaming = Income'   'Decentralized business and finance'   'Metaverse economy'

US $5 trillion

Value created

Web 1.0
Desktop
E-commerce

Web 2.0
Mobile
Sharing
Economy
Streaming

Web 2.5
Web 2 Infra
Web 3 Assets

Web 2.5–3.0   **Web X**
Hybrid or decentralized
Self sovereign

2030

Web3, AI and now the metaverse. Although we will later explore in more detail how the metaverse builds upon and brings these technologies together to focus on the customer experience, it is important to understand how we have got to this point of the metaverse in the technology evolution, and understand how the past can provide some indications and insights into what the metaverse could be in the future. Figure 1.3 outlines the technical evolution to the metaverse.

The technical developments in Figure 1.3 outline the evolution of the web from the early internet in the 1990s to Web3 and the metaverse today, but of course if we take a step back there have been many business revolutions driven by technological innovation dating back to the publication of Adam Smith's *Wealth of Nations* and the beginning of the first Industrial Revolution. All of these major business and industrial revolutions had significant technologies that fundamentally changed business, employment, economies of scale and pricing. The indications are that the metaverse as an immersive operating system, combined with AI, Web3 and 5G, could be the drivers for the next business revolution (see Figure 1.4).

FIGURE 1.4 The five business revolutions to the metaverse

Business revolution phase 1 – Industrial

The first industrial and business revolution introduced several technological and mechanical advances including manufacturing mechanization powered by steam engines, which enabled the rise of factories and mass production techniques. Some examples include innovations in textile machinery, such as the spinning jenny and power loom, which revolutionized the textile industry. The introduction of iron and steel production techniques significantly increased productivity and growth, but also impacted jobs as production was now divided into discrete tasks tooled by mass machinery. The overall impact of these developments was significant on businesses, global macro-economies and societies. Some of the key outcomes were urbanization, increased productivity, the introduction of economies of scale, reduced unit costs of production and market prices. These factors led to the growth of the middle class, and the shift from agrarian to industrial economies, ultimately laying the foundations for modern industrialized societies which would eventually evolve to incorporate more technological advances such as industrial robots, just-in-time processes and the limited introduction of mainframe computers.

Business revolution Phase 2 – Processing

The biggest jumps in industrialization, business and enterprise models, however, have by far come from the democratization and reduced cost of computing that resulted from the introduction of microcomputers. The microcomputer was first introduced in the 1970s and led to the increase in computers in homes and businesses, which would eventually result in widespread adoption. The microcomputer revolution had profound impacts on business and industrial productivity as they could now automate processes, improve productivity, and store and analyse data, information and knowledge more efficiently for re-use within business processes. In addition, new industries such as software development, IT services and electronics manufacturing emerged. These developments transformed communications, education, entertainment and even business governance and reporting, resulting in the empowerment of individuals, acceleration of innovation which paved the way for the internet revolution that followed.

Business revolution phase 3 – Internet

The democratization of communications and access to information, which was made possible by the introduction of the internet, can be described as the internet revolution. This revolution began in the 1990s and was made possible by the World Wide Web, which was invented by Sir Tim Berners-Lee in 1989, with the first website going online in 1991.

The internet led to the rise of the dot-com era in the late 1990s and early 2000s which saw the emergence of several internet-based companies and startups. E-commerce added payment capabilities to the internet thus enabling online shopping, which would eventually create a new dimension to global trade. The new capabilities that the internet introduced were key to the success of both established and new businesses and led to web-based technologies being incorporated into business models, and as a result industries like media, retail and finance were reshaped, and new digital industries were born. Some claim that the internet has made the world smaller and revolutionized communication, entertainment, education and person just in time processes to just in time processes person and person just in time processes to just in time processes business interactions, leading to a more interconnected and globalized world. Following these developments businesses were able to sell online and develop new platform businesses with the introduction of mobile and cloud computing. With the speed of development and adoption accelerated by open-source computing and business models, the outcome was the incorporation of remote workers across the globe into virtual work-forces, supported by global information systems and applications available for a relatively low-cost subscription.

Business revolution phase 4 – Information and platform

The platform revolution was made possible by the internet revolution and began in 1994 and 1995 with the emergence of the Amazon and eBay platforms. Platforms developed to include the shared model with the emergence of YouTube in 2005, Airbnb and Spotify in 2008, and Uber in 2010. These digital platforms enable interactions and transactions between consumers, producers and service providers, and as a result they have further disrupted traditional industries and transformed business models, providing greater access and convenience to a global market. However, these business models are based on a centralized model where the platform controls and monetizes the data generated on the platform in return for use.

These first four phases are the building blocks to Web2, Web3, AI and the metaverse, but they also provide the digital infrastructure for what could be the biggest industrial and business revolution to date – the metaverse incorporating AI and Web3.

Business revolution phase 5 – metaverse – Web2, Web3 and AI

The story of the metaverse revolution is still writing itself, but it is an operating system that can fundamentally change how we communicate, work, socialize and interact with businesses. We have seen how mobile phones, Web2 and social media have fundamentally changed communication and social aspects of our lives. The metaverse has the capability to incorporate the most powerful new technologies with a focus on customer experience and business, and, like many of the revolutions before, we expect increases in productivity and new business models to emerge. It has been forecast that up to 300 million jobs could be lost because of AI alone; however, on the other hand, it has also been forecast that millions of new jobs will be created. There is one difference, however; if access to the metaverse is needed for work, business and social activities then it becomes a universal right for consumers and businesses globally, and therefore access cannot be left to market forces alone to determine. Government policy and governance could hold the key to achieving a balanced success across socio-economic groups and geographies, but maybe the key to fairness and inclusivity in access lies in the re-balancing of solutions to incorporate wider social goals, objectives and priorities at the design and code stages.

How is the metaverse defined?

The truth is that the metaverse is still evolving and we don't know definitively what it will be yet, but we can use its current position of development and adoption combined with our understanding of how it will evolve to shape our definition of it. However, one of the most important components of the metaverse definition is its role as the new digital operating system, as this function will allow the metaverse to grow with the underlying technologies supporting the operating system.

Here, we outline some of the key attributes associated with the current metaverse definition:

1 **Persistence and consistency** – The environment is able to remember a user position and enables them to go back to that same position with things exactly as they were. We have seen this feature in the Apple Vision Pro where users can place an application and it will remain in that same place when they go back to it, but initially we expect this to be within specific platforms and ecosystem in line with the initial metaverse being embedded.

2 **Interoperability, inclusiveness and openness** – The metaverse should be accessible to users and providers across platforms and ecosystems and include freedom of movement across metaverses. The same laws on discrimination and accessibility that apply to the physical world should apply to the virtual world. The open metaverse will be critical as it increases in importance for work and daily activity, therefore becoming a universal right. However, interoperability is not expected in the initial phases of metaverse adoption.

3 **Immersive and 3D** – The capability to have a realistic experience including VR, MR and 3D-enabled virtual spaces, are key to providing lifelike virtual experiences comparable to the real world. This enables activities and services to be delivered online that previously could only be delivered in the physical world.

4 **Social, interactivity and collaboration** – The ability to interact, socialize and collaborate with other users with persistence and security.

Many leading figures from the world of technology, business and metaverse startups have begun to define the metaverse. Some of the key themes and features in those definitions include:

1 A collective virtual space which incorporates persistent virtual with physical reality.

2 An environment for the creation of content and interaction of users which represents the next generation of the internet.

3 A fully immersive digital virtual reality environment which blends with the physical world but extends its boundaries.

4 An evolution of the current internet but in 3D.

5 The physical environment and interaction point between people, businesses and AI.

An academic definition of the metaverse is 'the layer between you and reality' and a '3D virtual shared world where all activities can be carried out with the help of augmented and virtual reality services'.[1]

Many of the metaverse definitions have some common themes running through them, as they all talk about a virtual space, 3D, immersiveness and some mention persistence. What is clear from the current thinking on the metaverse is that although it is still in its early phases there is agreement that it has the potential to fundamentally change the way we interact with the people, organizations, machines, places, technology, AI environments, and digital and physical ecosystems around us.

In summary, some of the key features included in pre-existing definitions and discussions of the metaverse are:

1 Interoperability – If the metaverse will evolve as many different mini-metaverses across key industry and consumer verticals, then to get the holistic, complete metaverse experience interoperability and openness need to be included in the definition. The alternative would be like having several physical countries without the potential to travel between them. The opportunities for division of labour, specialization, international trade, sharing markets and consumer choice would be lost.

2 Digital ownership, portability, medium of exchange of digital assets, and their links to physical assets and the institutions and processes for asset recognition, trade, jurisdiction and recourse to legal resolution.

3 Economy, finance and business models will be key to establishing the metaverse economy. The size of the metaverse opportunity represents a significant percentage of global GDP, and therefore needs to be considered in wider macro- and microeconomic models

and policies. Some of the questions that would need to be considered include how will inflation in the metaverse impact wider inflation in the physical world? How will unemployment in the metaverse impact wider unemployment in the physical world? How will tokens in the metaverse impact global money supply?

4 Consolidation of key technologies. The technology operating system is key to this. The metaverse will not act as a stand-alone technology but will function as a new digital operating system bringing together different technologies including Web2, Web3, Mobile, IoT, fintech, cloud, edge and AI.

My definition, which reflects the current consensus of definitions but also takes in points 1–4 above, is:

> A digital world, which exists alongside the real world, and provides a digital operating system on which applications are built that provide a shared virtual reality experience, economy, business models and interoperability across users, AI ecosystems and communities.

The metaverse vision

The metaverse vision builds on the current definition of the use cases, applications and takes into account the value that will be built on the metaverse operating system. We expect this to encompass most areas of the economy and industry verticals.

Imagine a world where billions of people live their daily lives, shopping, socializing, working and interacting in digital communities either from the comfort of their homes, virtual digital workspaces, or on the move via mobile devices, and interact using a combination of virtual or physical hybrid realities, where both are combined seamlessly to maximize the experience and effectiveness.

A world where children from any geographic location or socio-economic group could access the curricula of the best universities in the world and participate and collaborate with fellow students across the globe, even on courses involving practical physical aspects, but now made possible through VR and MR technologies.

A world where the limits of current online business opportunities are extended to encompass services that are only delivered physically today, but in this future can be accessed globally by people from all locations. These people are able to use metaverse and Web3 capabilities like smart contracts to organize themselves into digital communities so that skills and resources can be combined to form flexible virtual business entities to supply market demands.

The metaverse landscape in this vision will include metaverse universities, metaverse businesses, more inclusive metaverse finance products, metaverse tourism.

However, some of the common questions that arise from the vision are:

1 Is there one overarching metaverse like the internet or many small metaverses?
2 Does the metaverse already exist?
3 What makes the metaverse different from the current internet?
4 How will the metaverse work alongside the physical world and the current internet?

Some things we hear about the metaverse are listed below:

- 'The metaverse is the internet in 3D' – What will a metaverse search engine look like?
- 'The metaverse is a tool to connect humans with the planet and can be a force for good.'
- 'The metaverse combines real and virtual worlds' – Is this the new foundation for hybrid working solutions and new levels of productivity?

The metaverse of the future will change the customer and business experience and make it easy to combine different technologies to support the customer experience and as a result it is expected to power new dimensions to the world of work, business and pleasure.

The metaverse benefits to consumers should be significant. The current internet and e-commerce have brought a lot of businesses online and enabled the creation of experiences where key functionalities like ordering and payments are embedded in the end-to-end customer journey. The metaverse is expected to significantly expand this to include more high-value goods where physically experiencing before purchase is at a premium, as well as other services which without VR and MR could not be provided online.

However, I expect that this is just the beginning as the metaverse is expected to usher in a new level of automation, with new AI workforces that interact with people using realistic personas and workplaces. This could include metaverse environments like industrial collaborative workplaces and retail stores with realistic environment options and AI sales assistants. I expect this combination of metaverse, AI, Web3 and fintech to provide the foundations of the next level of metaverse business growth and adoption.

Is the metaverse the next iteration of the internet?

The internet is a global network of interconnected computers and devices that communicate through standardized protocols. It functions through the transmission of data packets over various networks, such as ethernet or wireless connections. These packets are routed through routers, switches and servers, using TCP/IP protocols, all of which enable seamless communications and information exchanges globally.

The evolution of the internet started in the 1970s with email and the TCIP protocol which supported computer messaging. In the 1990s the internet progressed to the http protocol which enabled browsers to identify and interact with web pages using IP addresses, HTML webpages and java scripts. The evolution to Web3 required a web protocol that could build on the current internet and support the convergence of emerging technologies like MR, VR, AI, blockchain, IoT and fintech extends to encompass both real and virtual, internet search and activity that extends the scope of physical services available online. This is described as the progression to the 'internet of everything'.

There has been much discussion as to whether the metaverse is the next iteration of the internet, or whether the internet will evolve to become the search layer for the metaverse see Figure 1.5.

There has also been much discussion about the Spatial Web, which was described by the Spatial Web Foundation as 'a library of spaces, governing objects (people, places, things) under context control factors like locations, activities, and identities'. In addition, new protocols like the Hyper Space Transaction Protocol (HSTP) which allows parties to agree on person and IoT device ownership and enables IoT sensors to identify, localize and update on states at any time. This evolution of web protocols points to incorporation of Internet of Things devices and associated data in the metaverse, and an additional role in industrial processes and solutions.

FIGURE 1.5 Evolution of the internet to metaverse

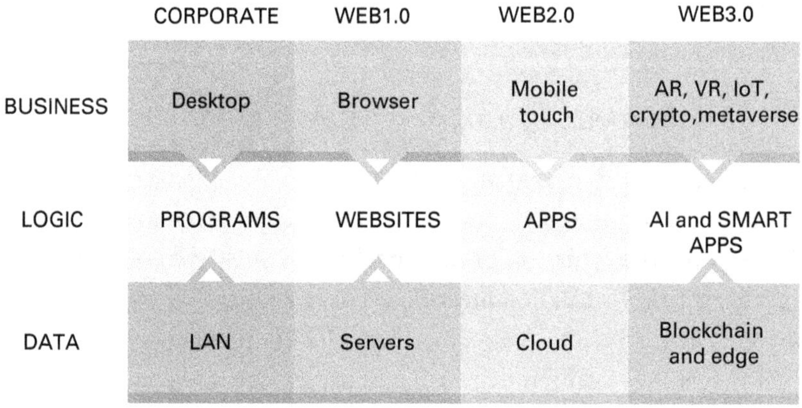

	CORPORATE	WEB1.0	WEB2.0	WEB3.0
BUSINESS	Desktop	Browser	Mobile touch	AR, VR, IoT, crypto, metaverse
LOGIC	PROGRAMS	WEBSITES	APPS	AI and SMART APPS
DATA	LAN	Servers	Cloud	Blockchain and edge

The Spatial Web can be described as the digital overlay of information and experiences on the physical world. It integrates MR and VR technologies, enabling the seamless blending of digital content and physical surroundings. The Spatial Web encompasses the interconnected network of spatially aware devices, sensors and platforms, allowing users to interact with virtual objects and information in a spatial context. The metaverse, on the other hand, refers to a collective virtual shared space where users engage in immersive experiences. The Spatial Web could serve as the technological foundation for the metaverse, providing the infrastructure and tools for users to access and navigate the metaverse with increased sensory capabilities.

However, the relationships between the internet and the metaverse are complex. The internet can be seen as the underlying infrastructure that enables the development and functioning of the metaverse and the current role of the internet can be summarized as a global network of interconnected devices that allows for the transfer of information and communication between users across the world. It provides the foundation for various online platforms, services and applications such as websites, social media platforms, online gaming, streaming services and more.

The metaverse, on the other hand, provides users with a virtual space, which is part of a network of spaces, where people can interact with a computer-generated environment and other users in real time. It incorporates 3D MR and VR and goes beyond the traditional 2D browsing experience of the internet to create immersive and interconnected virtual worlds and experiences.

It can be argued that the internet facilitates the connectivity and communication required for the metaverse to exist, and that without the internet, the metaverse would not be feasible or accessible on a global scale, but does this mean that the metaverse will not redefine or even replace the internet as we know it?

The current metaverse leverages internet technologies to deliver real-time interactions, high-quality graphics, immersive environments and seamless connectivity. However, it is important to note that the metaverse is in the early stages and as technology continues to advance, the relationship between the internet and the metaverse will likely become even more interconnected but with the metaverse leading the requirements and development roadmap, and ultimately becoming the interaction point for people and businesses and relegating the internet to underlying search enablers for legacy content. Below are some examples of how the internet and the metaverse contrast:

- **Internet access is by** computers, tablets, smartphones, wearables, IOT devices, with some more recent developments with AI

- **Metaverse** access is by VR, MR devices, smartphones, wearables, IoT devices with AI and natural language processes expected to be an important access method

- **Internet User Experience:** 2D screens using touch or mouse

- **Metaverse user experience:** Natural language, 3D and VR, AR UI/UX, AI
- **Internet persona capabilities for users:** profile pic, user ID
- **Metaverse persona capabilities for users** different personas, secured by decentralized digital identity solutions, in 3D.

The metaverse and the internet will for now coexist and work together; however, in the future, as the metaverse operating system evolves, it is possible that it will increasingly incorporate technologies to connect computers, digital online addresses with people and businesses more effectively leading to the evolution of internet protocols to metaverse ones, but in any event what is clear is that the internet will need to evolve from its current position.

Is the metaverse a new operating system?

The metaverse in its current phase of development is not functioning as a new operating system, but rather utilizes the existing ones. However, this is expected to change as adoption and focus on the customer experience and touch points grow, and the metaverse evolves to bring together technologies and specific applications focused on speed of development and smooth operations for metaverse that incorporates AI.

Some of the excitement surrounding the metaverse as an operating system is that at the moment there are a number of new technologies emerging that are operating in silos. Web2 largely operates under the platform business model, whereas Web3 is based on decentralized and self-sovereign models and does not easily integrate with Web2. AI is generating a lot of excitement but needs governance and a physical presence which are areas where metaverse as an operating system could help. Fintech, mobile and IoT are also in similar positions and AI in particular will need special attention within the current operating systems which focus on human developers. Given the significance and potential for AI to generate code and automate the development of applications in the future, operating systems will need to evolve to make AI the user, application programmer and customer, which will drive change and could position the metaverse at the centre of technology development.

Could the metaverse be the new operating system to pull these competing technologies together and focus them to align in the same direction to the benefit of consumers, businesses and even our planet?

The size of the metaverse opportunity and the proximity of the metaverse to the user suggests this could be the case in the future. The metaverse opportunity (which we will cover in the next chapter) is forecast to represent as much as $5 trillion by 2030, according to McKinsey. This would represent 4 per cent of global GDP by 2030 and it is expected to cover many industries and sectors of the economy, providing the economic drivers for significant future technology integrations providing the economic drivers while the demands of spatial computing, VR, MR and AI in the context of the metaverse functioning as the new web browser are expected to provide the technology drivers.[2]

How important is AI to the metaverse operating system?

How AI is used and incorporated in the experience is a key difference between the metaverse and the current internet.

The current internet is characterized by data and search, and this is largely done through browsers like Chrome and using search engines like Google and Bing. The prompts have so far largely been by text with the differentiators in performance mainly in the data tagging, search and retrieval. The natural evolution of this is to start using AI to turn data into intelligence – this journey has begun with Bing incorporating ChatGPT into their search, with Google following suit. Similarly, e-commerce and social media is largely text- and prompt-based. How will the metaverse differ?

On thing the metaverse will bring to the internet is immersive technologies including sensory. This, combined with 3D online personas, has the potential to enable AI to take on a human persona and interact with humans in a real setting using natural language to interact. This gives rise to the saying 'the metaverse is AI on earth' because the metaverse + AI can power the next generation of chatbots. These could interact with humans but with an AI-generated persona and in a very real setting. Imagine filmmakers speaking to their AI crew who turn instructions into animation in real time. AI and the metaverse have the potential to move the internet beyond the current search and e-commerce realm to become real life in another dimension with automated content and application generation.

This metaverse and AI dimension could be the next evolution of e-commerce where online scope is extended to retail stores which provide human-like services. AI lawyers could provide legal advice and draft contracts, armies of AI coders interact with visionaries to build new code for new application developments, AI doctors assess patient symptoms and provide medical advice, and AI customer service agents resolve queries. Technical developments like computers, mobiles and the cloud have changed the way we work, business models and pushed productivity forwards. However, this evolving AI and metaverse dimension has the potential to fundamentally change the current reality by bypassing the need for people completely replacing them with AI equivalents for certain tasks. With the metaverse also enabling further increases in global scaling by removing geographic boundaries and opening up the possibilities for new levels of service, cost and productivity optimizations. However, the human cost and social impacts will need to be assessed alongside the economic benefits.

In this scenario the internet evolves to become an immersive world where, rather than search, socialize and buy, people can actually do most of the things they do in the physical world as well and in some cases in a better way using AI to drive personalized experiences and smart interactions and the metaverse to remove travel and other physical barriers and restrictions. Some may say we can do most of this already, or even claim that they prefer to do some things in the physical world, but there are some examples where people do not have the choice. Below are some examples of groups that may be attracted to the virtual experience.

1 Disabled people can experience activities virtually in the metaverse that they physically cannot do. For example, running, hiking, climbing or sailing. This could provide a whole new dimension to their lives and if we combine this with socializing in the metaverse this could be a key market group.

2 Similarly, elderly people can enjoy virtual experiences in the metaverse they cannot physically experience, yet also relive past experiences. This could involve AI helping them to take on a metaverse persona with physical attributes like their younger selves which could enable them to relive sport or entertainment activities like dancing that they cannot do in the physical world. Over time as more data on a person is stored, AI could enable them to return to their younger selves in an environment of their choice, so that they can experience their past again.

3 People in poor and developing countries can enjoy experiences they cannot afford to physically travel to, and more importantly enjoy access to services like medical help or education they also cannot physically attend or afford. This attendance is enabled by the internet and the metaverse, but the affordability can come from AI. For example, AI teachers and lecturers should drive down the cost of education and make it cheaper, and AI doctors should drive down the cost of seeing a doctor; in both cases the learning capabilities of AI will improve the cost effectiveness and quality of the service. However, this places more importance on internet and mobile phone access as it becomes a right and critical to even more aspects of life than today.

4 Groups who want to use AI and the metaverse to interact with key figures from the past can travel back in time. The AI and metaverse dimension has the potential for these groups to have a conversation with key figures from the past like John F. Kennedy, Steve Jobs or Elvis Presley. This same technology could be effective as we go forwards to use data and photos and social media data to preserve most people's identities and views virtually and bring them back to life using AI and data. For example, if this technology had been in place 100 years ago, we could move from static pictures of historical figures to having an immersive interaction and conversation with our grandparents, and even discussing current events with them. This leads to the question as to whether our online virtual persona dies when our physical persona dies. It is possible that with AI and metaverse our virtual persona could live on?

Is the metaverse an industrial evolution or the next revolution?

There has been much discussion about how the metaverse will mature, and whether there will be a 'big bang' revolution where the metaverse will disrupt consumers and business over a short period of time, with massive investment driving the rapid development of the metaverse infrastructure and a universal protocol. This would be the revolution approach. The other possibility is for the metaverse to be born from the evolution of the internet and current technologies.

The metaverse is currently in the emerging stages where the initial investment has driven sufficient innovation and enough capabilities to support a limited number of early adopters who are currently trying the new functionality, but this is powered by limited hardware and software which operate across several closed metaverses with limited but persistent digital content. The fact that we are in this stage suggests that the metaverse will coexist with current technologies and be embedded in current platforms and experiences and evolve over time to become interoperable and then eventually offer a seamless and converged experience in the longer term.

There are, however, several key factors that may speed up the emergence of the metaverse and drive revolutionary advancement:

- The technological advances that are required to power the metaverse are emerging to the right level of maturity. Web2, Web3, AI, Cloud and Edge computing, as well as 5G and fibre connectivity, are providing the infrastructure and processing capabilities required for the first use cases and experiences on the metaverse to run.

- Businesses have reached the limit of their current automation boundaries and productivity levels, and to unlock more productivity not only do the new technologies need to be blended but the parameters of growth need to be expanded. This includes expansion of markets, increasing the workforce, increasing work times, removing boundaries and limitations of travel and travel times and expanding markets. The metaverse can potentially bring in these new automation boundary improvements and enable new levels of productivity.

- The digital economy is evolving – digital money, central banks are moving towards central bank digital currencies which will provide instant clearance between banks. The recent banking crisis highlighted that the past approaches to managing the economy cannot work and digital advances on the consumer and business are required. The metaverse economy may seal the move away from the current hybrid of Victorian paper semi-digital processes that sometimes operate in parallel with each other; for example, paper Know Your Customer (KYC) processing which runs alongside automated digital processes. The metaverse could be the catalyst to move to a new fully digital economy, but key to this will be new digital currencies, integration with real-time systems, reporting and action triggers.

- The digital citizens are now ready, and the millennial generation are ready for a fully digital immersive world to supplement the physical world! Online purchases are increasing, and many expect more embedded experiences as part of user and customer journeys.

- The industrial metaverse is ready for monetization, and the market for digital twins in supply chain, manufacturing and other heavy industry is increasing. We expect there to be over 30 billion IoT devices by 2030 and 3 billion of them transacting in the Economy of Things.

The metaverse is still in the early stages, and any combination of the drivers above could move the development level from evolution to a revolution, but the key indicator to watch will be the level of investment. The more investment the closer the emergence of the metaverse and impact will be to revolution.

Is there one metaverse or many?

There have many debates on whether the metaverse will be one or many, with some proponents arguing that there will be one metaverse and others arguing that the metaverse will be several metaverses which are interconnected and interoperable.

Since 2022 there have been headlines announcing many brands entering the metaverse, alongside news of real estate purchases often on different platforms. This would support the former view that indeed the metaverse will be made up of several mini-metaverses, and this will allow the metaverse to evolve and grow as incentives lead to more metaverses being set up, which could crucially mean that metaverse adoption can start now, with the current infrastructure and immersive technologies and grow organically.

There is also a school of thought that the metaverse needs to incorporate real-time persistent environments, interoperability and portability of assets across metaverse platforms and ecosystems and scalable immersive technologies that are able to support the processing and rendering required to support this and make a real difference from the current internet.

The definition of the metaverse also has significant implications for when it can start as a minimal viable internet rival, and also have implications as to how it will evolve and grow (See Figure 1.6), the investment required to complete it, and when and how the opportunity can and will be realized.

How will the metaverse evolve going forwards?

The current operating systems evolved over time from initially powering a laptop to run applications locally, to then incorporating networks, and now global cloud and internet infrastructures. I see the metaverse evolving in the same way.

Key things the metaverse must incorporate are:

1 Immersive and sensory technologies – to ensure that users can now have an enhanced online experience which provides sight, feel and sound close to real life. This is key to opening up the new use cases, e.g. metaverse concerts, metaverse surgeries procedures. (stage 1)

FIGURE 1.6 Three phases of metaverse evolution

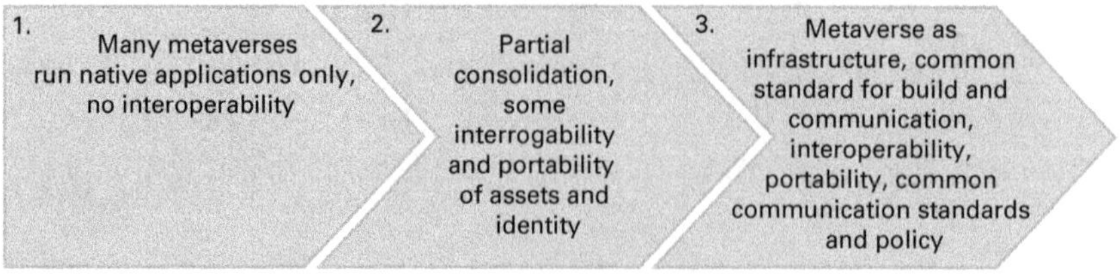

1. Many metaverses run native applications only, no interoperability

2. Partial consolidation, some interrogability and portability of assets and identity

3. Metaverse as infrastructure, common standard for build and communication, interoperability, portability, common communication standards and policy

2 An infrastructure and operating system standard to enable a common set of applications to be built. (stage 3)

3 Metaverse applications – to ensure that users have a touchpoint to access and use the metaverse. (stage 1 but will grow and evolve as we move to stage 3)

4 Interoperability – to ensure that users and the applications they use can move across different metaverse platforms and ecosystems and with minimal friction. Key to this will be interoperable digital identity. (stage 2)

5 Portability – so users can carry identities, value, assets and medium of exchange capabilities across ecosystems. (stage 2)

6 Embedded payments and financial products incorporated in metaverse consumer and business experiences. (stage 2)

7 Data and AI – provide insights, triggers and the basis for personalization. (stage 2)

The current position suggests that the metaverse will establish itself first as embedded metaverse in many different platforms, and by stage 3 the metaverse will become a consolidated infrastructure, an operating system for the virtual world like iOS and Android are for smartphones, before consolidation and open sourcing by stage 3.

Is the metaverse open or closed, centralized, decentralized or hybrid?

There is a view that for the metaverse to have true real-time, seamless and dynamic interoperability of digital identities across metaverse platforms it will need to be decentralized to provide the trust and self-sovereign capabilities required to do this at scale. This would require the metaverse to leverage some of the Web3 developments for decentralized digital identity, tokenization and portability of digital value across platforms. However, the user numbers, developer ecosystems required for scale are with the current Web2 platforms, for example Meta (previously known as Facebook) enjoying over 3 billion active users across their platforms, suggesting that the metaverse will need to exist within centralized Web2 platforms in the initial stages.

Therefore does the metaverse need to be Web3? Could the metaverse be built without Web3?

The metaverse does not need to be Web3 and could be built without it, but I think the more relevant question is around the most effective use of these technologies to progress the development of the metaverse.

It is clear that social media will be critical to the early access and adoption of the metaverse and can expose it immediately to billions of users. However, Web3 has some capabilities that are critical to the version of the metaverse being described by many which incorporates features like peer-to-peer transactions, tokenization of assets, NFTs, smart contracts and smart legal agreements, immutability, self-sovereign digital identity and Web3 wallets. These are potentially important to the metaverse as they are designed to work across an infrastructure which no one entity controls, and given the importance of the metaverse and the need for universal access, decentralized control as opposed to centralized could be key.

These factors suggest that the more probable route forwards will be a hybrid metaverse evolution where the social media and internet companies (Web2) leverage their massive user bases and ecosystems to embedded metaverse. However, in the longer term Web3 will play an important role in joining up the customer experience across embedded metaverses and provide the functionality to effectively store and port assets and value across them. It is possible in the longer term to see a metaverse with Web3 at the core of the infrastructure as we can expect many new entrants to the market which will grow and adapt to new business models, but this is unlikely in the initial stages.

Could the metaverse become a protocol with its own trust algorithm?

Some virtual worlds in the emerging metaverse have been built on public blockchains which employ consensus protocols to secure and validate transactions and data. These protocols enable decentralized networks to agree on the validity and order of transactions. Through mechanisms like Proof of Work (PoW), Proof of Stake (PoS) or Delegated Proof of Stake (DPoS), participants propose transactions, blocks are verified by nodes and agreed-upon blocks are added to the blockchain. This ensures transparency, security and immutability of transactions without relying on a central authority and ultimately provides trust. How could protocols be applied in the metaverse?

As the metaverse grows and demands more processing power, interoperability and automation, could a blockchain be developed specifically for the metaverse to form part of its core infrastructure? Where a blockchain is incorporated into the metaverse could a metaverse-specific consensus protocol be developed and implemented to secure the information, digital identity, transactions and other key events in the metaverse to ensure activity and protect against fraud, spoofing and deep fakes?

The metaverse protocol could build on some of the uses of consensus in Web3 with specific applications to the metaverse. For example, across public blockchains there are currently a number of consensus protocols, each providing slightly different applications of validations including PoW and PoS, and more recently there have been specific applications of consensus for specific problems like Proof of Reserves which was implemented to prove the level of reserves in crypto exchanges.

For the metaverse you could see specific metaverse applications like proof of identity, proof of data, proof of identity, proof of funds, proof of location, which could be critical when 'deepfake' is made more possible with the technology.

The application of blockchain and a specific metaverse protocol demonstrates the potential to provide automated governance and security to the metaverse. This could be a crucial step to build the confidence required to drive adoption of the metaverse by consumers and business and achieve scale in line with forecasts.

Is the metaverse already here?

As we have explored the metaverse in this chapter it is clear that the metaverse is not just about immersive technologies, environments and experiences, but rather about these combined with other key technologies to form the presentation layer for the metaverse. In this context the metaverse acts more like a framework, which powers an operating system and brings key technologies together so that new applications can be developed.

There are many platforms that have emerged that claim to have some metaverse features, some of which we listed earlier in this chapter, but leadership to date has been found in video games, which have already incorporated virtual worlds, immersive experiences, communities, social interactions, user-generated content and assets, and limited portability of digital assets. The elements of the metaverse in the video games include:

- Providing users with connected immersive experiences.
- Communities that go beyond gaming to include social interactions including messaging inside the game's virtual world.
- Some self-sovereign elements of digital identity and users can create new personas, which is linked to their identity.
- Community members can create content and assets, and there is some portability and persistence of these assets, although this is often confined to the game virtual world.
- Digital twins of real-world assets or people exist, e.g. players or land, but there is no scarcity of these assets beyond the game, as in theory infinite copies of the asset can be made and sold on other gaming platforms.
- The technology is maturing with Web3 NFTs, and virtual technologies used by many of the platforms.
- Some of the larger platforms like *Roblox* have several millions of users, and an economy where assets in the game can be earned, bought and sold, but this is limited to the game ecosystem.

The above highlights the emergence of the metaverse in its first phases. However, usability, scale and adoption are very limited and represent a fraction of the metaverse described early in the chapter. The progress so far suggests that the realization of the metaverse vision will be an evolutionary journey building on the Web2, Web3, Mobile, fintech and AI revolutions to establish the first phases of success and evolution together.

Notes

1 M Damar (2021) Metaverse shape of your life for future: A bibliometric snapshot, *Journal of Metaverse,* 2021, 1 (1), 1–8, dergipark.org.tr/en/pub/jmv/issue/67581/1051371 (archived at https://perma.cc/XC9C-Z2U6)

2 A Sarkar (2023) Metaverse to possibly create $5T in value by 2030, McKinscy Report, Cointelegraph, 7 January

02

The eight layers of the metaverse

The eight layers of the metaverse describe a holistic framework which brings together key enabling components required to develop, operate, grow, finance and govern a virtual world. Some of the technologies in these eight layers like CBDCs (central bank digital currencies), DeFi, DAOs, VR, MR are new, and in this framework, they will interoperate with more established technologies like mobile, open banking to power the metaverse. However, the bigger story could be about how the different components of the economy like banking, finance, business and technologies like Web3, Web2, AI come together in the metaverse under the direction of market forces and government policy.

It can be argued that we are moving to a point where we have several technologies that are making an impact on their own, but the real value now will be in the convergence of these technologies to shape the future of the customer and business experiences and drive new levels of productivity. This framework outlines the unique positioning of the metaverse to act as the catalyst to a new digital experience revolution and a point of focus for the required technology convergence.

The metaverse framework

The metaverse framework describes the metaverse in eight layers: 1) Experience, 2) Physical interface, 3) Finance, 4) Data, 5) Ecosystem, 6) Business, 7) Governance, legal and regulation and 8) Technology, and as layers 7 and 8 will run across all layers we will cover them in separate chapters.

These eight layers of the metaverse go beyond the typical description of the metaverse which largely focuses on the metaverse as an experience application (see Figure A.1 on page 245). Instead, outlining the capabilities that will be required for a virtual world running alongside the physical world we live in today, with policy, governance, government representations, laws, regulations, economy, business, finance, ecosystem, money; and given the stage we are at with the penetration of technology in the physical world, it is logical that technology will be at the core of all components of the metaverse.

In the sections below we describe each of the eight layers, with a deep dive into the technology of the metaverse.

Can the mobile phone number be the middleware of the metaverse?

One of the considerations is how users will move across metaverses and the different layers described in this model while ensuring that there is a legal person or entity that can legally contract, access financial services to transact, store value and finance assets and be held legally responsible for actions.

To achieve this will require digital identity and credentials which can be verified in real time including Know Your Customer (KYC) and Anti Money Laundering (AML). In the framework, we show the potential of the mobile phone number which already has processes in place for KYC and AML and could be used to associate metaverse activity with a physical person. To set up an equivalent system from first principles would be time consuming and complex, but extending the role of the mobile phone number to digital identity and the metaverse would be quick and leverage an established and trusted system.

I have already worked on similar approaches for IoT devices where virtual mobile phone numbers are issued to devices as part of their interoperable digital identities. Here the same approach could be extended to people, businesses, IoT devices and even AI to link virtual world activity back to a legal entity in the physical world.

Layer 1 – Experience

The metaverse experience layer is at the centre of the framework providing direct interaction with users and content, goods and services. It will act as a new immersive web browser at the centre of virtual world experiences, but with links to physical world capabilities to bridge the physical and virtual experiences.

What is the experience layer?

The metaverse experience layer can be described as the gateway to a new immersive experience. There has been much discussion about the ways in which we will access metaverse experiences and the technologies. Some of the technologies used to access metaverse experiences include smartphones, wallets, and VR and MR technologies, and the key going forwards will be to use the right access technology for the right use case, application and experience, and to lower barriers to entry by ensuring that the access devices with the largest footprints can be used as far as possible, which would place a lot of focus on the smartphone. I expect there will also be some consolidation as smartphones, MR and VR, headsets, headphones and wallets are all merged into one device, with applications incorporating core baseline technologies in the context of the new operating system for optimization on the new hardware devices.

The metaverse experience layer provides the enablers for users to interact with the metaverse. It encompasses technologies, platforms and interfaces that enhance immersion, facilitate social interactions and enable a wide range of activities. This layer includes XR headsets and glasses, haptic feedback devices and motion tracking systems, but I think given the size of the metaverse opportunity and its strategic positioning as a touch point to the customer, we can expect significant investment and innovation in the devices to access the metaverse. There has already been significant movement in this space with Meta, Google and now Apple all entering the market, and there are indications that many others Original Equipment Manufacturers (OEMs) will respond and follow given the market potential for access devices to merge with or replace smartphones and become the new evolution of the web browser revolutionizing the way we search for, access, create and monetize content and services and data.

What is clear is that the metaverse has the tools and enablers to fundamentally change the way we experience things, but as well as 3D and immersive layers, we expect the current 2D smartphone experiences to remain as the entry levels; especially where immersiveness adds little or no value. More fundamental changes at the experience layer can be achieved where the experience is proactive and shaped to your profile by AI, with digital agents able to add additional content, goods and services as required by interacting with other platforms on the user's behalf. It can be argued that the Apple Vision Pro product is a step in this direction.

What does the experience layer mean for businesses?

There are many business-use cases that are part of the industrial metaverse which draw on the experience layer to support business collaboration, communication, training, global workforce recruitment, retention and management, as well as retail, industrial predictive maintenance and digital twins.

We will cover in more detail the metaverse business opportunities in the next chapter, but some of the discussions for business are around 1) the new sales potential associated with expanding the potential market. This could include businesses that would only be feasible online with new immersive technologies. Also, 2) new business use cases that are made possible through the experience layer, which could be associated with the creator economy and other virtual world examples.

There are also enterprise use case benefits. For example, in manufacturing, the immersive experience capabilities of the metaverse could be used to physically inspect factory machinery, output and quality without the inspector travelling to the physical location. Another example that I have been personally working on is the virtual car showroom, where customers can experience the car and its performance, interior and software upgrades through XR. While the metaverse is relatively immature, businesses have started to use and explore the experience capabilities and some of the use cases include:

- Accenture are using the metaverse in recruitment, onboarding and training staff.
- Nike are using the metaverse to collaborate with other brands and sell digital products which are linked to physical products.
- Meta is using the metaverse to enhance user experience and launch new collaboration product sets on its social media platforms, with plans to use the technology to better join up the experiences across platforms.
- KIA and Fiat have introduced digital metaverse dealer showrooms so customers can more easily shop for cars from the comfort of their homes.

The above examples illustrate the metaverse experience layer as an opportunity for businesses and enterprise. For potential low-friction, large-scale market access through the experience layer combined with the automation and productivity capabilities by combining Web3, fintech and AI could help to redefine the productivity boundaries of businesses.

Layer 2 – Physical interface to the metaverse

The metaverse experience will not be limited to XR headsets and virtual world, but, as outlined in the metaverse definition in Chapter 1, it will need to exist alongside the physical world, and to a large extent the balance between physical and virtual worlds – the connection between them and how the interoperability evolves – will be a key factor in how much of our lives the metaverse can encompass.

What are Metaverse Experience Centres?

Metaverse Experience Centres (MXCs) could be the bridge between virtual and physical capabilities, with the potential to bring the virtual worlds to our high streets, where they would be operating as both:

- Showrooms in physical locations for people to experience services from the virtual world before they buy. For example, to experience the taste of champagne, a collectable NFT could be bought in a virtual world to access trying it at an MXC. MXC centres could also be useful where the hardware to access the experience is advanced, expensive or not yet available to the consumers and small businesses, and with little ability to afford the access device required. This could be particularly important where access is required for individuals to carry out work and businesses need to experience before investment.

- Collection centres where people can get physical goods and services already bought and owned in the digital world. This could include clothing, services like massage (where this was selected in a virtual environment but delivered in a physical environment) or digital items which require expensive 3D printing.

Could these MXCs change our reasons for interacting with retail locations? Could MXCs redefine the retail store? Could MXCs redefine the high street? Could they act as the bridge between online and physical retail?

What is clear is that virtual worlds and their digital assets will need physical locations where people can try and experience goods and services before buying them, and in some cases virtual communities will require a physical place to gather and interact with digital content, services and goods. MXCs have the potential to fulfil these intermediary functions between the virtual and physical worlds and provide new economic benefits like revitalizing high streets, which have lost business to online shopping by providing them a complimentary role and function.

Layer 3 – Metaverse finance

The metaverse finance layer will need to bring together the capabilities that have developed and matured in the dominant world of centralized finance. Some of the new automated and decentralized capabilities that have recently been developed under Web3 and decentralized finance initiatives provide new levels of interoperability, automation, liquidity, digital asset ownership and fractionalization have started to gain traction already in some metaverse platforms.

The metaverse as an operating system will be able to bring together Centralized Finance (CeFi) and Decentralized Finance (DeFi) solutions, and also enable new central and retail bank solutions like central bank digital currencies (CBDCs) and tokenized bank deposits to be incorporated in metaverse applications. This will allow the full range of finance capabilities to be embedded into metaverse experiences and user journeys. We will explore these in more depth when we explore the metaverse economies, currencies and regulation further in Chapter 7, but I have outlined the key components and working model in Figure 2.1.

CeFi and DeFi will coexist within the metaverse, offering different financial services. CeFi refers to traditional centralized financial institutions operating within the metaverse, providing services such as banking, loans and investment products. DeFi, on the other hand, involves decentralized platforms and protocols that enable peer-to-peer financial transactions, smart contracts and automated market-making.

FIGURE 2.1 Metaverse finance framework overview

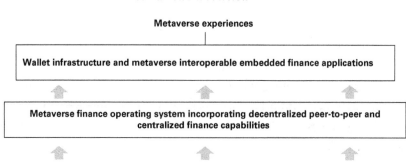

Open Banking and Embedded Finance play a crucial role in the metaverse's financial landscape. Open Banking allows users to securely share their financial data across different platforms, enabling seamless integration of financial services. Embedded finance involves integrating financial services directly into non-financial applications, allowing users to access financial products and services without leaving the metaverse environment.

Tokenized assets represent ownership within metaverse platforms. Tokens can be fungible or non-fungible, with NFTs (non-fungible tokens) representing unique and indivisible digital assets like virtual land or digital collectables. These tokens enable ownership, provenance and transferability of virtual assets, facilitating commerce and economic activities within the metaverse.

CBDCs and tokenized deposits can serve as the medium of exchange within the metaverse. Digital currencies issued by central banks can enable secure and efficient transactions, cross-border payments and provide stability to the metaverse economy. CBDCs can integrate seamlessly with the financial infrastructure of the metaverse, facilitating user interactions and transactions.

The financial capabilities within the metaverse have the potential to bring together virtual economies and real-world finance. They can support new forms of value creation, digital asset ownership and financial inclusion. However, it is crucial to ensure robust security measures, privacy protections and regulatory frameworks to safeguard user assets and maintain the integrity of the financial ecosystem within the metaverse. As the metaverse evolves, these finance capabilities will continue to shape and redefine how users engage with digital assets, conduct transactions and participate in metaverse virtual economies.

Layer 4 – Data in the metaverse

It can be argued that data will be the currency of the metaverse and without it there will be no metaverse and no AI operating within it. As a result data has been described as the 'life blood' of the virtual world and its economy. Over 90 per cent of data has been created over the last 10 years, and the metaverse is expected to increase this significantly further. So how will data be incorporated in the metaverse framework?

TABLE 2.1 Data generation levels 2020

Unit of Time	Amount of Data Records Generated	Year
Every second	7.7 million	2020
Every minute	463 million	2020
Every hour	27.8 billion	2020
Every day	668.5 billion	2020
Every year	243.5 ZB	2020

The rate of increase in data generated globally is increasing significantly

The IDC reported in 2020 that the global datasphere reached 59 zettabytes (ZB) in 2020 with 90 per cent of this data created between 2018 and 2020, and the size of the datasphere is forecast to double in size by 2026 with enterprise organizations largely driving the data increases, and the size reaching 175 ZB by 2025. Are these forecasts correct or could the actual size of the datasphere be significantly higher?

Given the advances in the emergence of the metaverse and AI, is this forecast correct or has AI and the metaverse changed the parameters?

The impact of the metaverse and AI on data generation and growth

Data generated by AI will be key to the personalization and automation of metaverse experiences, but to what extent will this impact the levels of data generated?

The size of the metaverse opportunity which could be as much as 5 per cent of global GDP over the next 10 years could hold some of the answers here, With this level of economic activity, the metaverse is expected to be one of the key drivers of data generation and a major factor contributor to the growth of personal, business, IoT and government data.

Meanwhile the relationship between the metaverse and AI could play an ever-increasing role in the datasphere. Generative AI, where algorithms use original data but in turn create AI-generated data could increase levels of data significantly and with the role of the metaverse as the interaction point between users and AI how much data will need to be stored in metaverse platforms and experiences?

Goldman Sachs forecasts that the impact of AI on global GDP could be as much as 7 per cent (or almost $7 trillion), which could also lift global productivity by 1.5 per cent. In the next two years Gartner forecasts that 30 per cent of outbound marketing messages from larger organizations will be generated by using AI data.

These growth statistics for the metaverse and AI in the data economy indicate that current forecasts for the growth and size of the global datasphere could be conservative, and that the metaverse data layer incorporating AI could become the significant driver of data growth in the future.

How does the metaverse data layer work?

The metaverse is expected to generate new levels of data directly from activities across virtual worlds and platforms, but experiences will also require data from the internet and other platforms like social media as well as business, enterprise and government data. This combination will serve to perpetuate the generation of data and the creation of metaverse initiated synthetic data which could lead to a much more significant acceleration in data growth than currently forecast (see Figure 2.2).

Data plays a fundamental role in the metaverse, serving as the lifeblood that fuels its functionality, personalization and immersive experiences. In the metaverse, data is generated and collected from various sources, including user interactions, virtual environments and IoT devices, among others. This data is then utilized in several ways to enhance metaverse experiences and functions.

FIGURE 2.2 Data in the metaverse

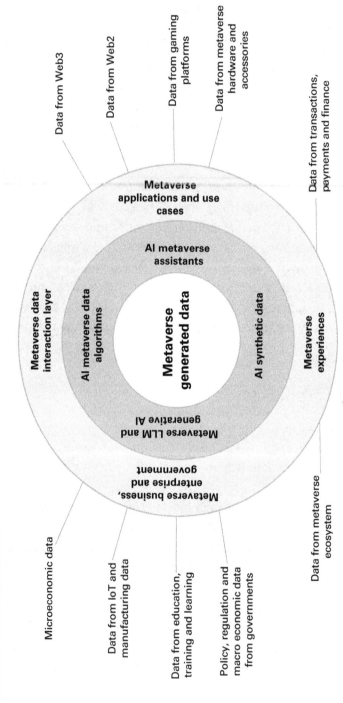

One of the most important functions of data is its role in personalization and the opportunities for data owners to monetize data. By capturing and analysing user data, platforms and applications can tailor content, recommendations and experiences to individual preferences and behaviours. This personalization fosters a more engaging and immersive environment, catering to the unique interests and needs of each user. Data powers the creation and optimization of virtual environments and objects. Designers and developers rely on data-driven insights to understand user behaviour, preferences and engagement patterns. This information helps in refining virtual landscapes, optimizing user interfaces and creating more compelling and interactive experiences within the metaverse.

Data also serves as a foundation for social interactions and community building in the metaverse. User data enables the identification of like-minded individuals, facilitating connections and fostering communities based on shared interests and experiences. Additionally, data-driven analytics can be used to understand social dynamics and behaviour patterns, allowing for the creation of richer and more meaningful social experiences, and with AI a real time dimension can be added to this.

Perhaps most exciting is the economic value that data creates and represents in the metaverse. Data created by users has a value to platforms, applications and AI and the metaverse functioning as a marketplace could play an important role in helping users to monetize it. Perhaps one of the most important areas to emerge is the link between user data and AI large language Models (LLMs). Could the metaverse functioning as a marketplace be the bridge between data and LLMs thereby providing a new route to monetization to metaverse platforms?

One area where I have looked at this is with IoT devices, 'Metaverse of Things' where essentially data created from IoT digital twins could be sold to LLMs. With billions of IoT devices in operation this could be an important source of data for AI, but also an important source of revenue for IoT. This could be just the beginning as data sold to LLMs grows to become an important new revenue stream for the metaverse.

On the experience side data-driven insights about user preferences, buying behaviour and trends can inform pricing, supply and demand dynamics, facilitating a more effective online economy.

However, it is essential to ensure privacy and security measures are in place to protect user data within the metaverse. Robust data governance frameworks, consent mechanisms and encryption techniques must be implemented to safeguard user privacy and instil trust in the metaverse ecosystem.

The impact of the metaverse on data generation

The metaverse is expected to contribute to the exponential growth of data generation with users in doing more things and spending more time using it. As a result, data creation is likely to surge, adding to the overall global datasphere and driving new solutions on how data is stored and used.

How does the economics of data in the metaverse work?

While the metaverse is still evolving we expect data to play an increasingly important role in the ecosystem model, and the consent and reward for the supply of data across people, business, governments and established platforms will be key to establishing the minimum viable data network (see Figure 2.3).

FIGURE 2.3 The metaverse data incentive model

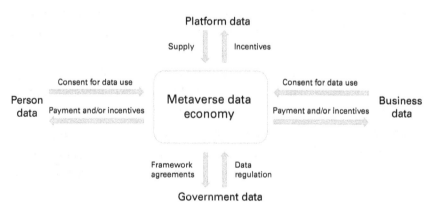

The Metaverse Data Economy (MDE) represents the flows of data from the different actors across users, consumers, producers, people, businesses and governments, but there is no consolidated design or technical architecture for this layer as yet, but rather data solutions are evolving as separate ecosystems. The current developments in Web2 and Web3 suggest that both technologies and ecosystems will play a role in the future MDE but there are core business model differences between them.

Web2 typically involves centralized platforms that collect, control and store user data, monetizing it through targeted advertising and selling data to third parties. Users often have limited control and transparency over their data, and little recourse to monetization.

In contrast, Web3 is about decentralized data, and the associated platform business models are largely around self-sovereign, user-centric data ownership with users able to directly monetize data they create. The Web3 platform models for data potentially provide users with greater control. Technologies like blockchain, smart contracts and Self-Sovereign Digital Identity (SSI) applications could also provide new improved automation in authenticating metaverse users and their data, incorporating new automated consent mechanisms and rewards for sharing data. Web3 models explore data monetization through concepts like personal data vaults, where users can selectively share and sell their data directly, fostering a more transparent and fair data economy that empowers individuals while preserving privacy and ownership rights.

Given the differences in platform data monetization models between Web2 and Web3 which is the better fit for the metaverse?

The Metaverse Data Incentive model in Figure 2.3 combines both Web2 and Web3 and utilizes SSI and tokenized reward to incentivize and automate the sharing data for metaverse users, which would include people, businesses and IoT devices, while also incorporating specific supply and reward agreements with Web2 platforms.

Recent legal ruling on platform data may be pointing to the use of MDEs in the future with Facebook, one of the biggest social media platforms recently facing regulatory scrutiny and legal challenges regarding its data handling practices. In 2022 the European Data Protection Board (EDPB) rejected the Irish DPC and Meta's bypass of the EU General Data Protection Regulation (GDPR), which now prohibits Meta's Facebook and Instagram platforms from using the personal data of users on its platform for advertising. This represents a significant challenge to the data monetization strategies of Meta and other Web2 platforms, but what does it mean for the metaverse?

These recent events, which have questioned the long-term viability of the current Web2 data monetization models, suggest that the long-term model for MDE could be more aligned with Web3 and SSI, and therefore well positioned for the metaverse.

Layer 5 – Ecosystems of the metaverse

In technology and business, we often refer to ecosystems to describe the interconnected workings and incentives of customers, suppliers, distributors, employees, partners and software developers. In the natural physical world, an ecosystem can be defined as a complex network or interconnected system of entities, organisms or components that interact and depend on each other for survival and growth. In the context of digital platforms, ecosystems are key to incentive users to join platform and monetize their engagements and ultimately they are a key performance indicator for platform health. With the emergence of the metaverse what is the role of ecosystems? How will the metaverse work with the ecosystems that have already been established by Web2 platforms and brands? Will the metaverse ecosystems be the same or will they function differently?

The basic components of digital platform ecosystems

The platform ecosystem at the most basic level has four main components, namely Platform, Users, Complementors and Governance. These four components interact and depend on each other within the platform ecosystem. The platform provides the infrastructure and sets the rules, while users and complementors contribute to the ecosystem's growth and value creation. Governance models ensure that interactions and transactions occur within a structured and regulated environment, fostering a sustainable and thriving ecosystem as shown in Figure 2.4.

FIGURE 2.4 The four components of the platform ecosystem

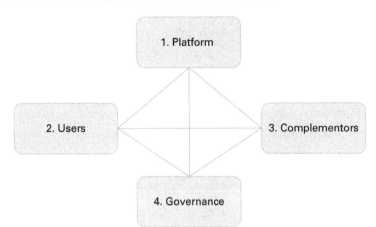

The Platform is the central component of the ecosystem, which serves as the foundation for interactions and transactions. The platform provides the infrastructure, tools and services to enable users and complementors to connect, collaborate and exchange value within the ecosystem.

Users are the individuals or organizations that utilize the platform and its services. Users can engage with the platform as consumers and/or producers, depending on the type of platform. They contribute to the ecosystem by creating demand, generating data and participating in transactions. More recently the rise of the creator economy has removed some of the distinction between consumers and producers as content creators are consuming the services of the platform to create content, and then to broadcast and in some cases monetize the content.

Complementors are third-party developers, businesses, individuals or other event platforms that create and offer complementary products, services or content that integrates with or enhance the platform. Complementors add value to the platform and ecosystem by expanding its functionality, providing specialized features or delivering additional offerings that attract and engage users.

Governance models provide the rules, policies, procedures and protocols that direct and manage the interactions, behaviours and relationships within the platform ecosystem and ensure alignment to wider regulations that apply to the platform. Governance also ensures fairness, transparency and compliance, and establishes guidelines for things like data usage, intellectual property rights, revenue sharing and dispute resolution. Effective governance promotes trust, collaboration and a level playing field for all participants.

In digital platform ecosystems, it is important to note that fundamentally the actors interact around activities and the architecture of the platform. The level of these interactions will determine the success of the platform. When looking at how the metaverse will evolve and operate there has been some discussion as to whether the metaverse will function as current platforms do with the four components described applying directly without changes, or whether the metaverse will give rise to new ecosystem models where users and AI linked to content, goods and services essentially form the basis of the new ecosystem model.

What are the key components of the metaverse ecosystem conceptually?

If we look at the metaverse as an operating system on which many platforms will be built, integrated and operated, then it is reasonable to assume that the four key components of the platform ecosystem will be part of the wider metaverse ecosystem and the metaverse will serve to aggregate many ecosystems to form its own macro-ecosystem. However, this view depends on how we expect the metaverse to develop. The metaverse as an 'ecosystem of ecosystems' aligns with one big all-encompassing metaverse which incorporates many capabilities, platforms, business, brands and their ecosystems. The metaverse's role as an operating system and browser in this scenario will act as an interoperable transport system between many ecosystems and their users, complementors and governance.

However, this ecosystem transporter role is more of an end game than a reflection of the current position, where many embedded-metaverses are developing and evolving with little interoperability; but what does this mean for the metaverse ecosystem components?

Current metaverse trends suggest that a phased approach to ecosystem development will evolve. The first phase will be characterized by discrete, independent metaverse platforms which will follow the standard platform ecosystem model. These ecosystems will continue to develop separately with specific ecosystem models. In this first phase we would include both new metaverse native platforms, as well as large Web2 platforms that are augmenting their existing platform capabilities with the metaverse.

The second phase of metaverse ecosystem development would align with the 'ecosystem of ecosystems' model which would see the metaverse function as an aggregator of ecosystems and interoperable transport layer between them, as described earlier, with AI agents linked to content, goods and services acting as the market maker.

In the second phase, the metaverse can be described as 'meta-ecosystem' that incorporates many other ecosystems associated with platforms, organizations, businesses and brands. But what is a meta-ecosystem and how does it operate?

Where the metaverse acts as a meta-ecosystem it functions as a macro-ecosystem that aggregates and incorporates several other ecosystems and an access point for a number of digital ecosystems, each with their own material, complementors and functionalities. In the meta-ecosystem, platforms, users and complementors are interoperable and work seamlessly with each other. AI could play a further role in dynamic management of ecosystem data, information, community as well as in driving Automatic Market Making (AMM) protocols across them, as shown in Figure 2.5.

In the meta-ecosystem value can be created both within each platform and across platforms at the macro layer. This could create new opportunities for complementors and creators, and give rise to new business models for the metaverse which considers this unique dynamic.

Layer 6 – The business of the metaverse

The metaverse is expected to provide new business opportunities, and at the same time challenge businesses to build on current business models associated with e-commerce, cloud, IoT, and Web2 and Web3 to incorporate the new metaverse dimension. Will the metaverse

FIGURE 2.5 The metaverse as a 'meta ecosystem'

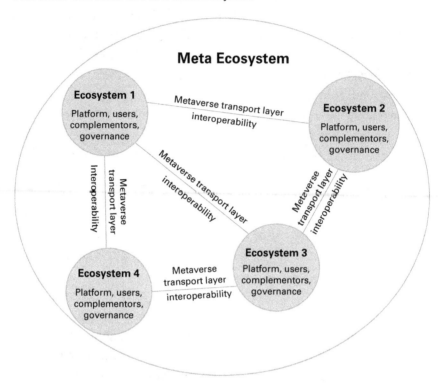

lead to a fundamental change in the business landscape, definition, business function and business models?

The metaverse can help us reimagine the ways in which businesses function and the areas in which they operate, but is the metaverse an opportunity for all businesses? If not, which businesses are best positioned for the opportunity? In this section we will explore the business of the metaverse and assess key business positioning considerations including the metaverse business architecture, feature set and value-added business positioning factors.

How important is the new metaverse technical operating system for business?

The size of the metaverse opportunity promises enormous potential for some existing and new businesses. For existing businesses, the metaverse can augment current value propositions by adding an immersive experience. In addition, the ability of the metaverse to remove key barriers to entering markets (such as the removal of geographic limitations) has the potential to power many new 'metaverse native' businesses.

If we imagine the metaverse as a new business Metaverse Operating System (MoS) that provides access to new markets it could represent an opportunity to gain competitive advantage. Their relative success in this case will be dependent on how effectively they utilize the MOS to access new markets and deliver new products and services in new metaverse markets. But what about new businesses?

The metaverse has the potential to attract many new businesses who are attracted by users, profits and new capabilities to bring their businesses online where this was previously only possible from physical locations. The incentive model could be like the Apple App Store but with broader cross-ecosystem impact and arguably even greater scale and impact given that the metaverse will be embedded across many platforms.

The App Store was launched in 2008 and created a significant opportunity for businesses by providing access to the Apple customer base for distribution and sale of applications. To achieve this the App Store provided simple solutions for discovering, purchasing and updating applications, as well as a global marketplace for developers to sell and monetize them. The App Store model has grown and in 2022 facilitated over $1.1 trillion in developer billings and sales and supported 4.8 million jobs across the US and Europe, with 29 per cent annual growth. Could the App Store business model be the blueprint for the metaverse business?

The business model for the App Store appears at first sight directly transferable to the metaverse as it incorporates 1) Content and services creation which provides the product and value proposition for the store. The quality of the content and services is directly related to the quality of the value proposition. 2) Rewards and incentives to creators, and here we assume that the higher the rewards and incentives the more content and services creators will supply to the marketplace. 3) Customer value proposition is directly related to the quality and quantity of the content but also to the customer experience, tools,

FIGURE 2.6 The business model for application marketplaces

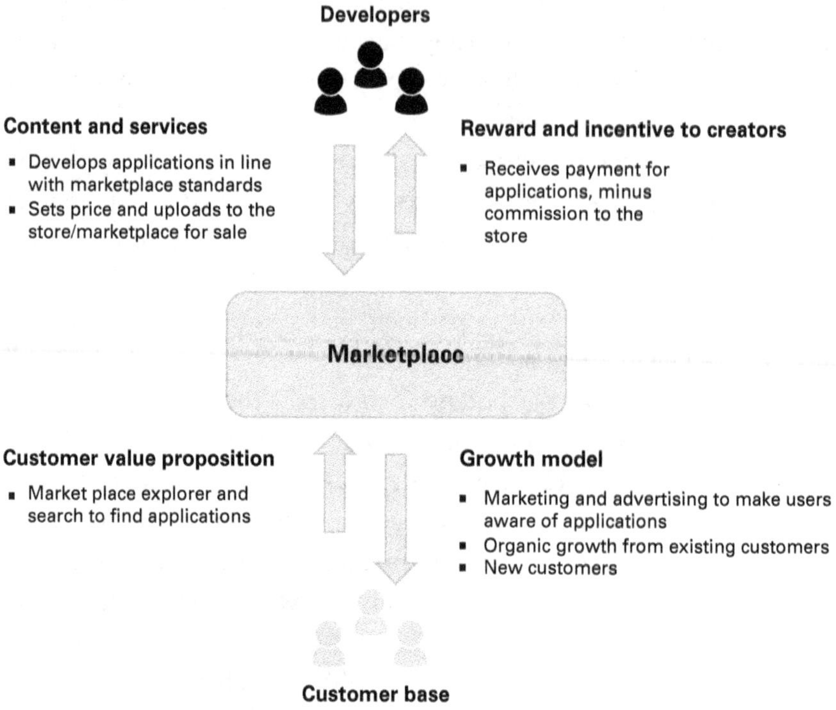

Developers

Content and services
- Develops applications in line with marketplace standards
- Sets price and uploads to the store/marketplace for sale

Reward and incentive to creators
- Receives payment for applications, minus commission to the store

Marketplace

Customer value proposition
- Market place explorer and search to find applications

Growth model
- Marketing and advertising to make users aware of applications
- Organic growth from existing customers
- New customers

Customer base

quality assurance, quality control, support and after-sales services that the marketplace provides to the users. 4) The growth model should include growth from existing customers buying more, and new customers and impact both sales and revenues; however, where ecosystem growth is the priority revenues may have to be foregone in the short term. However, the Apple business model does not currently incorporate interoperability across platforms. AI as a market maker with free market competition across platforms or decentralized operation and ownership of the marketplace may be critical for fast scale growth of metaverse business markets (See Figure 2.6).

Could the metaverse operating system create business opportunities as an aggregator of platforms?

The sum of the metaverse business model for the applications that will be built is beginning to look like an aggregation of the application exchange model. In this case the metaverse simply acts as a common set of immersive experience standards, and the developers work in the current application exchange ecosystem reward and incentives models. There is no metaverse marketplace and the value chain is business as usual.

Where the metaverse operating system acts as an aggregator of platform marketplaces for developers, the business model stays the same, and the metaverse role is limited, with much of the value remaining within the current ecosystems; but could the metaverse operating system on the software development market be more disruptive?

The potential for the metaverse to incorporate standards for development, to include customer touch point through web browser and application search on the operating system, and to disrupt the software development marketplace is significant.

The metaverse operating system has the potential to incentivize consumers, business and government developers to work to common standards, and extend this to combine government- as well as business-centric incentives to encourage cross-sector collaboration and applications with user's journeys seamlessly incorporating services across all key sectors. In this way the metaverse operating system should be able to interact with other platforms through integration, but also allow developers to collaborate and develop directly on the metaverse operating system.

In this context the metaverse utility and governance layers would provide users with access to metaverse applications and services across embedded metaverse platforms and experiences for a fee. The governance associated with this layer ensures legal, jurisdiction and regulatory alignment in real time, and the scope could be extended to incorporate taxes and subsidies. In this example, basic services would be made free of charge to some users where subsidies by the government are in place to fund them and these can be applied in real time. Web3 business enablers could play an important role in providing the technical solution to subsidize usage with self-sovereign frameworks providing the identity solutions, and a utility token being the medium of exchange to access applications and services, with smart contracts automatically implementing access rights, billing, taxes and subsidies in real time.

Metaverse users will typically access services embedded in metaverse user journeys and experiences via their personal space. The concept of a 'metaverse exchange' is the equivalent of the high street and retail park in the virtual world, providing enhanced search but also realistic XR experiences in line with the physical shopping experience. These capabilities would make retail and business interactions more aligned. Could the metaverse exchange replace the web browser with personalized and contextual search and interactions and create new opportunities for retail application developers? The answer is not yet clear, but where this level of application marketplace is t incorporated in the metaverse it has the potential to emerge as the application marketplace of application marketplaces, which according to Grand View Research is estimated at $230 billion in 2023 with a compound annual growth of over 13 per cent. This market is currently dominated by Apple, Google, Microsoft and Amazon and the immediate route to access metaverse applications will probably remain through these companies in the short term. However, with the emergence of open-source and the metaverse as an operating system and interaction point for users could change in the future creating more opportunity for application developers to sell directly to users, as well as providing a new more interoperable, joined up, direct and contextual way for users to access and embed applications and associated services (see Figure A.2 on page 246). This in turn could create new business opportunities.

How will the metaverse be split across consumer and business?

As we discussed, the metaverse platforms and ecosystems are expected to develop separately and independently initially but later interoperate with each other and then consolidate in the longer term to provide a converged virtual world and experiences. The potential size of combined global ecosystems across consumer and business could potentially create business opportunities that far exceed anything we are seeing on individual Web2 platforms today. But in this converged model, what will the metaverse landscape look like for businesses and consumers?

The metaverse can be viewed as the consumer, shared and industrial metaverses, where the shared metaverse represents new business areas and opportunities that cut across both. In addition, the AI metaverse describes the role of AI in embedded metaverses across industries and economies (see Figure A.3 on page 247).

1 Consumer metaverse – the immersive interaction points for consumers and suppliers. This includes retail, gaming, socializing, media, collaborating, fitness, travel, training and education. Here the addressable market is 7 billion people, with over 3 billion in developed economies with high-speed infrastructure.

2 Industrial metaverse – the immersive interaction points for business, heavy industry and enterprise. It includes digital twin, IoT, augmented reality manufacturing, augmented reality supply chain and immersive 3D manufacturing. It offers the opportunity for immersive collaboration and predictive maintenance. The addressable market is forecast to be a high as $500 billion by 2025.

3 Shared metaverse – the immersive interaction points between business to business, consumer to business and consumer to producer. Includes creator economy, producer economy, metaverse finance decentralized and centralized GIG economy. Within the metaverse, it builds on the model established by Web2 platforms to provide capabilities and infrastructure for consumers to become businesses, and for businesses to operate business models based on users being both producers and consumers.

4 AI metaverse – the AI capabilities and ecosystem underpinning the consumer, industrial and shared metaverses. We have previously described the 'metaverse as AI on earth'. Within the metaverse landscape data and AI are expected to be key enablers across all metaverses.

The metaverse is expected to play a key role for consumers and businesses in operating in the shared economy. This could even lead to virtual worlds and experiences being created that are digital copies of the real world, but in these cases like the physical world they will require governance, policy, regulation, banking and finance as well as legal and economic models to be implemented effectively. In this role the metaverse will mirror the real world in bringing together consumers and businesses.

Layer 7 – Governance legal and regulation

The governance, legal and regulation layer operates across all the other layers of the metaverse and will need to achieve the extension of current laws, regulations and polices to the virtual world. This is challenging as the virtual world is evolving and some like Web3 and AI do not have mature legal, policy and regulatory structures. In this section we will explore the fit of the current legal framework to the metaverse age, the key drivers and contributors required for change, the main challenges, and the potential and implications for monetization, taxation and regulation.

Is intellectual property in the metaverse a multifaceted problem?

Protection of trademarks and brands, ownerships and jurisdiction are only a few things that come to mind when one places the word metaverse next to IP. By nature, metaverse in its purest form removes geography. Simply put, there is no territory and no jurisdiction. Therefore, how can an owner enforce their rights in the metaverse?

In the same way, not only is there no territorial boundaries, but there is also a convergence between the digital and physical spheres. This can create further confusion as the rights of the owner in the physical world may not be easily transferrable and enforceable in the digital one, or vice versa. For example, since there is no set of established rules, it is unclear who will own and enforce rights over objects created in the metaverse. Will IP become a guarantee of creativity and freedom or a path to domination and digital servitude? It can be argued that the metaverse revolution is already happening and this will lead to IP being in greater demand and use, thus leading to a greater risk of infringement.

A potential issue on enforcement may be in finding accountable and responsible players to oversee the respect and uphold of IP rights in the metaverse. These could be the platform owners, the IP owners or even the regular users.

Another important question is around interoperability. Many of the current metaverse definitions describe it as one virtual identity providing seamless movement across metaverse worlds. This is currently not possible as user accounts exist in locked ecosystems protected by digital asset property rights. For this to change, interoperability would need to exist at the licence/operating system level. However, there is a danger that technology companies could become the vehicle to enforce and govern this rather than a legal framework. Part of the answer to how this will develop depends on the extent to which the current legal frameworks around the world can support the interoperability requirements in the metaverse.

While all these issues have persisted for decades outside the metaverse, they are now being brought to the forefront of discussions in the hope that they will be universally addressed.

Trademarking in the metaverse

Existing trademarks do not replicate the rights in the metaverse because they are only related to physical goods and services. Owners of trademarks must make specific trademarks applications that are applicable to the metaverse in the same way they file normal trademark applications with the relevant national authorities. However, those who file the applications should be careful not to choose the same classification categories for their virtual goods as they did for their physical ones, otherwise this would invalidate their claim. Based on the Nice Classification, most NFTs would fall under the category of class 42, digital tokens under class 36, while downloadable virtual goods would be part of class 9.

However, even if the trademark is successfully registered in the metaverse, this will still bring challenges to the creator, primarily from a jurisdictional view, as trademarks are confined to a territory. In case of infringement, the solution will be creating a new test to determine the applicable jurisdiction, considering factors such as the jurisdiction of the users or that of the infringer.

Plus, traceability, as we will see in more detail later, is a global issue at the level of the metaverse since some platforms are operated or used by anonymous accounts that require no prior ID verification.

What are the new challenges emerging from generative AI and the metaverse?

We have all seen the recent developments in AI, especially with the launch of ChatGPT. Generative AI is a new generation of machine-learning models, built on large scales of data and special algorithms to generate new and original content. As expected, these new models come with a range of challenges: IP infringement, privacy, misinformation and safety.

Most datasets on which the AI model is trained will be in the public domain or licensed, but this is not the case every time. While the input risk may be mitigated through the creation of special licences, the question remains for the output risk: can the content generated by the AI constitute an infringement as a derivative work based on the dataset used? All depends on the circumstances.

Some of these datasets may include personal information about individuals. When you process information about an individual, you are required not only to provide notice to them, but also have a legal basis for doing so. While there is an exception to the notice requirement under the GDPR (General Data Protection Regulation) rules, if the effort required for the notice is disproportionate to the aim, they still need to choose the legal basis for the processing carefully. One option may be legitimate interests. However, in choosing this path, the developers must weight their interests against those of individuals. Another derived challenge brought by privacy is the enforcement of data subject rights. If an individual whose data is part of the dataset requires you to delete their data, this may be impossible without having to completely redo the dataset and retrain the model, which can take weeks of significant computer power.

Another challenge is the potential for bias and misinformation. Datasets inevitably contain the bias of their writers, therefore training AI models on these sets has the undesirable effect of propagating the existing bias. Likewise, the fact that the output resembles the natural language of its creator makes it hard for the reader to spot information that is simply false. The AI does not (at least currently) have its own conscience to differentiate between what is right or wrong and can only produce output based on its training set by the developers. This flows into another challenge: safety. If AI is incapable of determining the good from the bad, it can easily be used for the wrong purposes (e.g. by asking it where to find guns). AI models deployed to the public such as ChatGPT must go through extensive safety evaluation processes, but the question remains about what would happen if a similar model did not in fact go through the same process and end up in the hands of the public.

Lastly, a more controversial issue is that of ownership. Who owns the content generated by the AI? Can AI be listed as a joint author? Now this seems to be a more philosophical than legal question. There is no known jurisdiction that accepts AI to be listed as an author and the more obvious answer is that the author of the AI will also be considered the author of what the AI generates. However, AI is still in its incipient stages and perhaps this position is likely to change in the future, allowing more advanced and independent AI to be collaborators.

How will the metaverse and law need to evolve in the future?

The metaverse is a complex concept that is still in its early stages, and as the technology evolves, new concepts will appear. Personal rights of avatars? Rights and liabilities of AI workers? Interoperability of objects? Universal law applications?

Once its shape starts to be defined more clearly, undoubtedly the regulations will follow, but most probably at a slower pace. We expect dimensions of the metaverse to evolve when the metaverse becomes a place for commercial activities and integrations with Web2, Web3 and AI speed up. However, given the removal of geography in the metaverse, there will have to be an international collective effort for harmonious use, and adoption at speed can only be achieved

if the metaverse and the use of AI operate with existing legal frameworks.

For now, users, creators, developers and investors are enjoying the
blurred lines, testing the limits of this technology which concurrently
tests the boundaries of existing laws and of those making them, but
for the metaverse to progress more certainty and clarity will be
needed.

Layer 8 – Technology in the metaverse

We are living in one of the most exciting technical phases in history,
with several revolutionary technologies maturing at the same time as
people are becoming more creative and ambitious. Some of the technologies that have grabbed the headlines over the past decade while
changing the technology and productivity landscapes include Web2,
Web3, 5G, AI, fintech, metaverse immersive technologies, cloud, and
edge computing; but how much more can the technology landscape
change with the metaverse?

It can be argued that the potential of technology for change is greater
now than in the early 2000s when Steve Jobs said the following, but
why is this important for technology in the metaverse?

FIGURE 2.7 Metaverse requirements overview

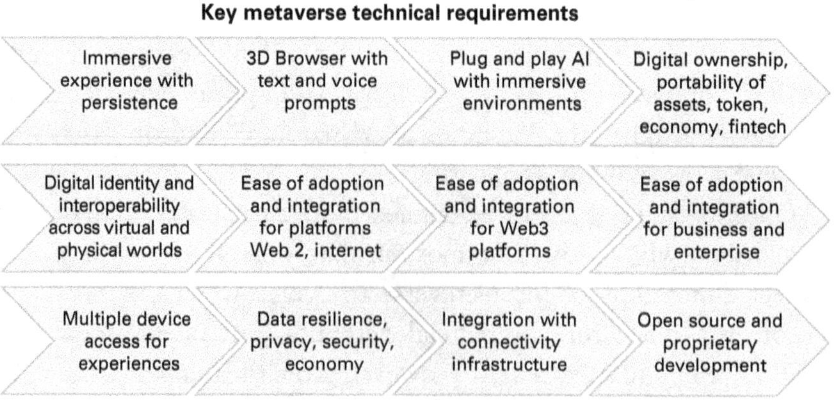

Key metaverse technical requirements

Immersive experience with persistence	3D Browser with text and voice prompts	Plug and play AI with immersive environments	Digital ownership, portability of assets, token, economy, fintech
Digital identity and interoperability across virtual and physical worlds	Ease of adoption and integration for platforms Web 2, internet	Ease of adoption and integration for Web3 platforms	Ease of adoption and integration for business and enterprise
Multiple device access for experiences	Data resilience, privacy, security, economy	Integration with connectivity infrastructure	Open source and proprietary development

Steve Jobs stated that 'Everything around you that you call life was made up by people who were no smarter than you. Maybe the most important thing: To shake off this erroneous notion that life is there, and you're just going to live in it versus embrace it, change it, improve it, make your mark upon it.'

What Steve was saying is that we should not be constrained by the systems, processes and technologies around us and should not be afraid to challenge and try to change things. One of the barriers to change historically has been access to technology but the metaverse and AI could change this and expand development capabilities to the masses and reduce barriers. For the metaverse technology model we describe the technologies that support the metaverse. We explore the role of the metaverse as new digital operating system enabling users to access a range of technologies and infrastructures required to develop and build new virtual world(s)and the role of AI and recent capabilities to automatically generate code and content to create a new dimension in technology development. When we consider the metaverse as an operating system some of the initial questions are 1) Should the metaverse operating system be open or closed? 2) What technologies will be included in, and support the operating system? 3) Why is this different?

What is clear is that the size of the metaverse opportunity is significant and as a result it will need to extend reach to many markets, industry sectors, and will need to integrate with and incorporate many of the technologies associated with them. This represents a significant widening in scope beyond the current focus on immersive XR and will require many more technological components to be considered.

While AI, Cloud, Web3 and mobile are significant technologies that have made their mark on the world, one can argue their true impact has been limited by how we interact, engage with them. Could the metaverse change this?

Should the metaverse be open-sourced?

The move to open-sourced software has played a significant role in providing the environment, tools, developer community, collaboration incentives, transparency and infrastructure for software developers to impact change across industries, use cases and geographies through software that is being used by millions of people, businesses and machines.

According to Githubs Octoverse 97 per cent of applications use open-source software and 90 per cent of companies are applying it or using it in some way. More recently we have seen all the major protocols in Web3 adopt open-source with innovation and development accelerating in this area. With the open-source momentum growing in mainstream and Web3 software, is open source the way forwards for metaverse development?

The first open-source kernel code was announced in 1991, followed by RedHat in 1993 and MSQL in 1995 as part of the emergence of open-source software and the Linux operating system which provided a powerful and open alternative to proprietary systems. In 1995 the Apache HTTP Server was launched, followed by the Mozilla web browser in 1998 extending open source to the web.

The early 2000s saw the rise of collaborative development communities and organizations promoting open source, such as the Free Software Foundation and the Open-Source Initiative and several enterprises embracing open-source technologies. The introduction of platforms like GitHub facilitated easy sharing, collaboration and version control for open-source projects, encouraging developer participation.

More recently open source has been at the centre of Bitcoin, Ethereum and all the major and Web3 protocols including the MetaMask wallet where they have enjoyed significant innovation and speed of development, and there are some AI protocols like Hugging Face which are open-sourced; however, it should be noted that some of the leading generative AI platform are not open source. Could open source be the key to speed up metaverse innovation and development?

We discussed in Chapter 1 the development of the metaverse initially as separate embedded metaverses across Web2 and Web3 platforms, but that eventually in the second phase there would be interoperability across the platforms, and then in the longer term there will be convergence and consolidation. This development life-cycle therefore indicates that open-source software will be required for speed of development and adoption and therefore dominate development.

However, given the size of the metaverse opportunity could it force a rethink of open-source software approaches and lead to one specifically for the metaverse?

The journey of open source for the metaverse has started and we list some interesting open-source projects in Table 2.2.

Table 2.2 provides a sample of open-sourced projects. What is interesting is that they have the potential for different areas of impact. This could be the key potential of open source, which can incentivize developers across different geographies, with different specializations, experiences, priorities and focus to come together to innovate and build different parts of the metaverse in parallel. The shared incentives where the rewards are spread globally across many developers rather than concentrated in a few large technology companies could be key in the metaverse development journey – but if we look at the potential of Apple user numbers to impact the metaverse growth, do we need both open source and proprietary approaches?

What are the key things metaverse technology needs to do to support all the layers of the framework?

Within the metaverse framework the technology layer works across all other layers and incorporates technologies that power the operating system. When we think of metaverse technology we normally think about VR and MR technologies and the headsets we use to access the applications, but within the framework the metaverse must support interoperability, finance, data and information, ecosystem and business, consumer, and government users virtually but over a global geography. The technology of the metaverse therefore needs to be more about how these technologies can be brought together with immersive technologies like VR and MR to support development of the embedded metaverses and virtual worlds and support the ecosystem and the applications that are built upon it. These require-

TABLE 2.2 A sample of metaverse open-sourced projects' potential impacts

Metaverse open-sourced project	Description	Potential impact
Webaverse	Open-source and browser-based Web3 metaverse engine aimed at developers that provides them with a metaverse engine, which can be hosted anywhere with Node JS v17, and provides them with the tools to build virtual world that can accessed through a range of devices including VR using a browser.	Lowers the complexity of virtual world set-up making it easier to drive adoption. Focus on creators and aims to 'shift the power from a few big tech companies to users and creators'.
Ethereal Engine (XREngine)	Open-sourced project that provides an end-to-end framework and tools and infrastructure for developers to build and deploy scalable 3D social applications with the tools to easily deploy AR, VR and XR.	Strong collaboration and interoperability potential as users can build their world, virtual worlds, games and social experiences and link them together.
JanusWeb	Open-source web framework for building social virtual reality experiences utilizing JavaScript and HTML, it provides developers with a framework and tools to create immersive 3D environments for desktop, mobile and VR devices.	It has the potential to drive adoption as it can be used to convert an existing 2D website into a 3D environment. This approach provides an upgrade path for over 1 billion websites on the internet to become part of the metaverse. Open-source could be critical in accelerating this capability and the associated adoption.
BlueJeans	Open-sourced video platform encouraging remote and mobile collaboration for large and small businesses. The company partnered with MootUp in 2021 to bring 'virtual events in the era of the metaverse with 3D, VR, and AR immersive environments, avatars, and AI chatbots'.	The project is business focused and supports collaboration on new metaverse business use cases. The potential to bring sections of the business community to the metaverse could have significant adoption impact.
Open Metaverse Interoperability Group	The Open Metaverse Interoperability Group, or OMI, has a mission to 'develop standards for the metaverse, ensuring that metaverse development is open and that metaverse apps, services, and platforms can easily integrate'.	Standards will be key to metaverse development and adoption.

ments have been important to the development of the metaverse role to bring together technologies for the development, management and interoperability of applications (See Figure 2.7).

This metaverse operating system is still being built but we are seeing some common technical approaches being adopted across early metaverse platforms and applications, and VR and MR, with initiatives like the Metaverse Standards Forum driving for an Open Metaverse. In this section we explore a conceptual metaverse technology architecture, and deep dive into the metaverse operating system.

The metaverse technology architecture

Technology architecture and design have evolved over time in response to the increasing complexity and demands of technological systems. Here are some key milestones in its evolution:

- Early computing and the birth of modern computing in the mid-20th century marked the beginning of technology architecture. Early systems focused on hardware design and programming languages.
- In the 1960s and 1970s, Monolithic systems and centralized mainframe systems dominated. Software and hardware were tightly integrated, and applications were built as monolithic structures.
- Client-server architecture in the 1980s brought the client-server model, where applications were divided into front-end clients and back-end servers. This allowed for more distributed processing and improved scalability.
- Web-based systems and the advent of the World Wide Web in the 1990s led to web-based architecture, enabling the delivery of applications over the internet. It facilitated the growth of e-commerce and online services.
- Service-oriented architecture (SOA) emerged in the early 2000s, promoting the modularization of applications into reusable services. This allowed for flexibility to incorporate system capabilities and interoperability across systems.

- Cloud computing emerged in the late 2000s introducing a shift towards scalable and on-demand computing resources around virtual machines and storage. It enabled the deployment of applications and services off-premises into virtual machines and virtual data centres, but more importantly enabled access from anywhere.

- Microservices and containerization architecture has emerged more recently enabling the development and deployment of applications as independent and lightweight components that can run in multiple environments.

These milestones reflect the progression towards more modular, scalable and distributed technology architectures, and this evolution is continuing even as new technologies and initiatives like Web3, AI, IoT and the metaverse are emerging, to drive the technology requirements forwards and push the automation boundary further.

The metaverse encompasses a range of advanced and emerging technologies for both the immersive and interactive digital environments, and the infrastructure, finance, data, interoperability and processing requirements. Some of these new technologies include XR, 3D graphics, haptic feedback, spatial audio, AI, Web3 and fintech.

In summary, XR capabilities includes VR which enables users to experience a fully immersive virtual environment, while AR overlays digital information onto the real world, and MR combines virtual and real elements, allowing users to interact with digital content in their physical surroundings, while 3D graphics provide realistic and visual representations of objects, environments and avatar on existing access devices like smart phones.

To support immersive experience capabilities haptic feedback and spatial audio provide sensory capabilities to enable realistic touch and sound sensations. AI provides intelligence, insight and automation of interaction and some services through natural language processing, computer vision and behaviour simulation. Finally, Web3 technology ensures transparency, security and decentralized control and portability of assets, transactions and identities. How can the metaverse technology architecture incorporate all these capabilities?

The technology architecture will need to address the requirements outlined in Figure 2.8 and must be designed to ensure these technologies and more in the future can be implemented flexibility and accommodate evolving user dynamics and core technologies, while ensuring that other platforms and the associated legacy and established technologies from the physical world can be incorporated and considered. Figure 2.8 outlines a view of the current technologies that could be considered in a metaverse technology architecture, but with focus on the operating system and application layers it provides flexibility in the use of the underlying system capabilities and leaves the door open for new technologies and innovations to be added in the future.

The metaverse technology architecture describes the metaverse technologies in three layers, where layer 1 describes the infrastructure, layer 2 the capabilities and layer 3 the operating system and applications. The metaverse brings together several technologies but

FIGURE 2.8 The metaverse technology architecture

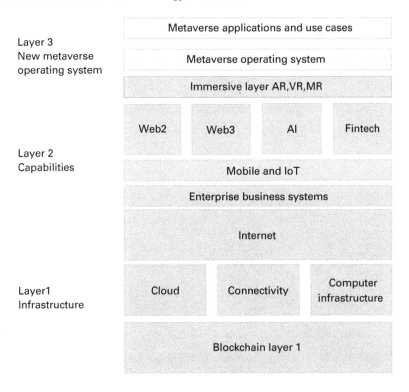

the key thing to note here is the metaverse can be seen as a technology framework and a new operating system with focus on supporting immersive use cases/applications. We expect the individual technology components in the architecture to change and/or evolve over time, and the metaverse operating system to evolve with it. In some cases, the metaverse will directly drive technology innovation and in others it will consume it, but key to understanding the metaverse technology architecture is that, overall, it must allow developers to incorporate established technologies within metaverse solutions and provide room for AI to play a role across all areas.

03

Opportunities of the metaverse

The digital revolution has changed the way we store and access information from siloed, paper documents and files to digital data-based world where people and businesses can access information, create content, buy and sell goods and services, and communicate with each other across the globe using mobile phones, internet technology and Web2 platforms. Our experiences have changed too, with mobile applications providing an access point to a wide range of services and as result of these developments the world is almost unrecognizable from the world of the 1980s, 1990s and even the early 2000s.

The mobile phone is now at the centre of the consumer and business experience and enabling them to shop, socialize, work, travel and learn using the internet and when this past 25-year period is reviewed in the context of history, I think it will go down as one of the biggest communications, social, business, economic and technological transformations. Some of the considerations around the metaverse centre on the role of the mobile phone as an access device, and the extent to which XR headsets and devices will be incorporated in the mobile phone, or even replace it. If the metaverse is indeed the new interaction point between people and content which will encompass communications and the mobile phone, what is the size of the metaverse opportunity?

Why is it important? How far can it take us beyond where we are now?

What is the metaverse opportunity?

Imagine a virtual world which when combined with the physical world forms a new experience dimension that enables truly realistic and immersive shopping experiences without physically shopping, travel without physically travelling, concerts and entertainment without physically attending, work without physically going to a physical work location, studying without physically attending, collaboration without physically meeting, but all with a very similar and comparable experience to the physical ones.

Imagine a world that removes the barriers of time, travel and physical presence from users, platforms and associated experiences.

Imagine a world where we could seamlessly transition from physical to virtual experiences without passwords and having to carry physical proofs of our identities. A world where AI assistants are able to establish or identities and verify credentials on our behalf.

Imagine a world where we have digital wallets that keep all of our identities and credentials, including educational, social, reputational, communication, banking, payments, finance and assets. This wallet would act as a digital key for authorization, access, and payments across virtual and physical ecosystems, and with users in full control.

Imagine a world where the geographic and social barriers to opportunity were removed, and a student from the most remote part of Africa or Asia can attend medical school at top universities without having to travel, and when they graduate, they could run a medical practice for people around the world providing services without physically meeting them.

The metaverse has the potential to reset the boundaries of opportunity enabling areas of the economy that are currently limited to physical interactions and processes to be brought online, and also for new business areas to be created which are only possible through the metaverse feature set, which we will describe in Chapter 6. As the metaverse enables more people, businesses, processes and activities to be brought online, and combined with new features, a new frontier of opportunity is being created, as shown in Figure 3.1.

I think that when there was particular excitement surrounding the metaverse in 2021, there was a belief that the opportunity would be

FIGURE 3.1 The metaverse opportunity breakdown

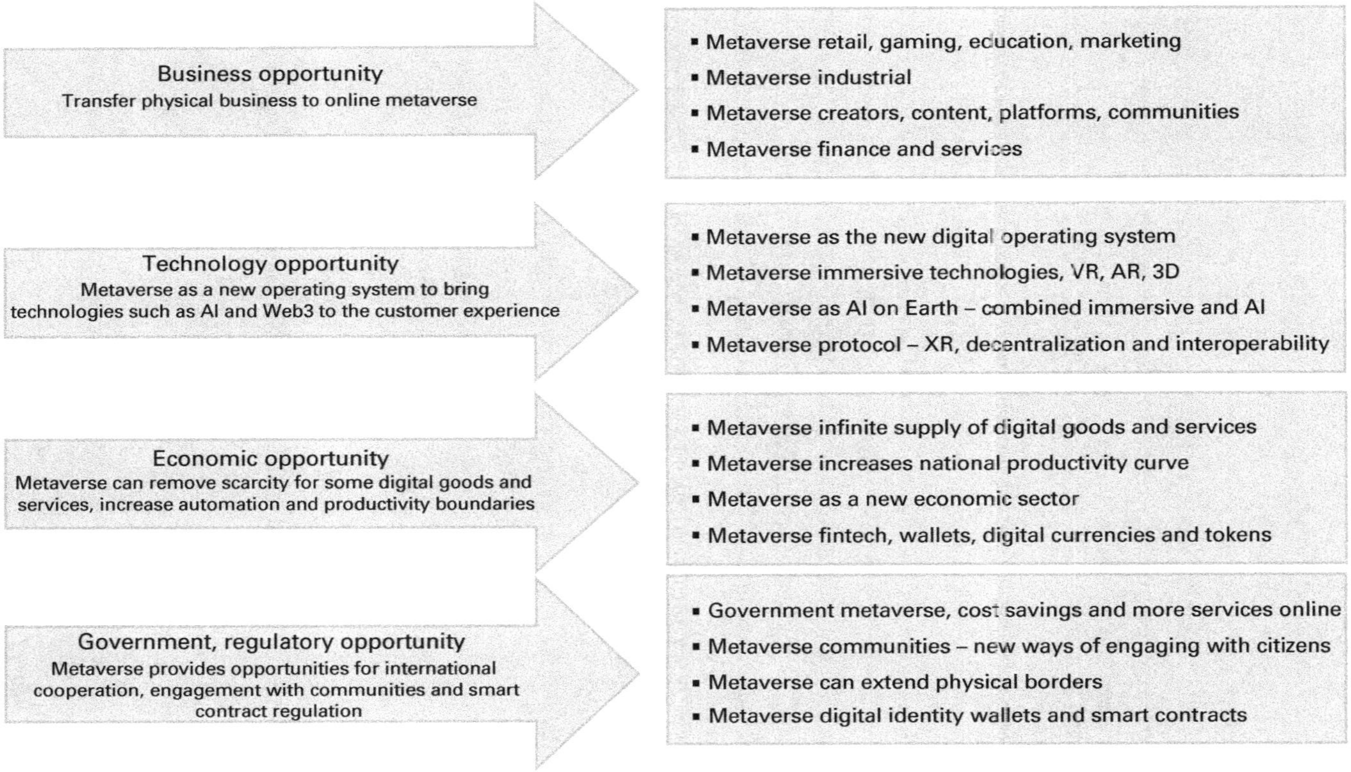

Business opportunity
Transfer physical business to online metaverse

- Metaverse retail, gaming, education, marketing
- Metaverse industrial
- Metaverse creators, content, platforms, communities
- Metaverse finance and services

Technology opportunity
Metaverse as a new operating system to bring technologies such as AI and Web3 to the customer experience

- Metaverse as the new digital operating system
- Metaverse immersive technologies, VR, AR, 3D
- Metaverse as AI on Earth – combined immersive and AI
- Metaverse protocol – XR, decentralization and interoperability

Economic opportunity
Metaverse can remove scarcity for some digital goods and services, increase automation and productivity boundaries

- Metaverse infinite supply of digital goods and services
- Metaverse increases national productivity curve
- Metaverse as a new economic sector
- Metaverse fintech, wallets, digital currencies and tokens

Government, regulatory opportunity
Metaverse provides opportunities for international cooperation, engagement with communities and smart contract regulation

- Government metaverse, cost savings and more services online
- Metaverse communities – new ways of engaging with citizens
- Metaverse can extend physical borders
- Metaverse digital identity wallets and smart contracts

directly related to virtual worlds and immersive technologies. However, as other technologies like Web3 and AI have evolved in parallel with the metaverse, it is clear that the value and the opportunity around the metaverse is associated with the convergence of technologies. As we explore the metaverse opportunity in this chapter, we will view the overall business, technology, economic, financial, government and social opportunities, with special focus on the interrelationship between the AI and metaverse opportunities.

How big is the metaverse business opportunity?

The metaverse business opportunity is expected to reach across manufacturing, retail, wholesale, advertising, sales and marketing. The new creator economy is of special interest given the metaverse ability to make AI accessible to creators of content, add new immersive features and connect them with customers. The size of the metaverse opportunity will largely depend on the level of transition from established solutions to new metaverse solutions and as a result metaverse growth calculations will need to factor these transition indicators into forecasting models.

While it is clear that the metaverse opportunity is significant, the transition will demand fundamental changes and reengineering of the very fabric of business, society, government and infrastructure to realize the full global opportunity. With some forecasts as high as $5

FIGURE 3.2 Factors impacting the metaverse opportunity sizing

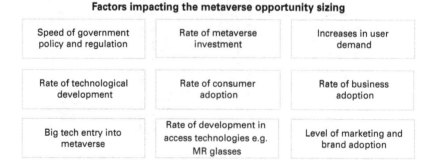

Factors impacting the metaverse opportunity sizing

Speed of government policy and regulation	Rate of metaverse investment	Increases in user demand
Rate of technological development	Rate of consumer adoption	Rate of business adoption
Big tech entry into metaverse	Rate of development in access technologies e.g. MR glasses	Level of marketing and brand adoption

FIGURE 3.3 The metaverse opportunity by category

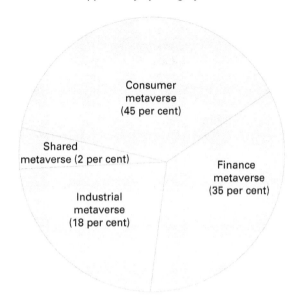

TABLE 3.1 Metaverse forecasts by business sector

Metaverse Business Area	2030 Forecast ($)	Source	My 2030 Forecast Model Outputs ($)	Reason Factors
Metaverse e-commerce and retail market	$128 billion	Skyquest	$500 billion	Addressable market size digital commerce $17.3 trillion by 2030. Increased incorporation of embedded metaverse experiences in existing and new retail experiences, new areas added to e-commerce by the metaverse, incorporation Web3 payments by metaverse supports 3–4 per cent of addressable market for metaverse retail.
Metaverse Gaming Market	$168 billion	Statistica	$140 billion	Addressable market size up to $665 billion. Forecast based on 21 per cent of the market. Again, embedded metaverse in existing gaming platforms and ecosystems makes this forecast on track, but our output model has reduced the forecast slightly as we expect some overlap and crowding out from social media where gaming tasks are included in social media market size and forecasts.

(continued)

TABLE 3.1 (Continued)

Metaverse Business Area	2030 Forecast ($)	Source	My 2030 Forecast Model Outputs ($)	Reason Factors
Industrial Metaverse Market	$172 billion	Grand View Research	$250 billion	The growth of IoT and the relationship between IoT data and digital twins as a source of data for AI LLMs indicates that a new market and driver for IoT and industrial metaverse digital twins is fast emerging. This incorporation of AI in industry and manufacturing is also expected to drive increased productivity and market size. We therefore expect a higher growth forecast due to the AI factor.
Metaverse in Finance Market	$14.29 billion	Virtue Market Research	$500 billion	The current scope of metaverse finance for this forecast includes virtual banks, insurance companies, investment firms and other financial institutions. However, our forecasting model also includes the ability of metaverse as an operating system to bring Web3 tokens, NFTs and bank tokenized deposits, and even retail CBDCs embedded in the customer and business experience. The global financial services industry is forecast to be worth $45,149 billion by 2031, and as an increasingly important operating system, interaction point for consumers and business, the location for setting up banking and finances branches and the new web browser the factors in our model indicate a much higher forecast for this sector.

(continued)

TABLE 3.1 (Continued)

Metaverse Business Area	2030 Forecast ($)	Source	My 2030 Forecast Model Outputs ($)	Reason Factors
Metaverse Advertising	$7.2 billion	Statistica	$28 billion	Addressable market is expected to exceed $500 billion by 2030 and the size of the metaverse market share will depend on the scope of the metaverse, transfer of advertising from existing channels to the metaverse and new advertising business that the metaverse can create. The attractiveness of the metaverse for advertising is dependent on metaverse adoption. Given the metaverse positioning as the new consumer and business interaction point for content, and the new web browser, and the new ways of advertising that 3D, virtual worlds and embedded advertising can offer, especially when in conjunction with data and AI, our model forecasts are higher.

trillion by 2030 for the size of the opportunity, we now must assess these estimates against our current models and the transition factors.

The key determining factors for metaverse growth include government regulation, rate of investment, user demand and access levels to drive overall rate of adoption (See Figure 3.2).

The opportunity size can also be broken down into the categories that will drive the opportunity including consumer, industrial, finance and shared metaverses, with the consumer and finance metaverses in our forecast models expected to drive significant opportunity (see Figure 3.3).

The opportunity drivers and outputs from our forecasting model can then be compared to other forecasts in Table 3.1 for the size of business opportunity across some of the key business areas.

Our model outputs as outlined in Table 3.1 estimate the metaverse opportunity at $1.3 trillion by 2030; however, other forecasts are significantly higher, and it is possible that the opportunity could land anywhere between these forecast ranges.

Our total forecast for metaverse opportunity across retail, gaming, industrial, finance and advertising is $1.4 trillion by 2030, but in almost all areas our forecasts are higher than the other metaverse forecasts, with the main factors driving our increased outlook being the following:

1 The metaverse role as the new interaction point and web browser for consumers, businesses and online, content, services and online retail.

2 The metaverse role as the new operating system that will be used to build the next generation of applications combining AR, VR, AI, Web3, Web2, fintech and other technologies. This will drive adoption and transition of current spending to the metaverse.

3 The metaverse role as the environment and interaction tool for AI for consumer and business experiences. With the size of the AI scope and market size forecast to increase this will also drive significant growth for the metaverse across these areas.

4 The relationship between the metaverse and AI is expected to be a key driver for growth. The metaverse is expected to provide the interaction capabilities and environments for AI to interact with people and businesses, and since the emergence of generative AI there is significant investment driving growth in this area which should in turn increase metaverse growth.

Metaverse e-commerce and retail market opportunity

The metaverse has the potential to not only change but more profoundly redefine e-commerce and retail, enabling new 3D and immersive experiences with AI-driven personalization and retail assistants to be combined with marketplaces that intuitively bring retail direct to your space. The metaverse can add new categories to e-retail which were previously only feasible for physical retail and grow the size of the existing e-commerce and retail markets. The opportunities for business, therefore, are the creation of bigger retail markets with wider scope, new support industries around metaverse

retail and e-commerce, new solutions and services which incorporate AI to drive experiences and market-making, as well as increased
embedding of finance in experiences. These metaverse technologies
may also help to lower retail barriers to entry by lowering costs,
removing geographic restrictions preventing access to retail technologies and markets, and helping to make goods and services that
were previously geography and physical retail channel specific more
broadly available via metaverse retail. This could then serve to
widen the opportunities to enter and succeed in metaverse retail.

The retail and e-commerce markets are forecast to be worth as
much as $17.3 trillion by 2030. However, factors expected to drive
the metaverse growth of this market included the following:

- Increased embedded retail metaverse experiences in platforms,
  applications and ecosystems, including social media. This is
  supported by the trend towards Super Applications (SuperApps)
  incorporating a range of functionalities in platforms.
- Incorporation of metaverse and Web3 payments and digital
  identity automation in retail and e-commerce to remove friction in
  payments and interoperability across retailers
- Growth in retail intuition and personalization driven by AI but
  triggered, manifested and executed in embedded metaverse
  experiences.

Incorporating these factors in our metaverse forecasting model and
working on a projection of 3–4 per cent of the addressable market,
our metaverse forecasting model calculates the size of the metaverse
retail and e-commerce markets at $500–550 billion by 2030. The size
of the opportunity will represent the beginning of a fundamental shift
in how and where consumers buy and sell, and how brands interact
with them. As discussed, the opportunities associated with this are
more than just market growth. For business, it could represent an
opportunity for new entrants to the market and new competition.

The metaverse gaming opportunity

The metaverse gaming market size is forecast to reach $665 billion
by 2030 according to Fortune Business, and with the metaverse

features seen as key to many areas of the gaming experience this market is also seen as a key growth area for the metaverse.[1] By adding metaverse features like VR, MR, virtual worlds, digital ownership and portability of gaming assets, incorporation of brands in gaming experiences, new immersive social interactions in game, as well as interoperability and portability of assets with other platforms.

However, our metaverse forecasting model calculates the size of the metaverse gaming opportunity at the lower end of current forecasts at $140 billion. This is in part due to some overlap and crowding out by social media and the wider entertainment industry.

The industrial metaverse opportunity

The industrial metaverse is growing and the market size is forecast to reach $170.12 billion by 2030, with a CAGR of 33.6 per cent between 2023 to 2030, according to a study by Grand View Research, with digital twins and simulations, and immersive training being key drivers.[2] However, our forecasting model values the industrial metaverse opportunity significantly higher at $250 billion by 2030 largely due to the expected role of IoT and digital twins actual and simulated data in AI large language models (AI LLMs) for businesses and enterprise.

AI is fast emerging as a critical success factor for enterprise and businesses, and while enterprises have been reluctant to share data with public AI LLMs, there has been a significant investment increase in enterprises developing their own LLMs. This reflects the view that enterprise and business AI LLMs will become a key battleground for competitive advantage in the future and metaverse digital twins will be a key input.

With the enterprise and business AI market expected to grow significantly, we have increased our industrial metaverse opportunity forecast accordingly to $250 billion by 2030 and expect that this could be revised upwards if AI adoption increases further.

The metaverse finance opportunity

The global financial services market size is forecast to reach $45,149 billion by 2031 and the metaverse is expected to provide increased opportunity to embed finance in customer experiences and drive more financial services online. In addition, the metaverse operating system will make it easier to incorporate fintech into applications, as well as Web3 finance providing the metaverse with an important role in financial applications and a significant potential growth area.

The current $14 billion forecast scope for metaverse finance includes virtual banks, insurance companies, investment firms and other financial institution. However, our forecasting model factored in the growth associated with the metaverse bringing in Web3 finance e including, tokens, NFTs, bank tokenized deposits and even retail CBDCs.

Banks are exploring strategies to expand activities in the metaverse to improve customer experience. Services planned include payments using XR to enable a more immersive online banking experience, incorporating virtual branches with AI assistants and agents to improve sales of financial products.

Banks have begun to use the metaverse as another channel for engaging with customers, similar to internet, social and mobile; however, the capabilities of the metaverse with AI and Web3 may provide an opportunity to provide new automated and tailored services in new ways that could fundamentally transform the sector.

There will be 5.6 billion people using digital wallets by 2030 according to Ark Invest.[3] With the metaverse functioning as an interaction point for consumers and businesses, and given its proximity to consumers, it can become the preferred location for setting up banking and financial services and virtual branches in the future, driving a forecast for this sector in our model of $500 billion which is higher than other forecasts.

The metaverse advertising opportunity

The global advertising market is expected to exceed $500 billion by 2030, and to an extent the size of the metaverse advertising market share will depend on overall metaverse adoption, the effectiveness of metaverse advertising features and the associated transfer of advertising from other channels to the metaverse and new metaverse native advertising revenues that will be created from new areas like the shared metaverse.

FIGURE 3.4 Consumer adoption drivers and the metaverse advertising opportunity

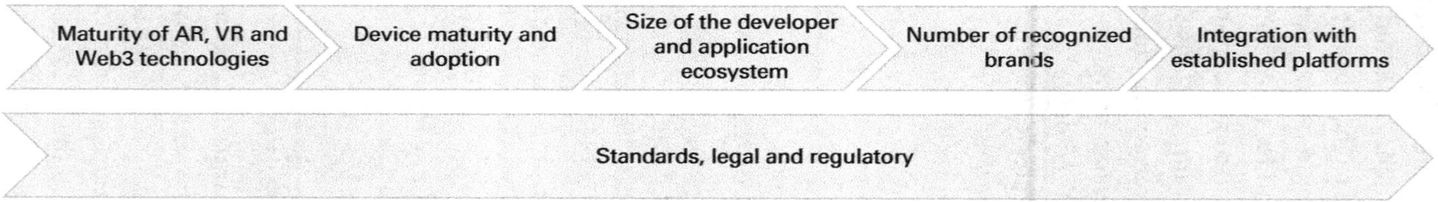

Maturity of AR, VR and Web3 technologies

Device maturity and adoption

Size of the developer and application ecosystem

Number of recognized brands

Integration with established platforms

Standards, legal and regulatory

Given the metaverse positioning as the new consumer and business interaction point for content, and the new web browser, combined with the new ways of advertising that XR, 3D, AI and virtual worlds indications are that the metaverse will play a significant future role in this sector. For example, AI and embedded advertising in metaverse experiences can focus products for more success to users with higher dwell times. Our forecasting model for 2030 is therefore projecting a metaverse advertising opportunity of $28 billion, which is also higher than current forecasts.

The size of the metaverse advertising opportunity is linked to adoption levels with the five main drivers to consumer metaverse adoption including 1) maturity of AR, MR and Web3 technologies; 2) device maturity and adoption; 3) size of the developer and application ecosystems; 4) number of recognized brands; 5) integration with established platforms, with AI integration and adoption of legal and regulatory standards also important factors (see Figure 3.4).

Where XR reaches mass market appeal this is expected to incentivize OEMS to increase supply, reducing price and making metaverse devices more affordable and increasing demand.

The introduction of more portable and lower-priced mixed reality headsets, which are needed to access immersive experiences, could be key to adoption, but smaller headsets which incorporate connectivity which could replace mobile phone use are also important considerations for growth. Meta and more recently Apple have entered the market, and their customer, user and developer ecosystems could be key to fast accelerated adoption. But more widespread devices will be needed at different price points for quality, convenience and to reduce the entry price point to replicate growth globally, especially in developing countries. However, another incentive to adoption could be government subsidies for headsets which could either be part of private sector initiated metaverse business models to grow users or wider government policy.

There is also expected to be a link between the level of industrial metaverse adoption and the consumer use where, for example, immersive technologies introduced into the workplace drive consumers to use the technology for personal use.

Big brands entering the metaverse and integration with big hyper-scale platforms will also promote awareness and trust. This will be critical to successful consumer adoption as brands are expected to attract consumers with new goods, services and experiences that exceed the current product offerings and help to incentivize customer transition to metaverse solutions.

The maturity of Web3 enablers like digital wallets, decentralized digital identity, and new payment and finance solutions like Open Banking will also be important to increase adoption. Nearly 70 per cent of the world's population is expected to have a digital wallet by 2030, and the incorporation of the wallet into the consumer metaverse will be key.

The opportunities associated with the metaverse as a new operating system

An operating system is a software that manages hardware and software resources and provides common services for programs and applications. The operating system in this context enables computers and devices to run common software and applications, use resources and infrastructure, and interact with each other and users (See Figure 3.5).

FIGURE 3.5 The metaverse operating system opportunity

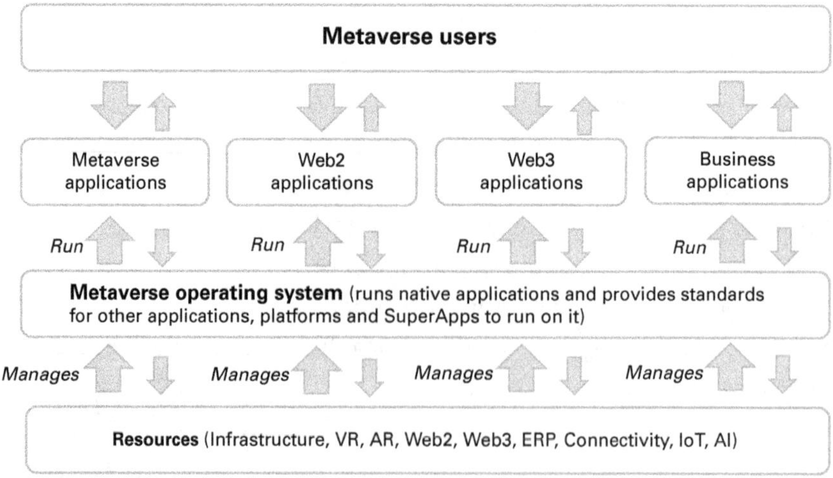

The key components of an operating system can vary, but the following have historically been the traditional components:

- The kernel is the core component of an operating system that provides services and manages the system resources. It interacts directly with the hardware and resources and performs tasks such as process management, memory management, device management and scheduling.
- The file system and management organize and manages files and storage and provides a structure for organizing files and enables programs to read, write and manage stored data.
- Device drivers enable the operating system to communicate and interact with devices and acts as intermediaries between the hardware devices and the operating system.
- The user interface is where users interact with the operating system through text, graphical interfaces, touch, voice and now AI.
- Process management where the operating system allocates system resources in line with its objectives and the performance selected.
- Memory management manages system memory for use by processes and applications.
- Networking components provides the protocols and services for connecting to networks, accessing remote resources and transferring data over network connections. Networking components include internet protocols like TCP/IP, and network device drivers and configuration utilities.
- Security components are responsible for protecting the system, data and user information from unauthorized access and threats. They include authentication, access control, encryption, firewalls, antivirus and other security measures.

But how can the metaverse function as an operating system? It must manage the interaction between resources, devices and applications. However, at the same time, many of the platforms, hardware devices and applications that interact with the metaverse already exist. In the initial stages of the metaverse operating system, there would need to be a dual role where the metaverse operating system can run the other major operating systems and set standards for them in the metaverse. In the medium term the native metaverse operating systems can be developed in line with interoperability, immersive, portability, persistence standards, and enable applications to access the many resources in the metaverse technology architecture (See Figure 3.5).

What is the wider opportunity for government and society?

The metaverse provides the capabilities to fundamentally change the way societies interact with each other and it can also provide governments, communities and other social groups with the potential to embed services at this new interaction point between people, business, IoT devices, AI which should increase data and participation

If we look more widely across society, could the metaverse present a once-in-a-generation opportunity to shape a new more interactive society without geographic boundaries, where people can choose their age, image, colour and location without physical limitations?

Can the metaverse redefine the limitations of scarcity for digital goods and services like education, and augment medical and social care with realistic immersive online options?

Can the metaverse reshape communities providing enablers to transform them into decentralized autonomous organizations (DAOs), providing the smart contracts and links to the collective digital identities, token economics, fintech and decentralized finance to add new economic and fundraising dimensions to support to the current position?

Can the metaverse help governments to get closer to citizens and better target services more efficiently? Can the metaverse provide an opportunity for governments to incorporate AI into government services and workforces?

Can the metaverse help governments to reduce the number of physical locations and expand the range of virtual services for ease of access?

While it is clear that the economic size of the metaverse opportunity will be significant, there are wider opportunities in technology,

Is the metaverse the key to equity?

Some of the features of the metaverse naturally lend the metaverse to removing some of the barriers to equality for developing countries and their citizens. For example, the metaverse can:

- Remove geography as a barrier to international trade.
- Create infinite digital assets removing the limitations of scarcity of resources in the digital economy.
- Increase education, training, and skills through immersive learning.
- Drive new levels of automation by providing an easy way for AI to be embedded in government services and private sector business processes and services.
- Open access to new virtual markets without the need for expensive manufacturing and transportation.

Could these metaverse features be the key to achieving greater equality? There is no doubt that the metaverse represents a significant opportunity to reset the boundaries of equality, but to achieve this first there needs to be equality of access to the internet and the devices required to access the metaverse. In addition to improving access to services the financial and business sectors will need to extend how they authenticate digital identity for KYC, AML and business and consumer credit scoring to incorporate credentials which are more aligned to the position in developing countries.

The above initiatives could allow developing countries to add a new virtual economic layer to their GDP and improve liquidity and investment improving business activity and employment, as well as improving productivity with the inclusion of AI from first principles.

To drive equality in developing countries is the first step to ensure an equitable metaverse?

Today's metaverse largely follows the structure of the current Web 2.0 internet where the majority of metaverse spaces, and the value chain contained within it, are owned by centralized entities.

There is, however, a growing movement to define and build a more equitable metaverse; one that ensures ownership and control of the value chain is decentralized among participants and where diversity, equity and inclusion are built into the foundations of the metaverse itself.

This chapter explores the concept of equity and the importance of embedding equity in the metaverse and examines the challenges and opportunities that this presents. By embracing equality-first principles, we have the potential to build a more inclusive co-reality that narrows the digital divide, empowers and enriches individuals and communities, and fosters meaningful and safe connections in immersive spaces.

An equitable metaverse is directly linked to equitable internet access, especially where access to the metaverse is needed, for work, education and to access financial services and conduct business. Ensuring national infrastructure for access, and support for this by governments remains a critical success factor going forwards.

Is equity the key to unlocking value in the metaverse?

Equality and equity are two concepts that are often discussed in the context of fairness and social justice. Equality represents a state where everyone is treated in the same way, without any distinction or bias. In a now ubiquitous illustration, equality is represented as an image of a row of individuals of different heights trying to watch a game over a fence. In the name of equality, each person is given the same size box to stand on. However, this approach doesn't consider the inherent differences in their heights, resulting in some still struggling to see over the fence while others have a clear view.

Equity, on the other hand, acknowledges and addresses the unique needs and circumstances of individuals, where, this time, everyone is provided with a different sized box based on their height. This approach ensures that everyone has an equitable opportunity to enjoy the game by providing them with the specific support they need to see over the fence.

The metaverse has the potential to remove inequality based on physical factors like gender, age, height, colour as in the metaverse people can create personas they are comfortable with and even have different personas for different metaverses. The human bias can also be mitigated, as the metaverse is also digital and therefore some of the barriers to equality which are based on human touch points and decision outputs are automatically removed. However, there has been much discussion about the data, code and AI algorithms which are building and operating the metaverse and AI which may contain inherent biases. For example, the data which fed into the LLMs supporting generative AI are largely using data collected in developing countries and may, therefore, create perpetual bias which will be amplified where AI in turn creates data based on it.

Addressing equity of data, code and AI therefore remains key to achieving metaverse equality, and to achieve this we need to get more data for developing countries and a wider number of different socioeconomic groups involved in developing the metaverse, AI and associated technologies.

An equity-first approach to building the metaverse is therefore important to ensure that a wider cross section of national and individual data, circumstances and digital needs are considered in the build and design.

The achievement of metaverse equity is critical to the wider goal of improving equality across developing countries and their citizens, but also to unlocking value in their economies by adding the virtual layer and markets.

Can the metaverse help to solve the digital divide?

The digital divide refers to the disparities in the understanding of, access to and use of digital technologies including devices such as laptops, smartphones and internet connectivity to engage in online society.

The technology and infrastructure needed to access the full metaverse further exacerbate the challenge. Current 3D immersive devices are cost prohibitive outside a small population of the world's richest economies. The base layer of infrastructure needed to power metaverse applications and low-latency experiences such as 5G networking are today prioritized in mostly urban areas.

Digital literacy is also a concern. The ability to explore, evaluate, use, share and create content online while understanding the basics of internet safety are key to generating and capturing the benefits of our digital age. Digital illiteracy affects employment, socialization, education and communication.

Addressing the digital divide becomes crucial for ensuring an inclusive and equitable metaverse. Failure to address the disparities in infrastructure, access to affordable devices and digital literacy can further marginalize already disadvantaged populations.

Policies and initiatives should aim to bridge these gaps to ensure that marginalized and underserved communities have equal opportunities to participate in and benefit from the new virtual economy.

Maybe AI holds part of the answer to this as the information, training and education that can be delivered could be a significant factor in improving digital literacy. In addition, governments can establish policies and regulations and collaborate with the private sector and international organizations to promote universal access to the metaverse, including broadband connectivity, affordable hardware and digital literacy programmes. This can ensure that marginalized communities have equal opportunities to benefit from metaverse platforms.

Public and private investments, subsidies and joint initiatives are needed to ensure availability and access to the appropriate metaverse infrastructure, including affordable hardware devices. Equitable and broader adoption of, and active participation in, the metaverse can only be sustained by providing low-cost connectivity to users and lower-cost alternatives to the high-priced headsets available today.

Digital literacy frameworks from international organizations can be leveraged by the public sector to benchmark digital capabilities of their citizens and shape widespread digital literacy programmes to ensure individuals have the skills to navigate and benefit from digital technologies and the metaverse. These programmes should be inclusive, targeting marginalized communities and bridging the digital skills gap.

Policies can promote the integration of metaverse technologies into educational curricula, fostering digital learning, creativity and critical thinking skills. This helps prepare future generations for the opportunities and challenges of the metaverse.

Can the metaverse start the journey to equality through individuals and communities?

In addition to closing the gap of the digital divide, attention must turn to how we generate shared prosperity for individuals and communities from a decentralized metaverse, and education could be the key.

The potential of the metaverse to contribute to wider improvements in society can be helped by providing access to education, economic and business opportunities and social inclusion.

The metaverse can offer individuals virtual classrooms and educational platforms that provide equal access to high-quality education regardless of geographical location or socio-economic background. Early versions of 'metaversities', digital twins of physical world university campuses, are now going online, providing immersive access to higher learning content and student socialization.

VR and MR are now being utilized to offer skill development programmes, vocational training and certifications. For instance, medical students can practise complex surgical procedures in a simulated environment, improving their skills and reducing the cost of traditional training methods.

By providing access to virtual training, workshops and skill-building experiences, the metaverse can empower individuals to gain the necessary competencies for participating in the digital economy.

Is equality in the metaverse linked to new economic opportunity?

Much like the internet, the metaverse will bring a whole new digital economy of new jobs, new enterprises and new roles.

New job markets are created that require skills in virtual reality development, 3D modelling, community management, digital marketing and more. This can create opportunities for job seekers to engage in emerging sectors. Individuals can start and run virtual businesses, leveraging their creativity, skills and digital assets.

Virtual marketplaces, virtual real estate and virtual goods creation can provide opportunities for entrepreneurship with lower overhead costs. New marketplaces have been created around 3D assets and digital products, and individual designers and creators make and sell their own virtual products for use in the metaverse. This enables individuals who may have struggled to find work in the physical world due to lack of opportunity, geographic exclusion, or credentials to generate income, start businesses and participate in the digital/virtual economy.

The pandemic accelerated existing trends in remote work and the metaverse further shapes the future of work, introducing new ways to facilitate interactive work collaboration and training and skills learning. This flexibility potentially opens up new job opportunities for individuals who face physical or geographical limitations.

The metaverse can also enable business collaboration across geographical boundaries, allowing entrepreneurs to network, form partnerships and access global markets and buyers. Entrepreneurs in the metaverse can take advantage of supply-side enablers (such as platform or world design) as well as the demand side (virtual experiences, virtual item trades, etc).

It is important to note that virtual environments can create a level playing field, minimizing biases and discrimination that may exist in physical spaces. As such, the metaverse represents an opportunity for underrepresented groups, such as women, minority communities or individuals with disabilities, to have equal opportunities and representation in the new economy.

How can the metaverse address financial inclusion?

Financial inclusion for marginalized individuals can also be addressed through the metaverse.

In the physical world, the use of mobile money services has been shown to have long-term effects on poverty reduction. The metaverse can mirror that model by enabling decentralized financial systems that enable peer-to-peer transactions, banking services and access to capital without relying on traditional intermediaries.

Virtual wallets, digital currencies and decentralized finance (DeFi) platforms can enable individuals with limited access to traditional banking systems to engage in financial activities, access credit, make transactions and build financial resilience, but maybe the expansion of digital wallet and extending financial digital identity frameworks to include credentials which are more aligned to developing countries are the most important. Wallets are expanding and can be easily downloaded to a mobile phone without the need for a traditional bank account. Some wallets are also able to operate across the crypto currency and traditional finance worlds, making them more flexible to use with wider access. Increasing the use of digital wallets could be therefore key to improving financial inclusion.

Building trust in digital transactions and safeguarding user data and assets are critical challenges that must be addressed to enable widespread financial inclusion in the metaverse.

Can the metaverse make local communities global?

The metaverse has the power to bring together people from diverse backgrounds, cultures and abilities. By creating an inclusive environment, it allows individuals to connect, share ideas and learn from one another.

Meaningful and safe experiences in the metaverse ensure that everyone, regardless of their race, gender, age or physical abilities, can actively participate and contribute without facing discrimination or exclusion.

Representation could be crucial and will play a vital role in shaping the metaverse. It is essential to ensure diverse representation across gender, race, ethnicity, age and ability to avoid perpetuating existing biases and stereotypes. Embracing diversity not only promotes equality but also enriches the metaverse by reflecting the real-world populations it serves. The concept of participatory design emphasizes involving diverse stakeholders, including marginalized communities, in the design and decision-making processes of technological systems. In the metaverse, this requires actively engaging individuals from different backgrounds, considering their needs and perspectives, and empowering them to shape the metaverse's structures, rules and governance.

Can the metaverse create safe space environments for social equality?

Just as in the physical world, emotional well-being is paramount in the metaverse. Providing meaningful experiences that foster positive emotions, personal growth and social connections can have a significant impact on the mental health and overall well-being of individuals. A safe environment free from harassment, abuse or toxic behaviour ensures that users feel respected, supported and comfortable while engaging in the metaverse.

Establishing clear and well-defined community guidelines is essential for setting behavioural expectations within the metaverse. Clearly communicating and enforcing these guidelines helps create a culture of respect and sets the tone for positive interactions. The use of reporting mechanisms and appropriate follow-up and action taken to address instances of antisocial behaviour ensures a safer environment for all users.

By treating antisocial behaviour seriously, implementing measures to address it and fostering a culture of respect and responsibility, the metaverse can become a safer and more inclusive space. Just as in the physical world, it is essential to create an environment where individuals feel protected, supported and empowered to fully enjoy the potential of the metaverse.

Is privacy and security the key to equality?

Ensuring privacy and security for users in the metaverse is crucial for fostering trust, protecting personal information and maintaining a safe environment.

Empowering users to protect themselves and maintain their safety within the metaverse is essential. By providing tools and features that allow users to block or mute individuals engaging in antisocial behaviour, control their privacy settings and manage who can interact with them, users can act with agency and take control over their virtual experiences.

Identity plays a significant role in the metaverse, shaping how individuals present themselves, interact with others and participate in virtual experiences. Users must be granted control over their own identity and what of and how their personal information is shared, and with whom.

Trusted identity systems can also help foster a sense of trust and accountability within the virtual space. For certain activities, such as virtual economies, online marketplaces or secure interactions, verifying the identity of users can enhance security and reduce fraudulent activities.

Personal data including user profile information, virtual identity, social interactions, preferences, interests and payment transactions provide valuable insight to platforms and applications to better tailor experiences, content and recommendations to individual users. Personal data protection measures are crucial to safeguard such information and prevent fraud or unauthorized access to a user's virtual assets.

It is crucial to prioritize user privacy and obtain informed consent for any data collection and usage within the metaverse. Clear privacy policies, transparent data practices and user-friendly privacy settings empower individuals to control their personal data and make informed choices about its sharing and use.

By prioritizing privacy and security measures in the design and operation of the metaverse, users can confidently engage in virtual experiences while maintaining control over their personal information. Striking the right balance between innovation and protection is key to building a trusted metaverse that respects user privacy and ensures a secure environment for all participants.

What are the key challenges to metaverse equality?

The top five challenges in building an equitable metaverse can be summarized as follows:

1 Access and connectivity: Ensuring equal access and connectivity to the metaverse for all individuals including addressing issues such

as the digital divide, affordability of internet access and availability of necessary devices. Bridging these gaps is crucial to prevent further exacerbation of existing inequalities.

2 Digital skills and literacy: Building an equitable metaverse requires addressing the disparity in digital skills and literacy. Providing opportunities for individuals to acquire the necessary skills to navigate and participate in the virtual world is essential. Accessible training programmes, educational resources and support for digital literacy initiatives can help overcome this challenge.

3 Inclusive design and representation: Designing the metaverse in an inclusive manner is crucial to ensure that diverse voices, experiences and identities are represented. It is essential to consider accessibility features for individuals with disabilities, avoid biases in algorithms and AI systems, and promote diverse cultural representation.

4 Privacy and security: Protecting personal data, ensuring user safety and preventing unauthorized access or abuse require robust security measures. Striking the right balance between protecting user privacy and providing a safe environment is crucial for building trust and promoting equitable participation.

5 Ethical and legal frameworks: Developing guidelines and regulations that promote fairness, accountability and responsible behaviour is crucial to prevent the metaverse from becoming a space where exploitation or discrimination can occur.

6 The speed at which developing countries can get their data included in AI models and have greater representation in the development of the underlying technology components. Without progress in these areas, there is the danger that opportunities associated with AI will not apply to developing countries and their citizens, and there will be biases inherent in the outputs.

Addressing these challenges requires collaboration among various stakeholders, including technology companies, policymakers, community organizations and users themselves. By working together to overcome these obstacles, it is possible to build a metaverse that fosters equity, inclusivity and ensures that everyone can fully participate and benefit from its opportunities.

How do we take the first steps towards an equitable metaverse?

By embracing the following emerging recommendations and fostering collaboration among stakeholders, we can build an equitable metaverse that promotes equal access, representation and participation for all, fostering a virtual world that reflects the values of inclusivity, fairness and respect.

Prioritize inclusive design principles to ensure accessibility and usability for all users, regardless of their abilities or technical expertise.

Promote diverse representation within the metaverse by actively supporting the participation of underrepresented groups to design experiences, define rules of conduct and establish inclusive governance structures.

Give users control over their personal data, privacy settings and virtual identities by providing transparent information about data practices, obtaining informed consent and prioritizing user autonomy.

Establish robust systems to prevent harassment, hate speech and inappropriate behaviour within the metaverse. Encourage reporting mechanisms and enforce clear guidelines and consequences for violations.

Foster collaboration among platform developers, policymakers, community organizations and users to shape the development of the metaverse. Engage in ongoing dialogue and solicit feedback to ensure diverse perspectives are considered.

These recommendations provide a foundation for building an equitable metaverse that promotes accessibility, representation, user empowerment, safety and collaboration. By implementing these principles, we can work towards creating a metaverse that embraces diversity and inclusion, enabling all individuals to participate and benefit equally from virtual experiences.

There is an opportunity to shape a metaverse that fosters positive change and paves the way for a more equitable digital future. The question is whether we can detach the metaverse and AI developments from some of the factors that have been blocking improvements in equality to date. To do this may be minimizing central intermediaries and automating decisions can be the answer. However, if this is the case, could Web3 be the key?

Notes

1 World Bank (2018) Nearly half the world lives on less than $5.50 a day, www.worldbank.org/en/news/press-release/2018/10/17/nearly-half-the-world-lives-on-less-than-550-a-day (archived at https://perma.cc/E7VL-64CQ)

2 United Nations (2021) ITU: 2.9 billion people still offline, www.un.org/en/delegate/itu-29-billion-people-still-offline (archived at https://perma.cc/B4HK-H2T5)

05

The metaverse transformation and new immersive revolution

Some argue that the history of modern business can be traced back over 3,000 years to India and China, and, as we explored in Chapter 1, since then we have witnessed many revolutions in business, with the internet, mobile phones, platform business models, and more recently the creator economy business model based on platforms and content creation. As we have explored in previous chapters, the metaverse has the power to fundamentally change the way people, businesses, AI and governments operate and interact with each other. However, there remain questions as to what extent the incorporation of immersive and virtual world capabilities that can remove geography and travel time, replace physical activities with virtual removing scarcity and embed AI capabilities can fundamentally transform business models from where we are now?

Despite the progress made so far to digitize processes, there remains paper documentation in many processes which result in hybrid business models with are based on paper document and digitized solutions. For example many ordering customer experiences require physical documents to be presented to prove identity. The metaverse has the potential to bring in fully digital business models and experiences as paper will not work at scale across virtual worlds and this could also help us drive more automation and reduce friction in existing business models. In this chapter we will explore the business transformation potential of the metaverse and the areas that have the most potential for disruption.

The components for transformation – the 4Cs of the metaverse

The metaverse can be broken down into four key capabilities – 1) Communicate, 2) Commerce, 3) Community and 4) Content – which are required to support the metaverse and must reach maturity to realize the full vision of the metaverse transformation; see Figure 5.1.

The components for transformation – metaverse interoperability

Interoperability provides capabilities for travel between different metaverse. It's needed for systems, devices, software, applications, and the overlaying virtual worlds and associated ecosystems to

FIGURE 5.1 The 4Cs supporting the metaverse transformation

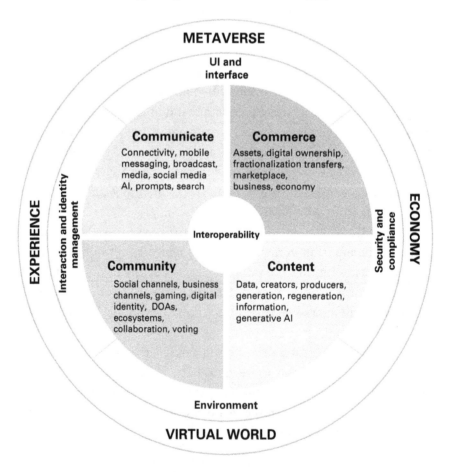

communicate, exchange data and work together effectively across each other for a borderless and joined up metaverse experience for users. For this to happen, the diverse systems and/or components need to be able to interact and operate together and share data seamlessly. However, this is difficult to retro fit and often requires standardized protocols, formats and interfaces to be developed early in the life cycle of each component.

Interoperability has been important to the growth and standardization of mobile telecommunications. For this sector, interoperability between communications service providers (CSPs) enables mobile networks to connect and communicate with each other seamlessly, something we experience when we travel and roam on other networks without any configuration to make calls, send messages and access services across various providers. This is all made possible because mobile networks have common standards and protocols which are interoperable.

The metaverse seems to be developing as many different virtual worlds. To bring them together and realize the opportunity that the metaverse offers, standardization of protocol and interoperability across virtual worlds will be key.

Interoperability is central to the metaverse providing capabilities for citizens of the metaverse to move across borders with their identity and assets. However, to bring standardization, it is important to understand what they will be moving across and the associated protocols and standardization that will be needed for interoperability. In Figure 5.1 we describe the 4Cs of the metaverse – Communicate, Commerce, Community and Content – which form the requirements for interoperability so that users can seamlessly navigate across them, and the virtual worlds built on them.

The components for transformation – metaverse communication

The ability to connect to the metaverse and communicate within it will be key to development and adoption. We saw in the evolution of the internet that faster mobile connectivity has been crucial to growth and adoption, enabling users to access online services and information at greater speed and convenience from a variety of devices including smartphones and IoT devices. Faster mobile connectivity has enabled new features, services and businesses to be launched including streaming, sharing economy platforms, social media, super applications and IoT models. Overall, this has accelerated the adoption of the internet and extended its reach to most sectors of the economy.

The metaverse will present new opportunities, but also new challenges for Communication Service Providers (CSPs) and others in the communications value chain. The most obvious change will be that the demands for data, content and immersive activity will translate to more demands for bandwidth. Although initial advances in the metaverse have been in gaming where the location point for interaction has largely been from the home, the future of the metaverse must incorporate mobile devices and the high bandwidth low-latency connectivity and communications solutions to support this. We will explore connectivity in the metaverse further in Chapter 8, but we provide a brief overview of the communication paths in Figure 5.2.

FIGURE 5.2 Making a call in the metaverse

Making a call in the metaverse

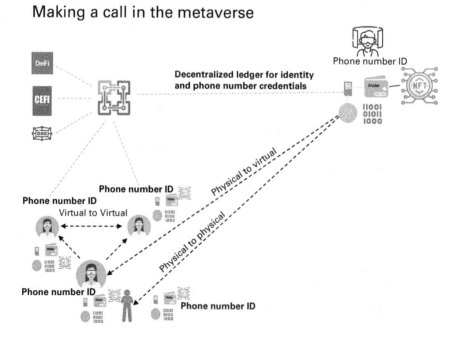

With over 90 per cent of the population owning a mobile phone, this will be key to accessing the metaverse at scale, and we expect more data to be generated and consumed as a result. However, the way we communicate may evolve from mobile phones to connected XR headsets, meaning that the device we use to access metaverse platforms will ultimately transition to headsets and force the innovation required to merge connectivity into XR headset, and make headsets more portable and mobile.

There are already several factors driving a rethink of communication including social media messaging; over-the-top (OTT) communications which delivers communication services over the internet; Decentralized Public Infrastructure Networks (DePINs) which enable mesh connectivity networks where each device serves as a node, relaying data to other devices, forming a peer-to-peer and decentralized communications, and 5G which provides fast low-latency mobile communications. But considering all of these drivers for change, what impact will the metaverse have on the communications industry?

There are two key areas of potential metaverse impacts on communications:

- Inter-metaverse communications including hologram calling. Here the metaverse will demand new features including new virtual environments, group and collaboration features, automated authentication and security, and shared calling experiences, where all parties in a call have a persistent, consistent shared experience. For example, this could be a social location, work environment or even an entertainment event like a concert.
- Digital identity credentials embedded in the communications infrastructure and experiences to lower the risk of fraud and deep fake.

Overall, being able to access virtual worlds in a fast seamless way whether at your home, business premises or on the move will be critical to the metaverse and require metaverse communications to incorporate new levels of fast, low-latency connectivity, mobile messaging, broadcast, media, with the incorporation of AI to support the experiences.

The components for transformation – metaverse commerce

The economic and business models of the metaverse have the potential to change and evolve from the current position and introduce new business streams, more markets, and bring together user and customer ecosystems. However, will the metaverse lead to a revolution for commerce or an evolution?

Much of the work to evolve the financial systems has already begun with the emergence and advancements in fintech and the Web3 token economy and DeFi, which are serving to expand the reach of embedded and contextual finance and change the ways in which digital assets can be owned, transferred, invested, exchanged and moved across platforms and ecosystems. Some of the questions commonly asked on this include how much more development will be needed to these solutions to meet the new commerce and finance demands of the metaverse?

Traditional business models are about producing goods or services through a structured and hierarchical approach. Customers play a pivotal role by purchasing products or services, but their involvement is often limited to transactional aspects. Feedback and engagement with customers may be limited, with decisions primarily driven by the company's internal processes and strategies rather than direct customer input.

FIGURE 5.3 Metaverse commerce

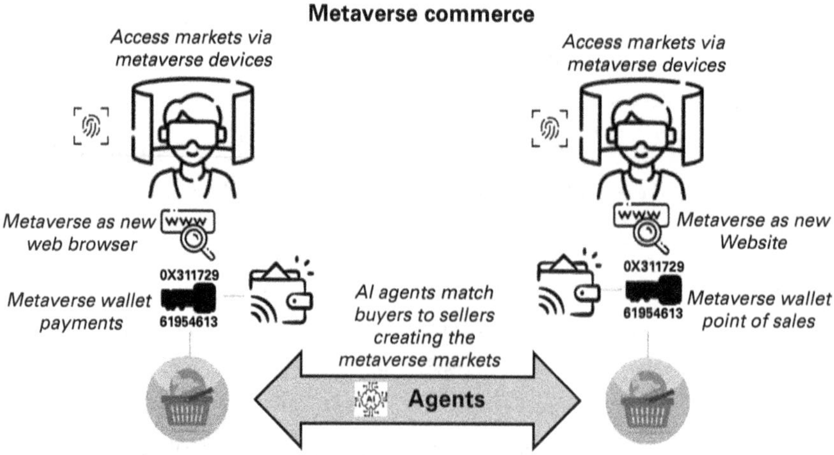

The recent platform business models revolve around facilitating interactions between users, connecting buyers and sellers or providers and consumers. Customers are not only consumers but also contribute as suppliers, creating a network effect. Data plays a crucial role by capturing user behaviour and preferences, enabling personalized experiences, targeted advertising and continuous improvement of the platform's value proposition, fostering user engagement and loyalty.

Web3 business models by contrast are based on decentralization of operation and ownership and control with users owning and controlling their data. In these models customers and users play an active role as participants and contributors to the network and engage in peer-to-peer transactions. Data and transactions are securely stored on the blockchain and associated layer 2 platforms. If the metaverse will incorporate Web3 capabilities how can this shape metaverse commerce?

As shown in Figure 5.3, commerce will either be user initiated proactively by AI-driven or by users. Therefore the metaverse commerce experience will become increasingly embedded, personalized and linked to a person's digital identity and data. All of this will become part of payments solutions, with users having the option to monetize their data in transactions. Wallets, smarts contracts and fintech can also be used to access commerce and further automate experiences.

In this model the web browser, mobile phone and applications are replaced by XR devices and AI assistants which embed these solutions in digital commerce solutions. Ownership of digital assets can be paired with physical assets or be completely digital.

Physical storefronts can be accessed normally, and for some goods the experiences can include XR in store and NFT gamification.

As well as physical and online stores, metaverse commerce will increasingly be embedded in social media and super applications, which incorporate immersive technologies, interoperability, portability of assets and AI.

The Apple and Meta approaches to the metaverse indicate there are three streams:

- Decentralized commerce – participation is based on tokens for ownership, utility and community. Examples include Decentraland and Sandbox.

- Immersive use cases and content – metaverse immersive layer is used to access and enable commerce associated with content, user applications and business solutions. The Apple example is integrating their Vision Pro headset with current applications and film content

- Social media– metaverse commerce is embedded in social media user journeys and community interactions. The main example here is Meta.

While the story of metaverse commerce is still evolving, a 2023 study by McKinsey found that '15 percent of company revenue will come from the metaverse in the coming years and 60 percent of consumers already using the metaverse prefer an immersive activity to a physical-world alternative',[1] and we expect the models for metaverse commerce to accelerate and evolve as the technology matures and adoption increases.

The components for transformation – metaverse and community

The history of human communities spans thousands of years, evolving from small tribes to large civilizations. The advent of the internet in the 1990s ushered in Web 2.0, enabling online social interactions and the formation of virtual communities. The rise of mobile phones in the early 2000s further expanded connectivity, allowing people to engage with communities anytime, from most locations globally. These technological advancements revolutionized community communications, breaking down geographical barriers and enabling global connections that were previously not possible. There have been significant impacts on the ways we form and interact within human communities which have more recently given rise to online communities on social media platforms. The platform model is now extending from messaging and sharing content to incorporate collaboration and generation of content, adding new creator dimensions to digital communities.

The digital factors may be increasing the role of communities online– over 4 billion people (more than 50 per cent of the world's population) belong to a social media platform, and these platforms have been successful in bringing people together around shared interests. More recently the role of digital communities has been extended to encompass user-generated content and provide enhanced user experiences, but what is the role and importance of community in the metaverse?

Business customers can be described as communities and when customers' interactions are on digital platforms these customers are targeted to engage more with the brand. Think also about universities, gyms and workplaces as communities; however, when considering these types of physical communities can they be transformed to the metaverse?

The metaverse can drive the next evolution of social connection, with the potential to take digital communities to the next level, with the incorporation of AI for personalized community experiences, removing geography and improving communication options. The output of this could serve to redefine consumer relationships and the community role in platform business models.

Some of the potential benefits of metaverse communities to businesses include:

- Direct access to customers, providing businesses with the ability to directly engage with customers and potential customers, and personalization of services. Interoperability could further provide the opportunity to do this across different virtual worlds and ecosystems.

- Reduced costs as communities can organize to provide peer-to-peer sales and promotion channels. At the same time, the success of platforms is typically measured by the size of their user bases and communities.

- Forums, marketplaces and rewards for content and data.

- Community loyalty which can extend beyond the scale and benefits of customer loyalty schemes through relationships with whole digital communities. This could reduce individual engagement efforts and introduce new economies of scale.

Is self-sovereign digital identity (SSI) key to the evolution of metaverse communities?

Communities have evolved over time to a point where they are now integral to the business and platform models of internet, social media and shared economy models. There have been a lot of questions as to how the metaverse could approach community, and the key could be in SSI and the ability of the metaverse to incorporate this into community models. For example, an education, job role or hobby that forms part of a user's digital identity could be used by AI to proactively suggest suitable communities. Web3 could then automate community management using the same smart contracts and Web3 tools as DAOs.

Ultimately the community layer of the metaverse can bring people closer together and ultimately enable communities to be more diverse.

SSI Communities will be a 'new customer growth channel' for business and enterprise. To optimize scalable customer engagement in the future, businesses will need to engage communities and do this through the metaverse. This could also include the management of internal communities, for example the metaverse can also help a business to connect their global divisions and workforces; see Table 5.1.

TABLE 5.1 Metaverse community functions and benefits

Function	Differences with metaverse
Connection and networking	Remove geography for more realistic meetings, with Web3 interactions can verification can be automated with decentralized identity and verifiable credentials. Interoperability.
Customer base and business market	Remove geography, community becomes the customer base and market, direct relationship with customers possible through Web3 digital identity and immersive metaverse communities, interoperability.

(continued)

TABLE 5.1 (Continued)

Function	Differences with metaverse
Share risk, insurance	More data generated from the consumer and industrial metaverses to feed into risk models. Self-funding and organized insurance models possible with metaverse and Web3. Specific metaverse insurance and risk products.
Decide on issues, advocacy and influence, manage organization	Remove geography, more immersive forums for people to organize themselves into communities, secure and automated voting and governance using Web3 digital identity and smart contracts.
Collaborate and innovate, knowledge and resource sharing	Remove geography, immersive collaboration forums, more possibilities to collaborate using immersive technologies on complex tasks previously only possible in a physical setting. Provenance of innovation activity with Web3.
Social and shared interests, social media	Remove geography, more immersive social and shared environments, interoperability between platforms, with Web3 self-sovereign control of identity credentials and data by users.
Crowd funding, DeFi and community-based financing	Metaverse communities combined with Web3 could support community-based financing of metaverse real estate and other assets. Decentralized finance through DAO financial institutions with Web3.
Data generation and feedback	More data related to users and their associated communities will be generated in the metaverse. With web digital identity, wallets and tokens the ability for users to sell data, and ensure personal data can be distinguished from AI-generated data when fed into AI learning models.

While communities have become important and integral to modern platforms, they can be seen as part of the DNA of the metaverse and at the centre of the associated social and business activities and the economic models. With AI, the explosion in data, the tools are in place to build dynamic, self-forming, flexible communities in the metaverse. However, there are questions as to whether communities can exist and flourish solely in the virtual world without a physical dimension. In the short term, the convergence of virtual and physical communities may be required; however, in the longer term the virtual metaverse is expected to be a key driver.

The components for transformation – metaverse and content

The consumption and generation of content can be seen as the life-blood of the shared metaverse and can be expected to build on the creator economies that have development in the current platform economies.

The metaverse XR will empower creators to develop more creative, interactive and immersive content. However, the introduction of AI to this will introduce greater levels of tooling and with it more intelligent content at greater scale and consistency. Some of the recent developments in AI include tools to generate video using text-to-video interfaces, and there are already developments to enable voice prompts. In the metaverse we expect that creators will work along-side AI-assisted tools for video editing, animation and even music creation to lower barriers and costs associated with content creation and improve the speed and quality

There are different types of content, including community-driven, personalized, customizable, democratic and collaborative, and we expect that AI tooling will impact all of them. One example is Meta's Polar which provides creators with features to design and distribute AR effects and filters seamlessly, without the need for coding, and the Presence Platform, which incorporates AI capabilities, enabling users to construct mixed reality experiences that seamlessly blend virtual content with the physical world. Additional tools include Promethean AI which helps creators to construct virtual worlds.

Creators who grasp the transformative potential of the metaverse will flourish by honing their craft, forging strong bonds with audiences, creating interactive and immersive content, and embracing the latest AI capabilities.

The metaverse has the potential to extend the boundaries of opportunity for creators by significantly disrupting the way creators generate content, and their ability to collaborate securely on the content creator journey and interact with content consumers. The creators that win as the metaverse develops will be the ones that understand how to maximize the AI tooling, and combine this most effectively with their creative skills, knowledge and capabilities.

In this content creation life cycle, the metaverse provides the canvass, professionals in the industry provide the direction and skill sets, but AI will be heavily involved in the content.

Can the metaverse impact the new interaction point and be the key to transformation?

The 4Cs of the metaverse support the four core capabilities 1) UI and interface, 2), Interaction and identity management 3) Security and compliance and 4) Environment, which we describe in the following sections.

1 **UI interface** (UI) for the metaverse will need to evolve significantly and we anticipate a shift towards more immersive, intuitive and seamless UI that integrate virtual and physical experiences. Gestural and voice-based interactions, haptic feedback and advanced XR technologies will also enhance user engagement. Additionally, AI-driven personalization and context-aware interfaces will enable UI to dynamically adapt to users' needs. The UI is also an important factor in how brands will utilize 3D designs in the metaverse, where they will no longer just 'see' the internet on computer monitors, but rather experience it through XR with 3D navigation to spaces like shops and corporate offices.

But could the metaverse force a fundamental rethink of how we interface with applications, services, content, businesses and governments?

One factor suggesting a fundamental rethink is the direction that current UI technologies are moving. XR headsets are converging with mobile phones, and when we consider SSI, digital wallets, AI agents along with natural language translation, could the metaverse UI be our voice, thoughts and hand gestures?

2 **Interaction and identity** are key to the metaverse and covers social media, social networking, business networking, collaboration, shared economy models and virtual businesses as well as peer-to-peer messaging and in some cases this could be linked with embedded payments. The ultimate

goals of interactions can be social or to create value and there has been focus on early consumer and industrial metaverse platforms on collaboration.

Interactions in the real world can be planned, unplanned, part of a group or peer to peer. In the metaverse, as well as providing more immersive experiences, there is the opportunity for Web3 to provide more peer-to-peer tools for interaction and for AI to drive these interactions, including business interactions for virtual business.

Gaming has led the way for metaverse user interactions, and the messaging and interactions have now extended to incorporate non-player characters (NPCs). From the other angle social media, messaging platforms and community forums have led the way in Web2 for interactions. It is logical for these to extend to the metaverse, adding new immersive features and potentially bringing significant adoption.

3 Security – As the metaverse develops there will be security and privacy concerns that will be key to adoption and trust. The lack of regulation has led to some uncertainty. One example of a potential threat from fraud in the metaverse is the use of different personas and avatars by one person. This creates the potential for a security risk and places emphasis on SSI and other security authentications solutions to manage these risks.

The metaverse will have to overcome its own unique challenges regarding identity and authentication, meaning that verification systems will also have to evolve; there are three main factors to cybersecurity in the metaverse which should be considered: 1) the cybersecurity of the hosting platform, 2) the cybersecurity of the property and 3) the cybersecurity of the users of the property. Some of the best practices for protecting against cyber-attacks in the metaverse centre on authentication solutions including encryption, 2FA, updating security and protocols and digital identity and the associated cryptographic authentication.

Environments are at the core of the metaverse proposition as the metaverse will excel at creating them and they are places where users will interact with metaverse ecosystems. There will also need to be environments to support specific metaverse applications. These immersive and diverse digital landscapes set the stage for social inter-actions, entertainment, commerce and collaborative experiences. Well-designed environments can evoke emotions, stimulate creativity and foster a sense of belonging, contributing to the overall engage-ment and success of the metaverse.

What is the role of ecosystems in metaverse-led transformation?

The metaverse has the potential to bring together the ecosystems of physical and virtual worlds. This could include consumers, busi-nesses, platforms, banks, financial institutions and fintech, and technology as well as the government and the public sector in new ways. Where peer-to-peer features are incorporated there is also the potential to remove layers of market markers, and fundamentally transform the ways in which people, businesses, machines and AI interact and carry out business.

Could the new metaverse ecosystems be the catalyst for new auto-mation in business processes, platform operations and customer experience?

The role of complementors have been key to platform growth and it can be argued that the successful growth of the largest digital plat-form ecosystems has been based on the contributions of complementors and the incentives that the platforms have provided to them. There has been some overlap with the emergence of the crea-tor economy which has expanded the traditional scope of complementors to encompass scenarios where users and customers can also be complementors. So, what is the role of complementors in the metaverse ecosystem and how does this differ to their role in plat-forms?

- In the context of a platform ecosystem, a complementor is an actor that creates a product, service or component that enhances or adds value to the platform. Complements are often created by third-party developers or businesses that integrate their offerings with the platform, extending its functionality, attracting users and driving engagement.

- The complementor role varies depending on the type of platform, industry and platform business model. With the social media platform ecosystem, users are content creators and consume content, and engage directly with each other, while developers create the applications and toolsets across different access devices and operating systems as complementors. In the sales e-commerce digital ecosystem, users can be either buyers or sellers, and in some cases both, and complementors provide third-party sales sometimes through over-the-top (OTT) application development, supply chain and logistics including last-mile delivery or payment processing.

- Complementors bring scope, scale and value propositions to the products and services associated with the platform and they can manage complex customer needs in response to market challenges. The right incentive models for complementors are important as they act as autonomous actors who invest time and resources only where it helps the value proposition and to capture value. Complementor activities often focus on the development of applications but also include collaboration across complementors, sales and business and user-acceptance testing.

- Within the context of the platform and wider metaverse ecosystems, innovation by actors like complementors who have historically been important to driving the resilience and response through knowledge sharing and rapid application development, will be key.

Could the role of AI as complementor in the metaverse be the key to transformation at scale?

As we move from platform ecosystems to metaverse ecosystems could AI provide toolsets to make the role of complementors more automated and productive? Taking this further in the metaverse could AI perform the complementor role in the future?

Recent developments in generative AI suggest that in the short to medium terms, some of the complementor functions could be performed by AI.

FIGURE 5.4 Metaverse ecosystem

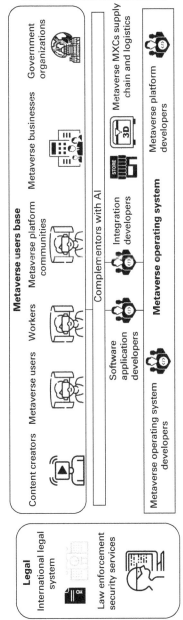

Metaverse ecosystem

In the future, users and other ecosystem actors may interact with metaverse AI complementors as a matter of course, which will execute the role based on self-learning algorithms through metaverse-based environments and experiences. Key to this will be the ability of the metaverse ecosystem to aggregate and interoperate across virtual, physical and hybrid users (See Figure 5.4).

The metaverse operating system is at the centre of the ecosystem acting as a foundation for interactions between technology and infrastructure providers including Web2, Web3 platforms, metaverse connectivity service providers, metaverse OEMs, cloud and infrastructure provides including hyperscalers, and the cyber security community. The metaverse operating system will provide incentives for these service providers to use the operating system and bring with them their customer demand, market access and financial opportunities.

Developers will build on the metaverse operating system to ensure core capabilities, toolsets and integration components are in place.

Between the operating system and complementors integration developers will ensure alignment with existing platforms to create incentives for complementors to build applications for users. This is a critical area of the ecosystem and key for metaverse adoption, with 77 per cent of internet users (3.59 billion people) actively using at least one of the Meta platforms and around 5 billion of them using social media platforms, as of 2023. The ability to ensure continued 'fit' for these platforms on the metaverse operating system becomes a key performance indicator and critical success factor.

The financial and legal components of the ecosystem include extension of the current legal system's extension to cover metaverse activity, and incorporation of law enforcement, banks and financial institutions in metaverse platforms and experiences.

Has the metaverse already begun to transform the ways in which ecosystems operate?

The metaverse is growing fast with several brands entering and establishing a presence, and we expect this trend to continue. At

the same time new companies will be formed specifically to operate in the metaverse with a key area of growth initially being in
the retail and infrastructure space. Eventually, these new companies will be involved in value creation with the number of
complementors increasing significantly.

The metaverse has the potential to bridge the gap between
consumers and brands in a more dynamic way across physical and
online experiences and in turn provide more opportunities for
brand interaction. This will enable brands to build deeper more
productive relationships with consumers and more importantly
contextualize the product and use it to consumer preferences. For
example, if a customer wants to listen to music on the beach or a
have a cocktail at a rooftop city bar, the metaverse can provide
brands with the relationship with the customer, but also data to
tailor their experiences to the consumers, virtual environment of
choice.

While the metaverse has been around in some form for a while,
household brands are now entering it in the expectation that the
opportunity could bring significant global value creation, competitive advantage and new touch points with consumers over the
next decade. Key to adoption will be how brands manage to
combine the metaverse with other consumer channels for the
benefit of their value propositions.

Can the metaverse ecosystem operations extend transformation to enterprise and business?

With so many businesses entering the metaverse there is still limited
business activity. The industrial metaverse is advanced and focuses on
the optimization of industrial and manufacturing production
processes, operations and maintenance using virtual immersive technologies, digital twins, collaboration tools and AI. Industrial
metaverse applications include predictive maintenance, online manufacturing simulation and digital twin virtual representations of
physical things (See Figure 5.5).

FIGURE 5.5 The enterprise, business and industrial metaverse ecosystems

Enterprise and business metaverse ecosystem

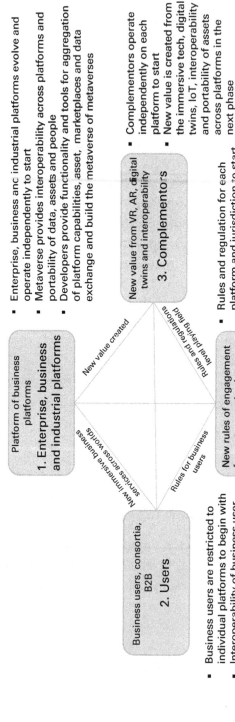

Platform of business platforms

1. Enterprise, business and industrial platforms

- Enterprise, business and industrial platforms evolve and operate independently to start
- Metaverse provides interoperability across platforms and portability of data, assets and people
- Developers provide functionality and tools for aggregation of platform capabilities, asset, marketplaces and data exchange and build the metaverse of metaverses

New value from VR, AR, digital twins and interoperability

3. Complementors

- Complementors operate independently on each platform to start
- New value is created from the immersive tech, digital twins, IoT, interoperability and portability of assets across platforms in the next phase

New value created

Rules and regulations level playing field

New immersive business services across worlds

Rules for business users

Business users, consortia, B2B

2. Users

- Business users are restricted to individual platforms to begin with
- Interoperability of business user journey across platforms
- Value propositions incorporating cross-platform journeys, experiences and capabilities

New rules of engagement for metaverse businesses

4. Governance

- Rules and regulation for each platform and jurisdiction to start
- Specific metaverse rules and regulation needed for metaverse
- Issues on trademarks, geographic tariffs and regulations are resolved, with specific metaverse governance

Digital twins technology can be used to create digital representations of production plants, heavy machinery which collects data from the physical counterpart which can then be simulated across different scenarios. Some manufacturers are already using digital twins to build virtual representations of factories, machinery and products in metaverse virtual environments.

The music industry is an example of an industry that has gone through major change in the ways in which its product is made, distributed and consumed. The metaverse has the potential to add immersive environments and moods to music, but with Web3 and AI it could go much further. The music video in the 1980s was a key step to evolve simply listening to music to watching and listening, and the music video format has remained largely intact to today, but what impact can the metaverse have?

The ability to bring immersive and sensory technology to music consumers, and combine this with AI to produce music, build communities as a customer base, and use metaverse platforms as a channel, and Web3 for trust and monetization has the potential to reshape the music business model for consumers; see Figure 5.6.

Are digital twins, IoT, Web3 and AI the keys to transforming manufacturing?

Digital twins are virtual representations of physical real-world objects, processes or systems across their life cycle. They are updated

FIGURE 5.6 New metaverse business model for music consumers

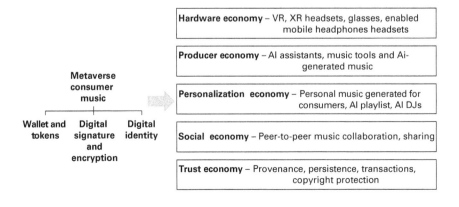

with real-time data from the physical counterpart. Digital twins have been used to model factories, product lines, machinery performance and resilience, product life cycles and even entire supply chains. However, the key difference with online simulations is the link to the physical counterpart real-time data. But do digital twins work?

IoT sensors related to the areas of functionality are fitted to the physical objects that the digital twins are being created from, and these sensors then produce data about the device and performance. The data is transmitted in real time to the digital twin solution to ensure real-time data updates to the virtual model which can be used to run simulations, analyse and model performance issues and improvements. Where the right outcome is modelled using the digital twin it can then be applied to the physical object, system or process. But what role can the metaverse play?

The metaverse operating system can provide more accessible VR, MR and 3D technologies to physical model physical objects, and support the incorporation of IoT. AI and Web3 will provide the tools for the convergence of wider data sets and validations with digital twin data. It will also provide a decentralized system of record as a basis for trusted collaborations within and across industries. This has the potential not only to scale digital twins for mass industry adoption, but also provide the foundations for secure, trusted cross-industry collaboration and a new high volume digital twin economy; see Figure 5.7.

FIGURE 5.7 Digital twins, AI and the metaverse

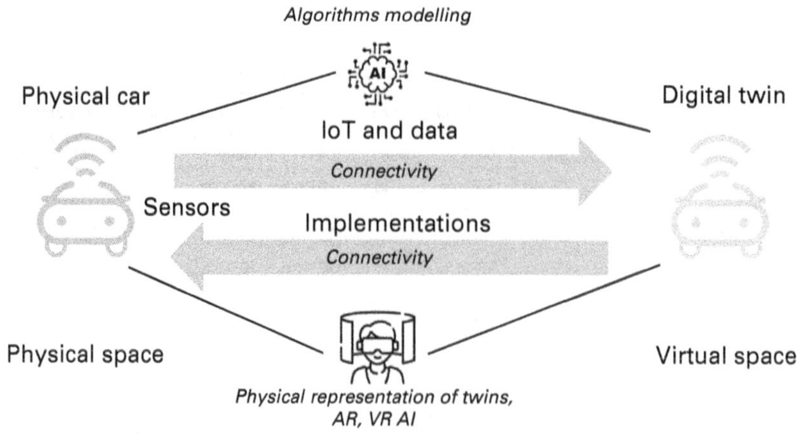

Algorithms modelling

Physical car

Digital twin

IoT and data

Connectivity

Sensors

Implementations

Connectivity

Physical space

Virtual space

Physical representation of twins,
AR, VR AI

Unlike simulations, digital twins are designed around a two-way flow which includes data from sensors on the device which flow to the digital twin solution, and then data from the model which flows back to the physical device and associated processes. This enables organizations to monitor and design assets in different scenarios and conditions in real time as part of industrial development processes, and experiment with changes to them. For example, new products can be prototyped, and manufacturers can model the impacts of use and predict when servicing and parts will be required. The metaverse provides the tools to experience the changes in different realistic environments before physical implementation.

Historically, digital twin solutions have been expensive; however, the explosion of AI, IoT, 5G and XR technologies which are expected to drive down costs. Adoption is growing fast, especially in retail, healthcare, construction and manufacturing. However, will IoT, Web3 and AI solutions impact digital twins?

Web3 provides trust, interoperable digital identities, wallets and smart contracts. It provides the digital toolset for IoT devices to automatically transact and monetize their data. This could be the key to unlocking cross-industry collaboration on digital twins, where devices from different owners and ecosystems within and across industries and value chains can share data to power new digital twin models, and which forms a new metaverse of things economy to support the monetization of data. This is the basis of the Pairpoint platform that I co-founded with Vodafone. It uses IoT to provide connectivity to IoT devices and Web3 to enable them with wallets and digital identities so that they can interoperate and transact with each other. STL partners recently forecast that by 2030 over 3 billion IoT devices will be transacting with each other, and this rate of transaction is expected to grow significantly. The metaverse of things has the potential to provide operating system capabilities for developers to combine digital twins with IoT, Web3 and AI to provide new digital twin-based industrial metaverse and enterprise solutions.

Why is the industrial metaverse important to business transformation?

The metaverse as a new industrial operating system will allow companies to combine technologies in a contextual way and link them across the value chain in ways that have previously not been possible. In addition, the potential to incorporate Web3 digital identities, wallets, combined with AI and open-source systems, with metaverse digital twins, VR and environment simulation could potentially fundamentally re-design of industrial processes with new levels of automation and the removal geographic boundaries. Digital twins are one of the most promising applications of the early industrial metaverse, and they are at the level of maturity for inclusion in production-level industrial processes. They are already helping businesses to improve processes, optimize operations and gain competitive advantage, but the industrial metaverse has the potential to help industry to extend digital twin solutions to include a greater level of immersive technologies and contextual environments. It has the potential to complement digital twins, and as an operating system the industrial metaverse could potentially quickly combine AI, Web3 and IoT with other industry solutions and applications to take the automation boundary further on the path towards Industry 5.0.

Closer exploration of the industrial metaverse technologies indicates that many of them align to the Industry 4.0; however, the metaverse enables the extension of Industry 4.0 to encompass people, business and machines as well as technologies providing the basis for disruptive solutions in industry. The metaverse and its ability to put people and AI at the forefront of industrial processes and solutions with digital twins removing geographic barriers has the potential to be a significant industrial enabler.

The metaverse as an operating system will be key to making the right combination of technologies available to industries, so that they can be combined in solutions to improve automation and extend automation boundaries. One of the exciting developments for the industrial metaverse will be the introduction of AI robotic digital workers (ARDW), which has the potential to operate most processes and enable employees to shift gears and begin moving to higher value-added tasks with the metaverse as their industrial web browser and collaboration tool.

Industry 5.0 focuses on people working alongside advanced technologies including AI-powered robots to increase resilience, but with sustainability targets included in addition to the usual profit, revenue and growth, is there a role for the metaverse?

The metaverse has the potential to provide immersive and collaborative technologies for people to interact with each other and AI, creating personas and environments to contextualize these engagements. In addition, the metaverse operating system can enable these key technologies to be accessed and incorporated in industrial processes and applications. The link to Web3 technologies could be key here. As we move to more automated processes secure dynamic digital identity and authentication across people and machines will be important. The provenance and trust in outputs will be the basis for real-time collaboration which Web3 blockchains can provide.

Can the shared metaverse transform the business landscape?

The creator economy in the metaverse is the economic activity that occurs within virtual worlds and other immersive digital environments. This includes selling virtual goods, services and experiences and creating and distributing digital content such as 3D models, music and videos.

The creator economy is worth over $100 billion with over 300 million creators worldwide, according to Intelligence Insider.[2] While brand sponsorship remains the key source of revenue for creators, some are now creating their own brands and products and using their platforms and influence to push sales. Creators typically include social media influencers, videographers, bloggers and other digital creatives in the creator economic model. Creators produce content which drives engagement across platforms, and in return creators are rewarded with direct payments by the platform or through advertising, but why is the metaverse important for creators?

FIGURE 5.8 The shared metaverse enabling creators access to tools and communities

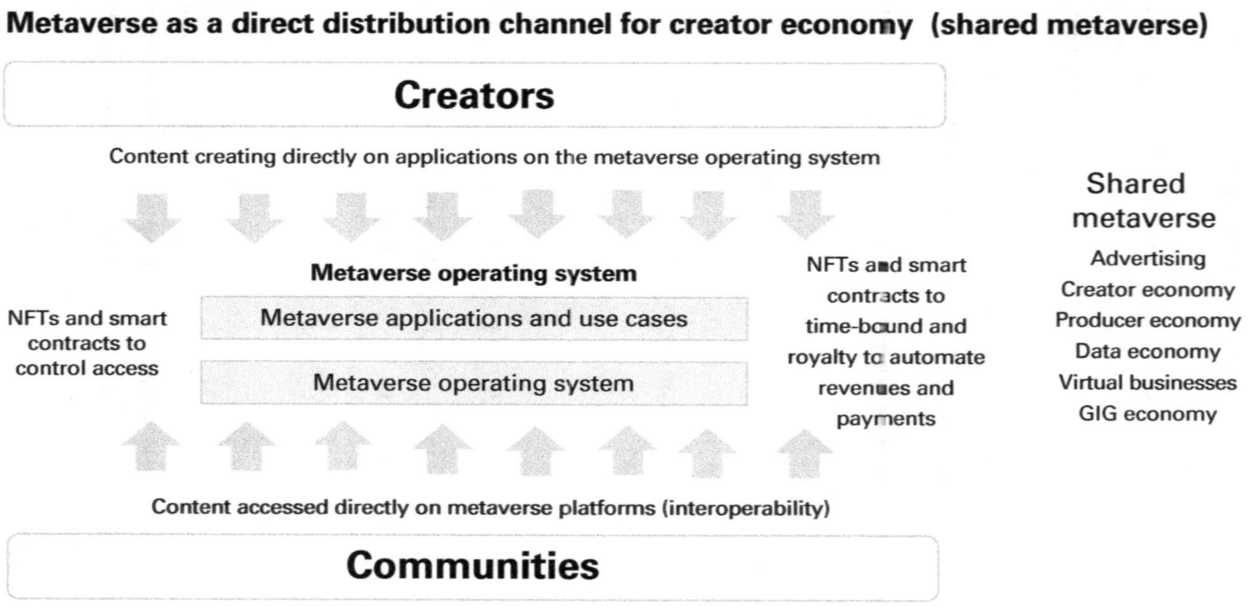

Metaverse as a direct distribution channel for creator economy (shared metaverse)

Creators

Content creating directly on applications on the metaverse operating system

Metaverse operating system

Metaverse applications and use cases

Metaverse operating system

NFTs and smart
contracts to
time-bound and
royalty to automate
revenues and
payments

NFTs and smart
contracts to
control access

Content accessed directly on metaverse platforms (interoperability)

Communities

Shared
metaverse

Advertising
Creator economy
Producer economy
Data economy
Virtual businesses
GIG economy

The metaverse has the potential to provide creators with the ability to include more immersive interactivity, and to combine more easily AI-generated content, but on platforms that include more decentralization, self-sovereignty and trustee consent, which could drive more power and opportunity to content creators. The creator economy is often associated with Web2 platforms who have used the creator content to provide the wider content on their platforms, and drive user growth and data monetization. Some of the leading platforms in this area include Facebook, YouTube, Instagram and TikTok which have developed a relatively new and diverse addition to the media and entertainment industry, which creates value around shared interests, information and beauty. However, in the metaverse the creator economy is expected to expand to include content created from the data generated from AI as well the creation of content to meet the new demand in the metaverse. As the popularity of the metaverse grows, it will reshape the creator economy into a multi-billion-dollar industry, surpassing its present market size leading to new ways to create, distribute, interact, engage and monetize creativity.

The metaverse has the potential to function as an aggregator channel for the creator economy, where creators can create their content using tools on the metaverse operating system, and then distribute through the metaverse directly to various channels linked to the metaverse. There is the possibility to include some innovations on Web3 like blockchain and NFTs, either to control access to the content or to use time-bound and royalty smart contracts with NFTs to automate control on revenues. This has the potential to grow the creator economy by making the content distribution interoperable, increase the addressable community base and remove intermediaries in distribution. But key to the creator economy is the interaction between creators and communities.

In Figure 5.8 creators can create directly on applications developed on the metaverse operating system, providing immersive technology, but also the ability to combine this with Web2, Web3 and AI. Distribution in this model can be peer to peer using Web3 platforms, direct to Web2 ecosystems or communities can access directly on metaverse application stores and embedded metaverse in super applications; interestingly Web3 smart contracts could be used to fully automate ownership, management, distribution and rewards across platforms.

FIGURE 5.9 The DAO operations model

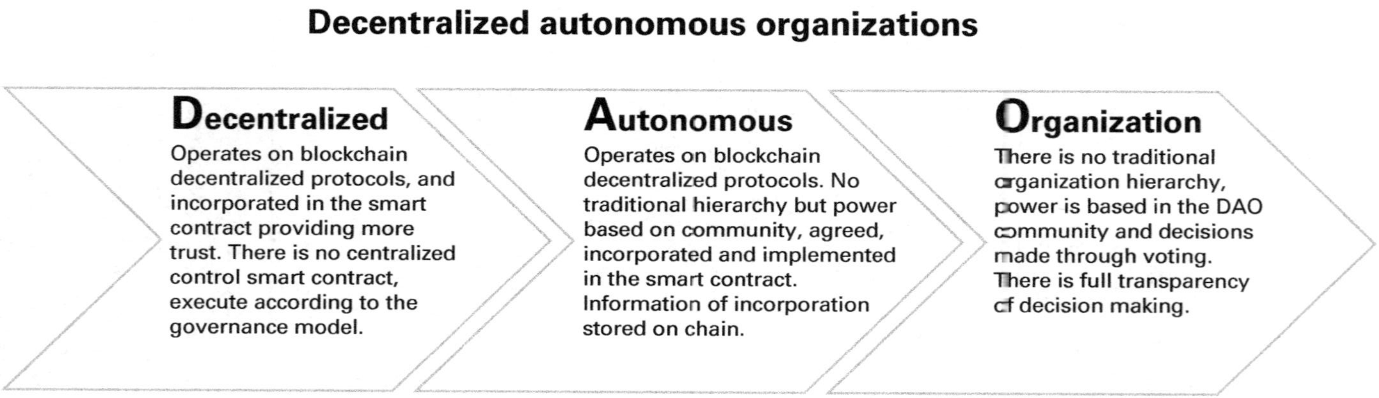

Decentralized autonomous organizations

Decentralized

Operates on blockchain decentralized protocols, and incorporated in the smart contract providing more trust. There is no centralized control smart contract, execute according to the governance model.

Autonomous

Operates on blockchain decentralized protocols. No traditional hierarchy but power based on community, agreed, incorporated and implemented in the smart contract. Information of incorporation stored on chain.

Organization

There is no traditional organization hierarchy, power is based in the DAO community and decisions made through voting. There is full transparency of decision making.

Ownership and use could be managed by smart contracts to turn creations and content into NFTs that represent ownership. Other smart contracts can automate turning the creator NFT it collateral for finance, bundling it with other assets as part of an asset pool, renting it, with royalty payment models and revenues, all automated within applications. This has the potential to bring new powerful automated toolsets to creators across platforms which can be applied across the shared metaverse.

Can Web3 decentralized autonomous organizations be the future of businesses in the metaverse?

Recently we have seen the transformation from sole traders, partnership to limited companies, public listed companies, to platform companies, but the common things that these companies' structures have in common are human managers, decision making and ownership. The recent emergence of the Web3 DAO disrupts the transitional model introducing community ownership, smart contract governance and collective decision making; so what is a DAO?

A DAO is a decentralized organization where members have a say in the decision-making process, and proposals are carried out automatically through smart contracts on a blockchain. The system is transparent, self-governing and provides incentives for owners and communities to participate in decision making and operations (see Figure 5.9).

DAOs can be used for a wide range of purposes, such as crowdfunding, investment management and community governance. They are seen as a promising solution for the problem of centralization and in some cases, management having alternative agendas and goals to owners, by introducing transparency and democracy in the business entity structures. DAOs emerged as DeFi gained popularity in 2021 and since then the DAO structure has been used for many decentralized projects; but are they suited to the metaverse?

- Metaverse financing: DAOs enable groups of individuals to come together to create financial DAOs which could be used for metaverse investment. Given the potential positioning of the metaverse with communities, DAO investment vehicles could be important for metaverse investment given the role of communities and new business models which will be more difficult to align to traditional financial products.

- Metaverse community participation in decision making: Anybody can join a DAO as long as they hold a certain number of the DAO's tokens. This gives them voting rights and they can be a part of the decision-making process in line with the DAO's governance structure. Members of the DAO can participate in the governance process, deciding the direction of the DAO and making sure that the rules are being followed. DAOs often issue regular updates, holding virtual meetings to keep members informed of decisions and changes. This could work well in the metaverse where decisions need to be made in a clear, transparent and fair way across geographies, ecosystems and platforms.

- Metaverse continuous improvement and innovation: Members of the DAO can propose ideas, and other members can vote on them. Proposals can include investment opportunities, changes to the rules, hiring new personnel or deciding on the usage of funds. These proposals receive votes from token holders, and they are executed when a predefined threshold of votes is reached. This could help to continuously improve the metaverse and foster an innovation culture.

- Movement in and out of metaverse virtual worlds: If a member wants to exit a DAO, they can sell their tokens. This does not affect the functionality of the DAO, as the tokens will simply be transferred to new owners who may continue to participate in the decision-making process.

The ability to embed objectives into DAOs for automatic execution through smart contracts has the potential for wider society objectives to be incorporated in metaverse business, as they can be written into the governance and executed without the possibility of interference. This could be environmental, regulatory and quality objectives.

Some states in the US like Wyoming and Vermont are amending their laws and corporate code to specifically acknowledge a DAO as a 'DAO LLC'. They are attempting to incentivize DAOs to register, but how will the metaverse jurisdiction do the same? There are many metaverse businesses that are registered and operating as DAOs and the relationship between the metaverse and Web3 means that DeFi is well positioned to finance them. While DAOs provide a structure for community governance and operations which aligns well with decentralized platforms, they are relatively unproven at scale where external shocks and political factors need to be assessed, analysed and factored into decisions. This raises wider questions about human involvement in the evolution of the metaverse vs AI, and in the initial stages while regulation, political factors and even the economics of the metaverse are immature, a mix of DAOs and businesses with human control will be required.

Can the virtual business be the future metaverse business entity?

In today's business landscape, ownership models were not created for online businesses and as a result they may include some legacy processes associated with physical banking and lack flexibility. In the metaverse where businesses will be digital first and operate in virtual environments serving people across the globe, are more flexible business and banking structures required?

In 2020 during the Covid pandemic when masses of people were being furloughed, but manufacturing and other activities were still required, I had the idea of the virtual business. These are flexible business entities that could be formed by people combining their digital identities temporarily to form a virtual business and their banks accounts or wallets to form a virtual bank account. The business terms and credentials would be secured on blockchain to provide trust and means to verify the business entity credentials, and the terms would be implemented by smart contracts. The virtual business would allow people to come together from any geography and profession or trade to meet business demands. In this model the blockchain and smart contract would replace the articles of incorporation, and the virtual bank account would replace the business bank account as

FIGURE 5.10 The virtual business model

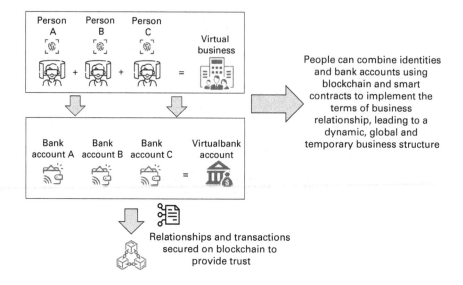

outlined in Figure 5.10. Given the metaverse provides virtual spaces and environments and interaction points, the virtual business is potentially a good fit for metaverse business entities.

The features of the virtual business include:

- Ability to merge the identities of people to form a temporary business relationship administered by smart contract.

- Division of profits written into smart contracts and executed legally by smart legal agreements.

- Finances operated using wallets and open banking, which are used to form virtual bank accounts, and which can be formed for a specific period of time to support the financial operations of a virtual business and the identities that are part of it.

- Automated Legal and HR supported by AI.

The virtual business enables any person or business from around the physical or virtual world to combine their identities to form a business to meet a business demand or realize a business opportunity. For the metaverse where geographic barriers are removed, and business opportunities could be time-bound, the virtual business could be the future business entity combining, Fintech, DeFi, DePIN, and mobile.

Can the metaverse Web3 and AI transform law and contracting?

There has been much discussion about how law will be applied and adjudicated in the metaverse, which legal jurisdictions will apply, how contracts will be formed dynamically to meet the expected interoperability across virtual worlds and how virtual worlds will work with physical court systems. One thing for sure is that the current manual legal and contracting solutions will struggle with the dynamic and real-time demands of the metaverse; but could Web3 hold some of the solution answers?

We have discussed smart contracts in a previous chapter, but the ability for them to self-execute terms which are encoded digitally and incorporate parameters fed by live real-time data has great potential to automate law. Smart contracts are designed to be secure, transparent and tamper-proof. They eliminate the need for intermediaries like lawyers, banks or brokers to enforce agreements; but could the future be to combine lawyers as inputs to the programming of smart contracts? Or could AI replace lawyers and provide legal inputs to smart contracts in the future?

A smart legal agreement is a legally binding document that is executed using a smart contract. It contains all the provisions and conditions of a traditional legal agreement, but instead of relying on intermediaries, it uses blockchain technology to execute automatically. They work by automatically executing pre-set terms and conditions when conditions are met. For example, if a contract is for the sale of a boat, the smart contract will release payment to the seller automatically when the boat is delivered, and the buyer confirms delivery. Smart legal agreements can also be programmed to self-execute when certain conditions are not met, such as cancelling the agreement and returning the payment if the seller does not deliver the boat within the specified time frame.

The global legal services industry is forecast to exceed $1.4 trillion by 2030 and as the metaverse grows so does the demand for automated legal solutions and smart legal agreements. There has been some progress by companies like Openlaw.io, an open-source platform that allows users to create, manage and execute legal agreements using smart contracts on the Ethereum blockchain, and ultimately provides a framework for users to create legally binding agreements that are transparent, secure and automatically executable and enforceable. It also offers tools for streamlined contract management, automated dispute resolution and robust governance mechanisms, which could be key to management of agreements in the metaverse; but can the demands be met without AI?

We have explored many ways in which the metaverse and AI can complement each other throughout the previous chapters, and in this case the metaverse could be 'AI in law'. The metaverse operating system providing developers and users with tools to combine AI in smart legal agreements, with AI providing the ability to incorporate complex scenarios, and even learning and precedence, in decision making with full real-time knowledge. There could even be a role for AI in adjudication of disputes, where AI legal assistants could make decisions based on legal rules, precedence and other factors like jurisdiction, but as with other areas of AI, the outputs will be as good as the data inputs and the fairness could be argued to be as good as the balance of data inputs and logic in the AI algorithms. The potential is there for AI and Web3 smart contracts to provide increased automation of law in the metaverse, but the journey is long, and the start should be measured and slow and grow with self-learning.

Notes

1 McKinsey and Company (2022) Value creation in the metaverse, www.mckinsey.com/capabilities/growth-marketing-and-sales/our-insights/value-creation-in-the-metaverse (archived at https://perma.cc/K4N4-P58P)

2 Jasmine Enberg (2023) 5 things to know about the creator economy in 2023, *Insider Intelligence*, www.insiderintelligence.com/content/5-things-know-about-creator-economy-2023 (archived at https://perma.cc/S8SU-V79E)

06

What is the future of metaverse business?

There has been a lot of focus on the metaverse experience and its ability to embed XR and 3D, in consumer products, services, games and platform experiences. Meta and Apple have demonstrated the potential of the embedded metaverse to increase monetization of existing content delivered in 3D and XR, and highlighted the potential revenues from metaverse generated content, but what is the full scope and potential of metaverse business?

The industrial metaverse is growing and gaining adoption in industries like manufacturing. There are new businesses being formed in the shared and AI metaverses which have significant potential to form new metaverse native industries and market verticals as we previously outlined in Chapter 2. However, we are now starting from the position of a limited metaverse for a relatively small number of users, and the one key to adoption will be easy access and usability, but also widespread availability to a device to access the metaverse which would be the mobile phone. Until these factors are addressed, the metaverse market size will remain small with limited demand.

On the supply side, businesses need to be able to embed metaverse capabilities into their business processes, products and services. This will require work not only on expanding the metaverse ecosystem, but also on incentivizing big hyper-scaler platforms to invest in incorporating metaverse capabilities.

Given the future positioning of the metaverse as the new web browser and interaction point between people, businesses and goods, services and content, it has the potential to function as an interactive cross-platform customer relationship management (CRM) system, but with a user-centric design and AI capabilities incorporated.

In this chapter we will explore the potential of the metaverse as a location to set up business, the relationship between the metaverse and physical retail, metaverse experiences, the metaverse as a platform aggregator, the industrial metaverse business models, and how the business of data could potentially function across all aspects of metaverse business.

Is the metaverse the new location for businesses to set up and operate?

Businesses have been going through significant transformation, and the drive to incorporate virtual and online capabilities accelerated significantly during the global Covid pandemic which saw record numbers of businesses add e-commerce, virtual work and collaboration capabilities. But how important is the metaverse as a channel and forum for businesses now?

The metaverse introduced the concept of the immersive virtual world to businesses, which has led to the emergence of new types of gaming, retail and virtual land platform businesses being set up. The current market trends suggest that immersive experiences are becoming important with over 171 VR users and a market size of $252 billion in 2022.[1] In addition many brands are now looking at the metaverse as a channel and opportunity to grow.

For brands the metaverse also offers new ways to communicate, interact, collaborate, build and maintain relationships with customers and users. Many global brands like Nike, Adidas, Gucci, Coca-Cola, Burberry and Louis Vuitton have now set up retail presences in the metaverse, mostly for marketing purposes, but some of them are now seeing the potential of immersive experience technologies like XR to help to sell high-value goods and reduce physical location costs.

Over 7 million people visited the Nikeland store in the metaverse in 2022, which demonstrates the impact of retail and marketing presence, but there are also wider considerations for the financial bottom line. For example, virtual options enabling the reduction in the number of physical locations required to service high-value goods sales like cars and luxury items, which could help many businesses move these areas fully online to realize significant cost savings.

When exploring whether the metaverse is a serious location for businesses to set up, we should, however, explore this in the context of changes in wider business patterns and behaviours. Online sales now make up over 25 per cent of total sales in markets like North America. In parallel over 25 per cent of professionals in North America and Europe now work from home, reducing the need for physical locations, while at the same increasing demand for improved virtual and immersive products.

The ways in which consumers want to engage and interact with business is also changing, with embedded finance now becoming a key differentiator for customer experience, and this is only expected to grow as platform businesses and super applications now increasingly incorporate finance and sales into customer journeys. These trends have served to place more importance on online and virtual capabilities, as well as the adoption of platform business models with focus on customer and user experiences.

The NFT also has the potential to provide digital ownership and portability of assets to business models which, when combined with metaverse experiences, have the potential to add new level of gamification. Some early examples, of the use of NFTs in business include art, music and collectables, and we are now seeing this extend to ticketing, transport and even rentals and leasing. But why is the NFT important to the metaverse?

The NFT could be the key to the business of the metaverse as they can be used to:

- **Incentivize the creation of metaverse content** – NFT royalty smart contracts like Ethereum ERC2981 can be used to incentivize development of content with the royalty distribution of creators guaranteed through this solution.

- **Manage and monetize access across metaverse experiences** – NFTs can be used to manage access to virtual worlds, with the NFT also determining the level of access and experience.

- **Store digital assets and provide a value for them which is transferable and can be financed.**

- **Prove and port digital ownership across different metaverses** – This includes assets bought or earned in gaming or social media virtual worlds, or real-world assets that are being represented digitally. This is the basis for asset interoperability across the virtual world.

In the relationship between the metaverse and the world of business, there has been a lot of emphasis on retail, gaming, collaboration and land. However, with the metaverse's role in providing the environments for AI to interact with people and businesses, the scope of metaverse businesses could be much boarder than previously thought. Some examples of future metaverse businesses are:

- AI interaction environment: This would include virtual call centres, government help centres, virtual medical centres, operation and support centres all powered by AI.

- Virtual entertainment: This can include immersive virtual concerts and conferences.

- Immersive interactive gaming – this includes new immersive graphics as well as VR and AR, with some elements of virtual world economics including asset personalization and portability.

- NFT sales and services: Many artists are already selling NFTs online. In the metaverse, these same assets and their related services can be embedded in virtual world experiences and customer/user journeys.

- Metaverse tokenized real estate: There are platforms already offering land and buildings for sale in virtual environments, and tokenized real estate is emerging as an option for real-world assets, but the tokenized solution could apply to virtual real estate, where they are tokenized then sold, leased or rented as part of new business models.

- Virtual retail: The metaverse has the potential to add many goods and services that are not currently sold online, and to provide a better experience for those that are. Almost anything that can be sold in the real world can have a digital version which can be sold in the metaverse.

- Virtual education: The metaverse can provide a realistic 'hand-on' education service globally to anyone who can access it, potentially extending the boundaries of universities and large established educational establishments and introducing new online markets to small service businesses like therapists who were limited to local areas but through the metaverse can now provide a global service.

Is connecting the metaverse experience to physical retail locations a business opportunity?

We briefly discussed the role of Metaverse Experience Centres (MXCs) in Chapter 2, where consumer and business users can experience metaverse products and services, but now we explore the extent to which these MXCs can change our reasons for interacting with retail locations and regenerate high streets and retail parks which have lost to online. Could MXCs redefine the very purpose of the retail store? Could MXCs redefine the boundary between physical and virtual worlds?

There are arguments that the metaverse, like many previous innovations before it, will be less of a substitute for physical locations and more complementary, helping physical retail locations to optimize the relation with the consumer. The concept of MXCs could support this, but is the metaverse different to the past?

Gartner predicts significant growth in the time that people spend in the metaverse, forecasting that 'by 2026 25 per cent of people will spend at least 1 hour per day', and that for enterprises it will provide 'the ability to expand and enhance their business models in unprecedented ways by moving from digital business to metaverse business, and as a result 30 per cent of the organizations in the world will have products and services ready for the metaverse by 2026'.[2]

At the same time UBS forecasts that up to 100,000 retail stores (up to 50,000 in the US alone) could be lost globally in the next few years.[3] However, the global market for smart retail is projected to reach $48.2 billion, with Europe being the largest regional market for smart retail and the US emerging as the fastest growing regional market.[4] Will MXCs be positive or negative for smart retail?

Retailers are starting to incorporate immersive technologies like XR, as well as AI and IoT into retail solutions to improve shopping experience. At the same time, they are incorporating them into the back-end supply chain, inventory management, and to further expand online offerings. In addition, several retailers are looking at incorporating IoT and metaverse immersive technologies to provide physical retail experiences without friction, for example Amazon Go shopping without checkout. Along with significant investment in retail, online growth, and an increased focus on customer engagement and experience, IoT and the metaverse could provide the right start for the introduction of MXCs. As many retail brands have begun to enter the metaverse we have started to see much higher dwell times for these brands (the time that consumers stay interacted).

Historically, a key challenge to adoption of customer online purchases is the preference to physically view, feel and touch the goods, so the introduction of XR in the context of MXCs can help to remove these barriers by enabling customers to experience the product, without a physical interaction. Although there are still low adoption rates for XR in retail there is significant potential, especially in cases where customers cannot go to physical stores. MXCs could be an important step towards getting over the preference for physical interaction in retail.

Overall one of the key objectives of the metaverse is to provide realistic experiences in the digital world which should enable us to shift more physical activity online. To do this, key physical experiences will need to be identified and XR substitutes created to expand the range of goods and services available online and create new market opportunities.

What is the role of the metaverse as a channel for retail and brands?

When considering the metaverse as a channel for retail, it is important to explore the ways in which the physical and virtual worlds can complement each other in channel strategies and how MXCs can act as a bridge between them.

The metaverse will build on and augment current digital channels like email, messaging, chatrooms and social media, but incorporate immersive technologies. Many retailers and brands could see this as an opportunity to improve products, processes and experiences and go to market in a more efficient and effective way. The metaverse provides an improved solution for users to interact with content. The consumer feedback for product improvements could be almost immediate, rather than the longer lead times we have today. Smartphones will be key to adoption and interaction with brands and retail in the metaverse and the evolution of current smartphones to incorporate XR capabilities will be key. In the meantime, MXCs could be the middle ground between the physical and metaverse channels.

We should, however, caution that while the metaverse is expected to increasingly emerge as a channel, it will not completely replace the physical ones, but rather solutions like MXCs are expected to evolve with them.

Can MXCs help metaverse businesses to attract and manage talent?

From a business perspective the combination of physical and virtual environments made possible by MXCs could provide the functionality for many more companies to expand their talent pools, extending the range of jobs and tasks overall that can be performed at home as part of the workforce. For example, companies could use MXCs to set up new global locations where new employees could participate in work tasks in real time using immersive technologies and digital twins with other locations across the globe. It should be noted that some big companies already have the capability to do this, but the scale is limited due to the cost; however, the metaverse has the potential to scale this up, extending the potential workforce to include new locations, gig workers and virtual businesses. MXCs could also lead to significant improvements in productivity as they have the potential to remove geographic and physical barriers in workforce-related business processes, in turn lowering the costs associated with switching between locations. There are, however, some limitations with the current XR and 3D technologies unable to replicate emotional prompts, read body language and handle random events. Work behaviours and culture both evolve in physical locations, but maybe these present challenges create new opportunities for management and AI to improve.

The metaverse's ability to help businesses redefine the possibilities of workforce participation and remove the barriers of geography could result in more concentration of activity in fewer locations, and inadvertently expand the role and size of big cities that have the infrastructure and scale to support MXCs. There could be a social cost to MXCs if not phased in with the right level of government policy and planning, as failure to implement MXCs at scale without wider policy considerations could further drive migration of people and jobs to cities and away from rural areas and exclude developing countries that lack of digital infrastructure to support them.

This trend is already beginning with some big global cities like Dubai, Shanghai and Guangzhou launching campaigns as part of strategies to become metaverse hubs and attract metaverse businesses and talent, in return for massive investment in infrastructure, friendly regulatory and tax incentives, and even funding for platforms, established brands and startups to locate. These could become ideal locations to experiment with among enthusiastic early adopters.

MXCs can also help businesses to redefine what a workforce is and who can be a part of it, building on some on the foundations and progress made during the Covid pandemic which accelerated online business.

Is 3D printing a metaverse business?

3D printing or additive manufacturing is a process of creating three-dimensional objects by depositing successive layers of material as part of the printing process. The 3D printing solutions enable complex items to be designed, stored, transmitted and consumed in digital format for printing anywhere on a digital printer including in the home or business or anywhere printers are available. 3D printing technology has started to impact manufacturing. Customized complete objects or parts consisting of various materials, ranging from plastics, metals, ceramics and even living tissue can be created by simply printing them. Manufacturing by 3D printing could increase productivity in the industrial metaverse. However, it may have a greater impact in the consumer metaverse as a bridge between the physical and virtual. Completely digitally owned goods can be printed in the home forming a complete end-to-end supply chain from metaverse business to consumer. Or they could be printed in MXCs for assembly and distribution using conventional collection or last-mile delivery solutions. 3D printing could therefore be critical to the supply chain for the metaverse where a physical output is required.

Makerverse is a startup company using 3D printing as part of its additive manufacturing metaverse business. They have created a platform that allows users to share 3D models in a virtual environment or consumer-standard models on the platform, and then print them using a 3D printer in the real world. This platform is demonstrating the potential to greatly reduce the barriers to entry for 3D printing by making it more accessible, but more importantly they are incorporating 3D printing into their metaverse business model and using it to bridge virtual and physical world experiences.

3D printing promises huge potential for healthcare and is even evolving to include bioprinting which is an additive manufacturing process like 3D printing that uses a digital file as a blueprint to print an object layer by layer. But unlike 3D printing, bioprinters print with cells and biomaterials, based on liquid and gel-based materials, and can additionally perform non-contact droplet printing, which can be used to create organ-like structures that allow living cells to multiply.

In Figure 6.1, I outline how the healthcare metaverse can be used to design products in healthcare printed on 3D and bioprinters, either through industrial MXCs or on premises with 3D printers.

The metaverse healthcare model illustrates the potential of the metaverse experience and collaboration capabilities in a business-to-business context. Healthcare organizations can select off-the-shelf medical design and files. They could also use the 3D and immersive technologies of the metaverse for design and prototyping, collaboration, simulation and customization and personalization. All these activities could also in the future be assisted by AI.

Once the design is finalized the file could then be consumed and 3D or bioprinted either in an industrial MXC or a local on-premises 3D printer for low complexity standardized designs. Where printing is on-premises the metaverse provides an end-to-end supply chain; however, where a MXC is involved there is still a requirement for conventional last-mile delivery or collection solutions. We assume here that bioprinting will not be available for local printing and will only be available to be printed in industrial MXCs where the appropriate heavy printing machinery is available as well as industrial testing processes.

For this, healthcare 3D printing business models are a great example that may be replicated across other use cases. Some examples include:

- Virtual showrooms where users can use immersive technology to experience products that can be 3D printed via a MXC or on an on-premises 3D printer. This could also extend to replacement parts of new product assembly like furniture, where in this case the metaverse could also allow the user to personalize some parts of the furniture in the printing file.

- Digital prototyping and collaborative designs where immersive and collaborative technology could be used for people to work together on a design and use 3D printing to view the physical design at any aspect of the design and build life cycle.

FIGURE 6.1 Metaverse healthcare business supply chain flow incorporating 3D printing

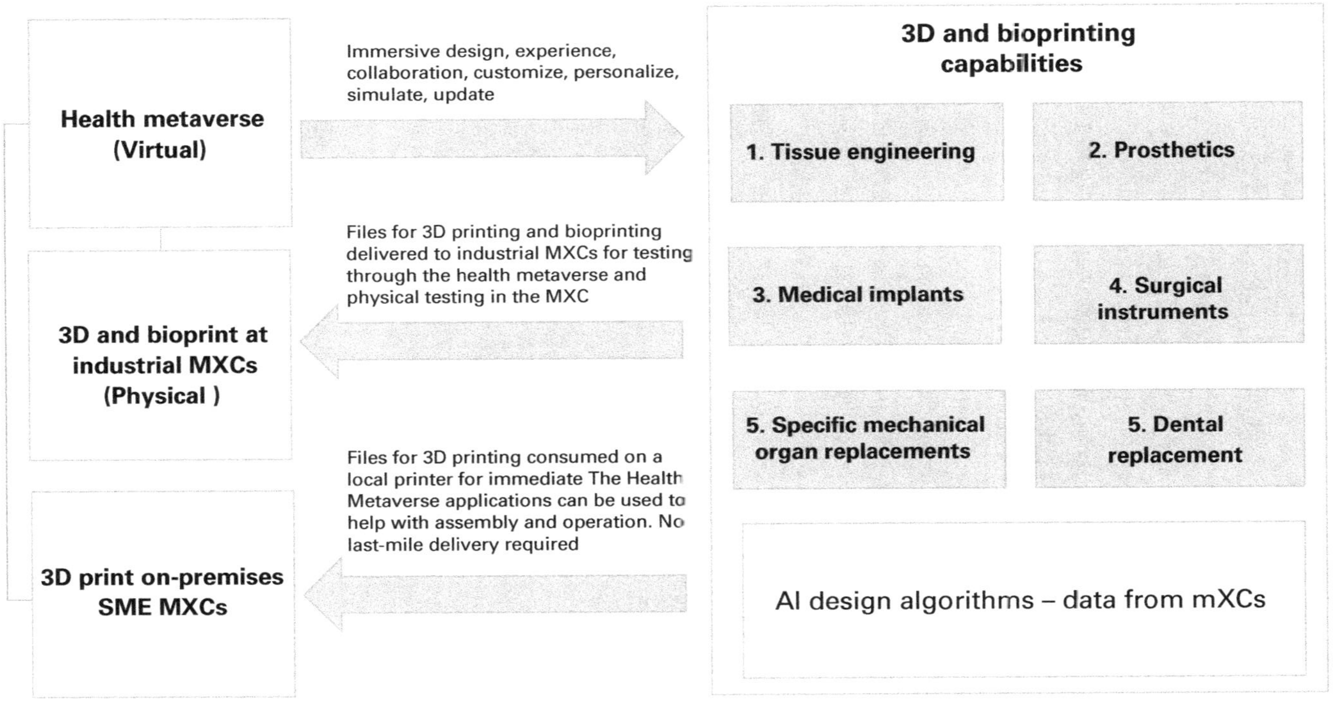

3D and bioprinting capabilities

1. Tissue engineering	2. Prosthetics
3. Medical implants	4. Surgical instruments
5. Specific mechanical organ replacements	5. Dental replacement

AI design algorithms – data from mXCs

Health metaverse (Virtual)

Immersive design, experience, collaboration, customize, personalize, simulate, update

3D and bioprint at industrial MXCs (Physical)

Files for 3D printing and bioprinting delivered to industrial MXCs for testing through the health metaverse and physical testing in the MXC

3D print on-premises SME MXCs

Files for 3D printing consumed on a local printer for immediate The Health Metaverse applications can be used to help with assembly and operation. No last-mile delivery required

What is the role of business in the consumer metaverse?

The consumer metaverse can be defined as the sum of metaverse goods, applications, services and experiences that are available to consumers through digital marketplaces or MXCs. These goods, applications, services and experiences can be further broken down into retail, gaming and social experiences and services which can be available either through direct or indirect channels.

Consumers are mostly using smartphones and games consoles to access a metaverse, and recent surveys indicate that they prefer physical stores to virtual ones, which represents a challenge for the consumer metaverse.

However, there are indications that consumer metaverse adoption is starting to move in the right direction, with some studies finding that one in four consumers globally are interested in virtual experiences,[5] with up to 50 per cent of consumers wanting to become active users. There are also forecasting that '25 per cent of consumers are expected to spend at least one hour a day in the metaverse by 2026', with '88 million VR/MR device shipments are expected in 2026'.[6]

These statistics support the view that consumers will shape the metaverse; but what does this mean and how will the consumer metaverse transition start?

The metaverse has the potential to provide capabilities that can fundamentally change what is possible in user interactions and experience. In turn, it can fundamentally change consumer attitudes and behaviours, and move the boundaries of when, where and how they will interact with suppliers to buy, learn, earn, socialize, collaborate and experience. Ultimately the metaverse may enable us to rethink the very definition of consumer.

Gaming has led the way for consumers in the metaverse, briefly discussed in Chapter 2 with many gaming platforms boasting high numbers of subscribers who are able to grow their own profiles, earn as well as play, own as well as spend and enjoy general content but also personalize their online personas, collaborate and build relationships within the gaming community, and experience different levels of immersiveness depending on preferences and the value this brings.

Could gaming be an example of the business model for the consumer metaverse?

The gaming industry has enjoyed consistent growth with consumers engaging with gaming platforms and ecosystems. These provide them with direct engagement incorporating interactive competition, collaboration and commerce. Now with the immersive 3D capabilities of the metaverse, as well as Web3 and AI the gaming platform can become sovereign economies that will eventually interoperate (see Figure 6.2).

Gaming consumers have digital identities on their platforms, and in some platforms use crypto wallets and private keys to securely transact. This allows the platform to engage with the consumer player for data, sales and personalization, which is the basis for the gaming consumer economy which includes game application sales, subscriptions, play to earn, game asset sales and marketplaces.

There are indications that personalization is emerging as a key differentiator in gaming with personalized in-game assets and personalized experiences using AI being key. There are also signs that social media and gaming are converging with social gaming increasing where users can play friends and others in communities.

Gaming platforms have been developing and growing largely independently but the metaverse operating systems provides capabilities for interoperability of play, assets, ownership and exchange. This could be

FIGURE 6.2 Gaming business model for consumers in the metaverse

a model for other consumer applications to grow and do business in the metaverse which has the potential to bring significantly more revenues to gaming.

How can the consumer metaverse business grow?

The five main drivers to consumer metaverse adoption includes 1) maturity of XR and Web3 technologies, 2) device maturity, availability, price and adoption levels, 3) size of the developer and application ecosystems, 4) number of recognized brands and businesses operating 5) availability of metaverse capabilities on established platforms, with wider compliance with industry standards, laws and regulations also important factors see Figure 6.3.

When XR achieves mass market appeal, this is expected to incentivize OEMS to increase supply, reduce prices and make metaverse access devices more affordable which in turn will increase demand.

The introduction of more portable and lower-priced mixed reality headsets which are needed to access the immersive experience could be a key factor to adoption. Meta and more recently Apple have entered the market, and their ecosystems will be key to initial growth in adoption, but more devices will be needed at different price points to reduce the entry price point. However, business and government subsidies for headsets could play a role but will still require supply to be increased.

There is also expected to be a link between the industrial and the consumer metaverses where, for example, immersive technologies are introduced into business processes that can then transition from the workforce to personal consumer use.

Big brands entering the metaverse and integration with big hyper-scaled platforms will promote trust. They will be critical to successful consumer adoption. They are expected to attract consumers with new goods and products experiences that exceed the current offerings and help to transition their customer base to the metaverse.

The maturity of Web3 enablers like digital wallets, SSI, and new payment and finance solutions like open banking and the token economy will also be important to provide the features required for

FIGURE 6.3   Six drivers for consumer metaverse adoption

6 Drivers for consumer metaverse adoption

1. Maturity of AR, VR and Web3 technologies

2. Device maturity and adoption

3. Size of the developer and application ecosystem

4. Number of recognized brands

5. Integration with established platforms

6. Standards, legal and regulatory

adoption. Nearly 70 per cent of the world's population is expected to have a digital wallet by 2030, and the incorporation of the wallet into the consumer metaverse will be key.

How important is retail to the business of the consumer metaverse?

The retail metaverse has been described as 'experience before you buy' adding new immersive and sensory features that can make more goods, services and experiences available to purchase online. The retail metaverse can become the new high street, retail park and business park. It's expected to grow and be physically present as the high street continues to decline largely fuelled by the economics of online vs physical. This trend could be accelerated further with further retail volumes able to be transacted online in the metaverse.

Online retail has increased over 200 per cent over the past decade, with e-commerce increasing over 50 per cent during the Covid pandemic. At the same time, the number of physical retail stores has been falling rapidly over the next few years, which will lead to an increase in e-commerce sales. What does this mean for the retail metaverse?

We have previously discussed in Chapter 2 the emergence of MXCs and how this could help to reshape the high streets and wider physical retail experience where online and physical retail journeys converge to omnichannel shopping to improve overall customer experience. In this new world where metaverse retail and physical retail work together, consumers may discover products and services online and purchase physically where they can touch, feel and see in more detail. The metaverse has a role to support the in-store experience with VR and AR but could also remove the need for the physical step completely.

The current retail model has been limited by the frequency of direct engagement with customers. The metaverse has the potential to enable retailers to reach consumers in new, more personalized ways which were previously unavailable. The metaverse is also showing signs that it could support retail customer journeys with more touch points. Metaverse immersive retail environments combined with AI retail assistants can provide realistic, personalized and high-quality customer experiences and service at times, days, dates and frequencies that were previously not possible. This includes customer engagement outside retail experiences through virtual environments, digital content or through MR. Some of the XR features that are being piloted in physical stores include magic mirrors, interactive windows, smart fitting rooms, virtual reality displays in store and beacons, all of which demonstrate the potential for the metaverse to add value to the retail experience in physical locations.

The retail metaverse which builds on e-commerce is a logical next step for businesses. It follows the approach that there will not be one all-encompassing metaverse but rather several embedded metaverses. The idea of retail businesses adding and augmenting their current physical and online shopping experiences with virtual ones would make sense for high-value goods like cars, luxury clothing and branded goods where returns justify expenditure.

The metaverse could also change the retail business model from design, produce and sell to one where retailers can interact with consumers to personalize goods, services and experiences and then manufacture or create those products. Examples of this include Nike's 'Nike by You' product. This is an example of a retailer using the metaverse capabilities to redefine retail and innovate their retail product development business model. The retail metaverse is amplifying the incentive for retailers with Technavio forecasting that the metaverse fashion market to reach $6 billion by 2026.[7]

The significance of the metaverse retail opportunity is supported by the growing importance of Generation Z consumers who were born and shaped in the digital age between 1996 and 2006. Gen Z will make up nearly 30 per cent of the global population and 27 per cent of the workforce by 2025 and have the highest adoption rates for tech-enabled shopping. As the retail landscape changes and the metaverse maturity grows this could be an important factor for change and transition to virtual experiences.

Key platforms operating in the metaverse

There are many consumer platforms that have launched in the metaverse with varying value propositions and approaches, all utilizing different features of the metaverse. Some are focused on Web3 and virtual world features while others focus more on 3D and XR; however, their presence demonstrates investment in metaverse as a place for business. Key platforms include:

- **Obsessar:** Startup metaverse retail platform using the metaverse to re-invent the e-commerce experience and empower brands and retailers to tell their stories and showcase their products using VR capabilities and applications. In this platform users can quickly create 3D virtual stores to sell digital products, experiences and services, or enable users to experience digital twins of physical products and have them delivered if they purchase them.

- **Tiliaverse:** Startup metaverse real estate platform which uses metaverse immersive VR technology to create a virtual world and sell real estate using Web3 NFT for digital ownership. For example, users can purchase places of personal significance like their childhood home through NFTs, but digital ownership is also part of community building as owners are also automatically part of the wider ecosystem.

- **Decentraland:** Startup metaverse virtual world platform where users can buy, sell and develop virtual land on the platform using the native MANA cryptocurrency. The platform is a DAO governed by smart contracts with decisions made by the community. Land is limited on the platform. Metaverse technologies and Web3 are used to provide users with tokenized ownership and community smart contracts. Users can use metaverse 3D technologies to create virtual buildings and experiences on the land, with the platform providing wider community events.

- **Sandbox:** Startup virtual gaming platform incorporating metaverse and blockchain technologies where users can buy, sell and create digital assets using the Sandbox cryptocurrency SAND and the platform earns utility revenues from these transactions, and some assets. Ownership is represented in NFTs; for example, the Sandbox avatar creation system allows players to create their avatars with unique appearances, clothing and accessories owned as NFTs and the associated marketplace allows users to upload, publish and sell their NFT creations. The platform interfaces with consumer wallets which can be used to utilize some of the platform features and support ownership and transactions. The platform is a DAO governed by smart contracts with decisions made by the community.

- **Axie Infinity:** Startup metaverse gaming platform where users can buy actors in the game called 'Axies' and use them to battle, explore and breed with other Axies. Users own their Axies in the form of NFTs and use them to combat other creatures in the game. They can resell them or even 'play-to-earn' where the platform rewards users with tokens that can be exchanged for money in return for playing and achieving play targets. The platform is a DAO governed by smart contracts with decisions made by the community.

- **Gala:** Startup gaming metaverse platform where users can 'play to earn' through games hosted on distributed network. Players are rewarded in Gala tokens which can then be exchanged peer to peer or on the Gala marketplace for NFTs, music and collectables.

- **Bloktopia:** Startup metaverse virtual gaming, educational, social experience and entertainment hub, which is designed as a decentralized VR skyscraper made of 21 floors which enables users to own and develop virtual real estate. There are events and advertising which can create opportunities for brands and influences to showcase their products to the Bloktopia ecosystem.

- **Highstreet:** Startup metaverse which provides users with a play-and-earn open-world metaverse that incorporates shopping, gaming, NFTs, traditional brands and crypto brands. Users can play to earn by completing quests, attending social events, socializing with players and shopping for NFTs from real-world brands. Highstreet bridges the physical and digital worlds with a massively multiplayer online role-playing game (MMORPG), where brands can use the merchant portal to seamlessly integrate and build their presence in the Highstreet virtual world. Highstreet

World is built natively with 3D Unity and Web3 technology. High Street provides real products with additional utilities by turning them into in-game items.

- **Fortnite:** One of the largest open-world concept games on the market today with over 250 million average monthly users who operate within the Fortnite virtual world, it began as an on-island survival game in 2017, where 100 players are dropped from a flying bus and must fight to be the last player standing. Players can collect resources and weapons, build structures and work together or against each other to survive in the game. The game incorporates some key metaverse features including user-generated content, real-time, multiplayer experience, cross-platform interoperability and real-time social interactions. There is no fee to play, but players can buy items, such as skins and emotes, by exchanging money for 'V Bucks' which is the currency used in the game. The game does not include VR support; however, Unreal Engine 3D technology is incorporated in the user interface so this could be available in the future

- **Roblox:** A metaverse virtual gaming platform which enables users to create, share and play games and experiences, within a diverse and interconnected virtual world. It provides a vast array of tools and building blocks for users to design their own games, avatars and interactive environments. Users can explore and interact with the creations of others, join multiplayer games and engage in social interactions, and VR via Meta Quest. Owned by Roblox Corporation, the platform had over 214 million monthly active users in 2023, and over $2 billion in revenue.

These examples demonstrate the momentum from both startups and established brands to utilize virtual world capabilities in the metaverse, but for the metaverse to scale the growth of metaverse retail will be key. However, adoption will depend on how easy metaverse retail experiences are to access, the value that these experiences add to the consumer over existing e-commerce and any improvements in productivity that can be realized.

FIGURE 6.4 Metaverse industrial operating system

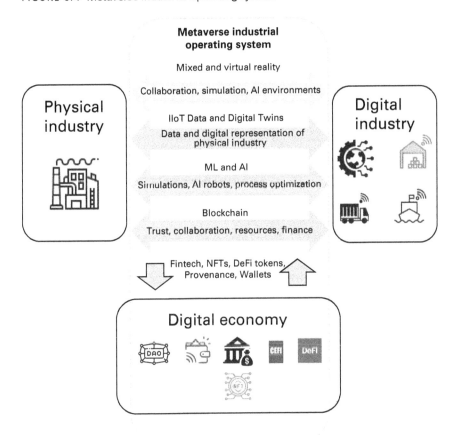

The key to these productivity and cost improvements could be the introduction of AI. For example, could the in-store assistants in metaverse enable cost reductions for in-store staff and online support?

What is the business of the industrial metaverse?

A number of analysts are forecasting that there will be significant use of the metaverse in the manufacturing industry by 2030.

The industrial metaverse can be described as the virtual world with immersive and 3D capabilities utilized within an industrial context to help improve processes, operations efficiency, quality, and reduce costs (see Figure 6.4).

And within the industrial metaverse digital twins can act as a digital version of physical assets and a bridge to the benefits of the digital world enabling designs, simulations and analysis at lower cost.

Using XR to blend physical, digital and AI to drive new efficiencies, the metaverse can enable industries to cut costs, act more sustainably, improve the work experience and accelerate operations by moving expensive, time-consuming activities into fully virtual environments. Within these spaces, enterprises and public sector agencies can test and optimize their systems, processes and infrastructure to identify and address issues before committing time and resources to the real physical processes and operations.

There are many examples of digital twins being used in industry, especially in conjunction with IoT. Vehicle and aeroplane OEMs are early adopters of digital twin technology and among the biggest users. Some examples include:

- BMW, which has over 30 digital twins of physical factories.
- Boeing, which uses digital twins to optimize aircraft design and cargo load balancing.
- Unilever, which uses digital twins of heavy manufacturing equipment to simulate and optimize the production process.
- Siemens, which is using digital twins to design and continuously improve its factories and production-line processes.

The use of digital twins also extends beyond OEMS, where for example some real estate companies are using it for architectural designs, modelling improvements before building, and there has even been discussion about extending this to include smart city design and management. In addition, healthcare providers are using digital twins to monitor medical equipment in the context of healthcare processes, but this could extend to incorporate the finance and insurance of medical equipment.

The business model for the industrial metaverse can be summarized as bringing lower costs of change and improvements in productivity through digital twins and AI.

What is the business of the shared metaverse?

Statista Insights suggest 15 per cent of the digital economy has already shifted to the metaverse and is projected to include 700 million people worldwide by 2030.[8]

The shared metaverse is the economic activity at the intersection of the consumer and industrial metaverses and includes things like the GIG economy, producer economy, creator economy, content economy, data economy, virtual businesses, advertising, and the embedded versions of these in applications to form new super applications. These areas can be seen as the new areas of business activity, productivity and growth that have begun to emerge in Web2 but can also be seen as being driven by the metaverse, Web3 and AI in the future. The consumer metaverse includes the creator economy, producer economy, metaverse finance and the GIG economy (see Figure 6.5).

FIGURE 6.5 The shared metaverse economy

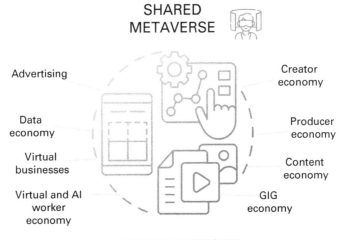

The metaverse and the business of content economy

Content is at the centre of the platform economy and a key point of competition across them. As we discussed in Chapter 1, in some platform business models content is generated by users for a share of consumption and in others it is generated not for monetary reward but rather the content generator is rewarded with followers and likes by other users of the platform which can later, when the critical mass is reached, be transformed into leverage and influence in return for sponsorship or influencer payments. This is the essence of the new content economy where core models differ, but the overarching principles of providing incentives for content-generation remain.

In this context the content economy can be described as the new emerging ecosystem where content creation, distribution and consumption take place, and as well as digital platforms as described above, it also encompasses industries such as media, entertainment and publishing. So what is the relationship between the content economy and the shared metaverse?

One of the key roles of the shared metaverse will be to enable interoperability across content platforms. The metaverse in this case will act as middleware so that user and content creator identities, wallets can work, and revenues received across all platforms. Some of this can be achieved through interoperability integrations and AI agents; however, the metaverse's ability to incorporate Web3 decentralized capabilities could enable self-sovereign models where the content creator creates and owns content but can then make this available across platforms and receive revenues directly. For example, if a content creator makes their video into an NFT linked to their identity, they could either sell the NFT linked to the content outright or use time-bound and royalty smart contracts to get revenues each time the content is used, with blockchain helping to execute and manage this in real time.

When we look at the metaverse as a platforms aggregator it provides the following functionality to content creators:

- Operating system to combine new technologies like Web3, MR, VR and AI to produce content.

- New virtual environments for content to be created and consumed.
- Extension of the digital content boundary to move further into the physical world for consumption incorporating more immersive, sensory and touch into content.
- Interaction points for direct engagement with content consumers on the metaverse space.
- Distribution across platforms but with Web3 self-sovereign models available.
- Ability to incorporate Web3 wallets, tokens, smart contracts, provenance of creation, trust and consensus in content business models.

The above describes a whole new content economy and the foundation enablers for content creators to access new tools including AI to create content, new self-sovereign ownership models, distribution and reach to global content consumers, and realize revenues from tokens like NFTs. The major shift here being that the shared metaverse can drive more power and revenue earning potential to content creators than the current position across centralized platforms, therefore opening alternative pathways for creators to earn money and become independent entrepreneurs.

One use case that has received attention is video and film production where there has been much focus on the use of AI and XR to create new films. However, the ability for the metaverse to combine tokenized movie financing, smart contracts for distribution and revenue management with global metaverse distribution and superior XR and 3D capabilities has the potential to significantly disrupt the film business model.

The metaverse and the business of producer economy

The producer economy refers to a system where individuals actively create and contribute to the production of goods and services, as well as content, which we covered earlier. It can be described as a shift from the model where consumers just consume to a more dynamic model where they are part of the value creation and can be both consumers and producers, in some cases producing as they consume. In this economy, individuals can showcase their skills, expertise and creativity to produce and monetize their offerings, often through platforms and marketplaces. The producer economy empowers individuals to become entrepreneurs, influencers, artists or content creators, fostering innovation, collaboration and economic opportunities; but what is the relationship between producers and the shared metaverse?

The metaverse has the ability to remove scarcity of some resources, for example land in the metaverse, and remove some limitations like geography and time which open up new opportunities for production. We have seen some of this with metaverse land sales, but this could be only the beginning as metaverse clothing, art and music can all have scarcity controlled by the producer rather than limitations of the resource itself. This combined with new models for digital ownership of goods and services like NFTs has the potential to impact demand, supply and ownership aspects of the current economic model. With scarcity of resources and supply and demand at the centre of current economic models, the metaverse's ability to create a limitless supply of resources demands new economic thinking but can also present new opportunities for producers.

The metaverse and the business of gig economy

The gig economy is a market where people's resources and labour are the products which are made available peer to peer using platforms. The services provided include temporary freelance work assignments, where individuals offer their skills and services on a project-by-project basis, or a combination of skills and resources to meet an agreed deliverable. Transitioning the gig economy to the metaverse could enable more services to be provided across more platforms and marketplaces, and for closer collaboration of gig workers with AI and the new AI workforce that is expected. Could the gig economy in the future focus on skills to complement and use AI tools and workers?

In the metaverse, individuals could offer their virtual skills and services such as virtual event planning, virtual assistance and virtual design. All of which would provide specific skillsets needed for metaverse businesses, but if we take a wider look across the shared metaverse, gig workers with interoperable metaverse digital identities and wallets could link their identities with AI robots and employ AI tools to offer services in both the consumer and industrial metaverses as part of new virtual businesses. In this context the gig economy operates across people and AI to form temporary businesses to provide services in the metaverse. Transitioning the gig economy to the metaverse can unlock new avenues for freelancers, expand the scope of remote work and encourage economic growth.

The metaverse and the business of advertising economy

The advertising economy brings together industries involved in creating, delivering and monetizing advertising content. Its current size is substantial, with global advertising spending exceeding $800 billion annually. How will the advertising economy evolve in the shared metaverse?

The metaverse's spatial and social elements provide new opportunities for contextual and targeted advertising, enhancing the current brand-consumer relationships. The metaverse is also expected to increase dwell time and provide additional metrics, analytics and more detailed insights into engagement and the overall impact of advertising campaigns.

The metaverse provides businesses and advertisers with new ways to interact with customers within the context of their normal activities, routines and entertainment in ways that would not be possible without the metaverse and its ability to incorporate AI. Businesses and advertisers promote products and services to new customers across geographies with pinpoint personalization combining profile data combined with real-time data and in 3D. This includes virtual items, MR and VR showrooms and other 3D marketing experiences, but maybe the question we should be asking is what is advertising in the metaverse and how will it change?

Advertising can be defined as an industry used to call the attention of the public to something, typically a product or service. This takes forward the functional evolution of advertising from awareness to matching assistants or personal CRMs.

AI will be critical but so will user activity across platforms and key to unlocking the opportunity to this evolution will be access to historical and real-time user data, enabling brands to engage with users through virtual and contextual product placements, interactive branded experiences and personalized advertisements tailored to individual data and predictions of needs.

The advertising economy in the shared metaverse has the potential to redefine advertising and move it from awareness to digital assistant matching goods and services to customer needs, requirements and ambitions, adding value as an enabler and moving the point of competition to closeness of match to customer needs and revolutionizing the way brands connect with consumers in a digitally immersive environment.

The business of the AI metaverse

There is significant interest in the future role of AI and the potential of the technology to fundamentally change the current business, consumer and social landscapes. There has been much discussion that AI could replace as many as 300 million jobs, but how will it do this? Many of these jobs will require human interactions and the metaverse will be required to provide an immersive environment, experience and toolset for AI to interact. In this context the metaverse can be described as 'AI on Earth' as it will be the technologies that gives AI a persona and the automated tools for digital identity, authentication, portability of value, payments and transactions. In other words, the metaverse could be the technology that makes AI real, but what is generative AI?

The development of AI has witnessed key milestones. Early milestones include the development of symbolic AI and expert systems in the 1950s and 1960s. The advent of machine learning in the 1980s and 1990s brought about considerable progress. Breakthroughs such as the introduction of deep learning and neural networks in the 2000s propelled AI further. The development of generative AI, with milestones like GANs and VAEs, enabled the creation of realistic content. Recent milestones include the emergence of advanced language models like GPT-3, pushing the boundaries of natural language understanding. These milestones collectively shaped the evolution of AI, paving the way for increasingly intelligent and capable systems.

AI has immense potential to transform businesses across various sectors. It can automate routine tasks, improve efficiency and enable data-driven decision making. AI-powered solutions can enhance customer service through chatbots, personalize marketing campaigns, optimize supply chains and improve product development processes. While AI may automate certain job functions, its impact on overall employment is complex. While some jobs may be replaced, new jobs will also emerge in AI development, data analysis and managing AI systems. The World Economic Forum[9] estimated that by 2025, AI could displace around 85 million jobs, with job displacement potentially increasing to 300 million by 2030 according to Goldman Sachs, but there are also estimates that AI could create as many as 97 million new jobs globally by 2025, but will AI chatbots be the workforce in the metaverse and how creative can AI get?

There has been significant discussion on the extent to which AI can perform even creative tasks like video generation, editing and coding, and there have been projections that there will be few professional areas that AI will not participate in.

So far AI has demonstrated its ability to perform various creative tasks, expanding its role beyond traditional analytical functions. Some practical examples of AI performing creative tasks include art and music generation: AI algorithms can create original artwork, generate music compositions and even mimic the styles of renowned artists or musicians, highlighting capabilities to reproduce creativity in visual and auditory domains.

FIGURE 6.6 The metaverse business positioning quadrant

Well positioned for metaverse

Immersive value added (high)

- Gaming
  - Entertainment and concerts
    - Metaverse universities
  - Immersive remote medical procedures
- Virtual showrooms of high-value goods
  - Virtual workplace
  - Metaverse car specialist remote
- Metaverse social media
    - Metaverse car specialist remote
      fixing
    - Metaverse wind farm design
    - Metaverse car assembly line

Metaverse geography impact (high)

Metaverse geography impact (low)

Immersive value added (low)

AI can generate written content, including news articles, product descriptions and social media posts. It can assist in automated content curation, summarization and even creative storytelling. In design and fashion, AI-powered systems can generate innovative designs, logos and fashion concepts by analysing existing trends, patterns and user preferences, offering fresh and innovative ideas.

AI algorithms can automatically enhance and modify images or videos, applying filters, adjusting colours and even generating realistic deepfake videos, pushing the boundaries of visual creativity. But how can AI and the metaverse work together?

AI can bring significant benefits to the metaverse by enhancing user experiences, enabling intelligent interactions and facilitating immersive virtual environments. Practical examples include:

- Personalized avatars: AI can generate realistic and personalized avatars based on user preferences, appearance and behaviour, enhancing user identity and immersion in the metaverse.

- Intelligent NPCs: AI-powered non-player characters (NPCs) can exhibit advanced behaviour, speech and decision making, providing more engaging and dynamic interactions for users within the virtual world.

- Real-time translation: AI can enable real-time translation of different languages, breaking down language barriers within the metaverse and fostering global communication and collaboration.

- Content-generation: AI algorithms can generate procedural content, such as landscapes, buildings and objects, making the metaverse vast and diverse, while reducing the burden of manual content creation.

AI can help detect and mitigate bad online behaviour, hate speech and inappropriate content, creating a safer and more inclusive environment for metaverse users.

AI algorithms can analyse user behaviour, preferences and interactions to provide tailored recommendations for virtual events, activities and connections in the metaverse. In addition, AI's capabilities can enrich the metaverse by enhancing realism, personalization, communication, content creation, moderation and user engagement, creating a more immersive and dynamic virtual experience.

The key lies in upskilling and reskilling the workforce to adapt to the evolving demands of the AI-powered economy, ensuring a smooth transition and unlocking the full potential of AI in business.

How can businesses position for the metaverse

The metaverse is emerging and adoption is increasing across the consumer, industrial and shared metaverses, and there are now many examples of business using the metaverse including:

- Car manufacturers using the metaverse for customers to try new car features before they buy them (industrial metaverse).
- Car manufacturers using an AR and tech specialist persona to help service centres remotely fix complex issues with cars rather than physically sending an expert (industrial metaverse).
- Car manufacturers using digital twins and AI to optimize assembly plants (industrial metaverse).
- Management consultancies and technology companies using the metaverse to train their staff (industrial metaverse).
- Retail stores using the metaverse to provide a place for customers to sample high-value goods before they buy them online (commercial metaverse).
- Wind farm manufacturers using metaverse and digital twins to generate simulation data, so they can build the wind farm first virtually and then optimize it before building the physical structure. (industrial metaverse)

The above indicates that new consumer, business and shared economy models are evolving and there is much discussion that the metaverse could be the catalyst to drive new opportunities and help us to re-draw the consumer, business and new economy landscapes.

With so many headlines about the metaverse many business leaders are thinking about how they should approach the metaverse, and many are trying to determine if there is an opportunity for their business. For example, can their business easily transform into a metaverse business or is a new business or business model needed. How businesses position themselves in the metaverse is key to the value they will get from it.

In Figure 6.6 we use both immersive value and the impact of geography to help businesses assess the level of benefits that the metaverse can bring to their business. Where the value added from immersive experience is high, and the impact of removing geography is high the business is well placed to benefit from implementing metaverse technologies. To provide more insight we also overlay some of the examples of consumer, industrial and shared metaverse use cases discussed in previous sections.

The use cases in the upper right quadrant of Figure 6.6 are the ones that are well positioned to benefit and succeed in the metaverse. This includes metaverse education which has the potential to extend the university campus boundary beyond the current physical and online to include new metaverse universities. These could be accessed and attended by anyone across the globe, with AR and VR providing a realistic campus, interactions with the university community, and immersive capabilities to enable 'hands on' courses like science, medicine and engineering. This has the potential to significantly increase the supply of educational courses which following the laws of economics should lower the price and the barriers to entry. Other use cases include gaming, virtual showrooms, virtual workplaces, digital twins building design, metaverse social media, remote repairs and predictive maintenance. We should also consider that some platforms and applications could merge these use cases with the emergence of super applications. Some considerations and questions are now outlined:

- Metaverse social media. How will social media evolve to the metaverse? Will the metaverse become just an immersive layer? Will decentralization of social media be a key factor as users will want control and data from social media becomes a currency? How will the metaverse and Web3 work with the evolution of some social media to become SuperApps?

- Entertainment metaverse. How does this work with the social media metaverse? How does it combine with physical entertainment? How does this work with AI and AI-generated film and movie content? Will AI be making the entertainment in the metaverse? Is there going to be a creative algorithm?

- Messaging apps. Will they extend to message in games, and across different platforms? How will in-metaverse e-messaging differ from today? Will the messages just be of a higher fidelity, or will the messaging have to evolve to fit in and operate with the features of the metaverse, e.g. across different virtual worlds and ecosystems? How important will Web3 be? Will NFT be the ownership of the messaging and Web3 the security?

The metaverse business architecture

Some of the most successful platform businesses have merged over the last 15 years, and now command billion of users, including Facebook (3 billion), YouTube (2.5 billion), WhatsApp (2 billion), Instagram (2 billion), WeChat (1.3 billion) and TikTok (1 billion), and in addition companies like Google, Airbnb, Spotify, Uber and Netflix have changed the business landscape. But can the metaverse have a similar impact for business?

The metaverse and its ability as an operating system to act as a new digital interface for businesses to access and incorporate a range of technologies presents significant opportunities for business. These include new metaverse business solutions and customer experiences, as well as a distribution channel to the metaverse business and consumer ecosystem. This, combined with the core feature set of the metaverse, provides new capabilities for companies to create specific new products and experiences for the virtual world. Could this be the enabler for the next generation of global metaverse platform businesses?

To be successful in the metaverse, businesses need to understand the unique characteristics of virtual environments and create experiences that are tailored to them. This means thinking about things like interactivity, socialization and immersion and finding ways to leverage these qualities to create experiences that are both engaging and profitable.

The metaverse presents a huge opportunity for businesses to create new revenue streams and engage with customers in innovative ways. However, it will require a shift in mindset and a willingness to experiment with new business models and technologies. Companies that can do this effectively will be well positioned to succeed in the digital world of the future.

The metaverse positioning quadrant can be used by businesses to quickly assess positioning and impact of the metaverse, and in Figure 6.7 we outline the metaverse business architecture which lists key metaverse business components for consideration ranging from metaverse manufacturing to metaverse finance.

For example, a business using the metaverse to enable customers to experience high-value goods before ordering and allowing users to access these goods using an NFT, and provided discounts for data, and used the data to collaborate with customers on future designs would also incorporate capability 2.

FIGURE 6.7 The metaverse business architecture

Metaverse business architecture

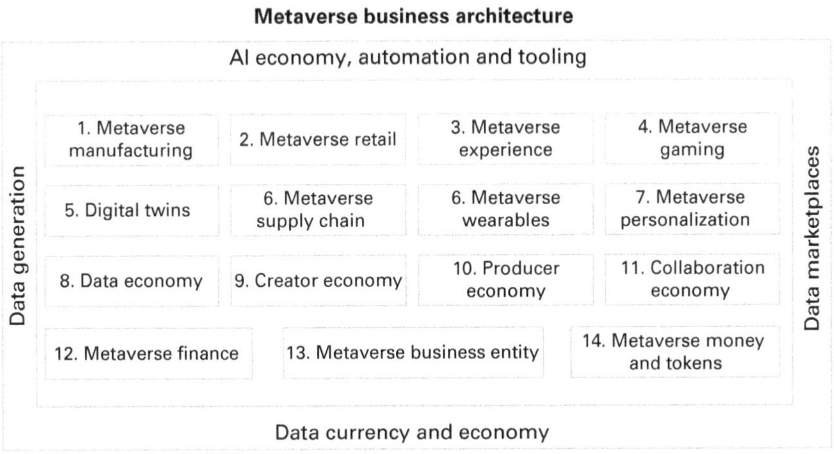

FIGURE 6.8 The metaverse business feature catalogue

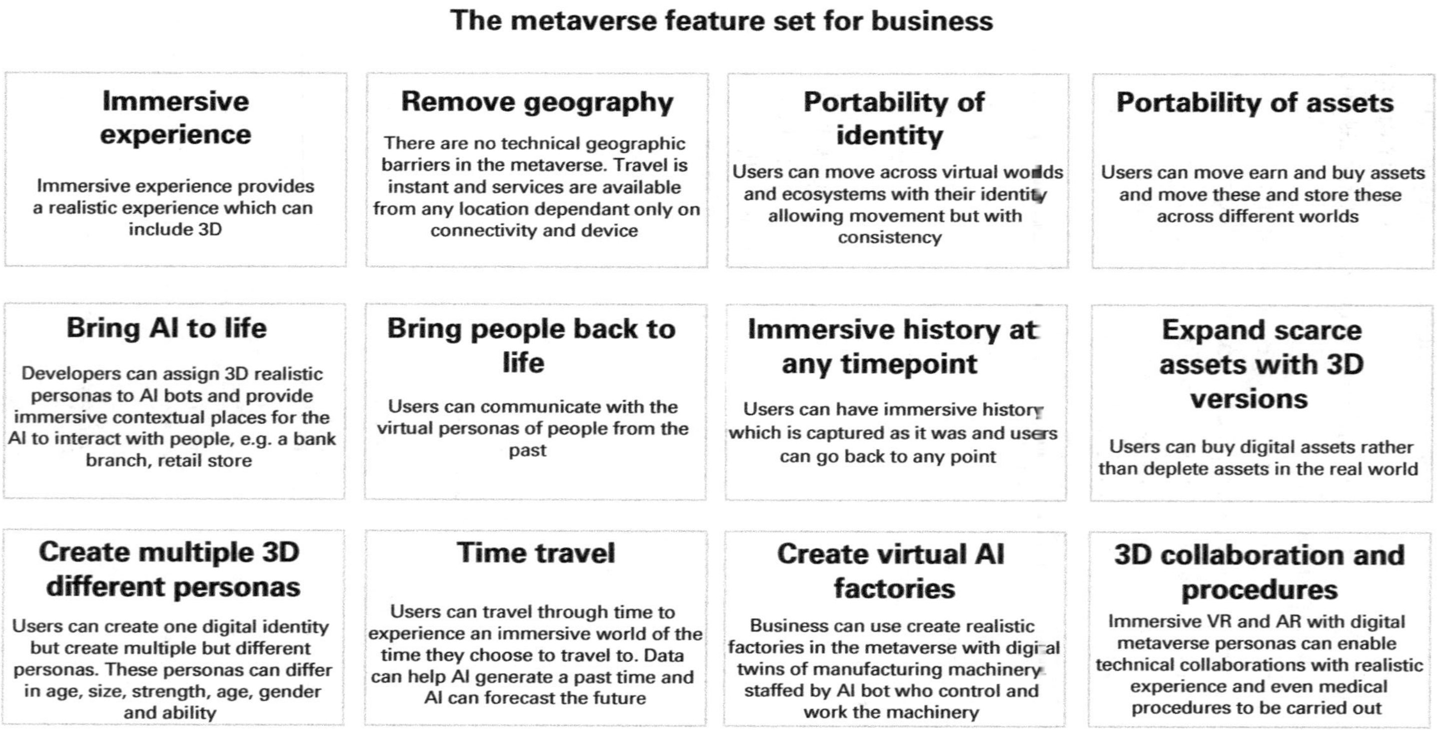

The metaverse feature set for business

Immersive experience

Immersive experience provides a realistic experience which can include 3D

Remove geography

There are no technical geographic barriers in the metaverse. Travel is instant and services are available from any location dependant only on connectivity and device

Portability of assets

Users can move earn and buy assets and move these and store these across different worlds

Bring AI to life

Developers can assign 3D realistic personas to AI bots and provide immersive contextual places for the AI to interact with people, e.g. a bank branch, retail store

Bring people back to life

Users can communicate with the virtual personas of people from the past

Portability of identity

Users can move across virtual worlds and ecosystems with their identity allowing movement but with consistency

Expand scarce assets with 3D versions

Users can buy digital assets rather than deplete assets in the real world

Create multiple 3D different personas

Users can create one digital identity but create multiple but different personas. These personas can differ in age, size, strength, age, gender and ability

Time travel

Users can travel through time to experience an immersive world of the time they choose to travel to. Data can help AI generate a past time and AI can forecast the future

Immersive history at any timepoint

Users can have immersive history which is captured as it was and users can go back to any point

Create virtual AI factories

Business can use create realistic factories in the metaverse with digital twins of manufacturing machinery staffed by AI bot who control and work the machinery

3D collaboration and procedures

Immersive VR and AR with digital metaverse personas can enable technical collaborations with realistic experience and even medical procedures to be carried out

The metaverse business feature catalogue

The metaverse offers several features to businesses that can be incorporated in business models and their associated value propositions. The most obvious feature is immersive capabilities and experiences which will allow business to incorporate 3D, VR and AR. This has the potential to strengthen their online capabilities and enable businesses to offer things online that were not previously possible. There can also be a shift in cost as some things which previously had to be physical can be substituted by virtual metaverse experiences. The potential of immersive experience has is to reset the business capabilities boundary both internally and external. As well as being able to provide new immersive customer experiences, businesses can have virtual offices, virtual workplaces, virtual collaborations and virtual training which can improve cost efficiency.

Another key feature is the removal of geographic barrier. A product or service could be delivered by online immersive technology. The importance of physical location is removed, and this could open new business opportunity and provide opportunities for growth, cost reduction or both.

The metaverse operating system's ability to incorporate Web3 brings self-sovereign digital identity linked to wallets, tokens, the ability for new digital ownership, interoperability of identity and portability of assets. These are all key features for businesses to unlock the metaverse economy.

Some other exciting features for businesses include the ability to provide the environment and interaction capabilities to bring AI to life. This could be important for businesses as incorporation of AI increasingly becomes a key point of competitive advantage. In thinking about the increased use of AI, the metaverse can provide the realistic interaction and environment that 'brings AI to life'. The metaverse as a key enabler to bring AI to life in the context of business models, processes and operations could be a key business feature.

Some of the metaverse features which could lead to new businesses include the ability of the metaverse immersive capabilities combined with AI to bring people back to life in virtual form. We have seen some of this recently with a Steve Jobs generated by AI and using past data to help generate answers to current problems. With AI and the metaverse this can be very realistic and use real data from someone's social media and internet data to generate their responses. The same approach could be used to enable someone to experience different periods of history in a realistic and immersive way. Figure 6.8 lists 12 metaverse features for business.

Some of the functions that these metaverse features support include:

- Convergence of technology framework to harness for experience – a framework to bring together a collection of technologies to support new immersive experiences and business interactions.
- Bridge to join platforms and ecosystems – across interoperability and consistency of identity and portability of value across ecosystems and platforms.
- Immersive and multisensory experience and data.
- The middleware to the established and Web3 economies.
- A supplier of data to AI.
- Replaces physical geography with new non-time-limited digital geography.

How will metaverse businesses evolve?

One vision for metaverse businesses is built on speed, flexibility, interoperability and lower barriers to entry. With these features anyone can become a metaverse business, and create new digital businesses, including new flexible virtual businesses and bank accounts based on digital identities and smart contracts.

This vision is based on Web3 capabilities. Could the metaverse see new organizations which build on the Web2.0 platforms, and Web3 protocols and smart contract organizations including DAOs? Could they bring us new metaverse organizations which operate as communities?

In the metaverse interoperability will be key and the customer bases will become communities. How effectively business can build, manage and monetize communities will be key to their success.

We have explored and seen many new businesses emerging where immersive features and removal of geography are key differentiators, as well as where new levels of automation, interaction and the associated data are key to the business model. These new metaverse businesses could include retail, insurance, gaming, entertainment, virtual real estate, digital supply chain and logistics, manufacturing and digital twins, financial services including MetaFi and new virtual AI banking assistants and personal branches, and MXCs. Some examples of business opportunities are listed below:

1 Business services to generate virtual personas and personalized virtual environments and metaverse personal spaces using AI and personal data with consent.

2 Digital identity and consent trustee services to ensure agreement for data to be used and monetized.

3 Virtual experiences for the disabled or elderly with the ability to experience things they cannot physically experience.

4 Virtual education delivered in the metaverse by AI.

5 Bring key figures and family back from the dead into a digital metaverse persona. The technology and business solution could potentially enable Elvis and Michael Jackson to perform again in virtual concerts.

This list represents the beginning of the business journey, and as the metaverse evolves we expect much more.

Notes

1 Jasmine Katatikarn (2024) Virtual reality statistics: The ultimate list in 2024, *Academy of Animation in Art*, academyofanimatedart.com/virtual-reality-statistics/ (archived at https://perma.cc/7QB2-7NFP)

2 Gartner (2022) Gartner predicts 25 per cent of people will spend at least one hour per day in the metaverse by 2026, www.gartner.com/en/newsroom/press-releases/2022-02-07-gartner-predicts-25-percent-of-people-will-spend-at-least-one-hour-per-day-in-the-metaverse-by-2026 (archived at https://perma.cc/EH5T-HCDE)

3 C Kennedy (2020) UBS estimates 100,000 more retail stores will close by 2025, www.loopnet.co.uk/learn/ubs-estimates-100000-more-retail-stores-will-close-by-2025/174318906/ (archived at https://perma.cc/3RWG-DUUP)

4 PR Newswire (2022) Global smart retail market to reach $48.2 billion by 2025, www.prnewswire.com/news-releases/global-smart-retail-market-to-reach-48-2-billion-by-2025--301510678.html (archived at https://perma.cc/37KH-B6YZ)

5 Dynata (2022) Global consumer trends: the new experience economy, www.dynata.com/content/GCT_The-New-Experience-Economy.pdf (archived at https://perma.cc/TLY9-R74K)

6 F Bonelli and R MacSweeney (2022) How meeting customers in the metaverse can unlock lasting value, EY, www.ey.com/en_uk/consumer-products-retail/meet-customers-in-the-metaverse-to-unlock-lasting-value (archived at https://perma.cc/6VV6-SUVD)

7 Technavio (n.d.) Metaverse in fashion market size, share | growth industry analysis 2026, www.technavio.com/report/metaverse-in-fashion-market-industry-analysis (archived at https://perma.cc/EY7E-8UFU)

8 Martin Armstrong (2023) This chart shows how big the metaverse market could become, *World Economic Forum*, www.weforum.org/agenda/2023/02/chart-metaverse-market-growth-digital-economy/ (archived at https://perma.cc/RR2U-M6T6)

9 World Economic Forum (2020) Recession and automation changes our future of work, but there are jobs coming, report says, www.weforum.org/press/2020/10/recession-and-automation-changes-our-future-of-work-but-there-are-jobs-coming-report-says-52c5162fce/ (archived at https://perma.cc/KGU8-75YS)

07

Metaverse economics, currencies and regulation

The metaverse GDP is potentially positioned in the coming years to be a major player in global economics with a larger share of global GDP than Japan and Germany, and a key contributor to growth, so how will the economics of the metaverse emerge?

Will the metaverse have its own currency and economic policy? What will be the impact for businesses operating in the metaverse? Will the metaverse economy be a token-based economy? How will national fiat currencies need to adapt to incorporate metaverse economic activity? Will central bank digital currencies (CBDCs) evolve to become the currencies of the metaverse? Will data become a universal currency, and if so will NFTs be the unit of exchange? How will macroeconomic policy adapt to cover the metaverse? What regulation will be needed for the metaverse economy? How do you manage inflation, interest rates, money supply, finance, banking and taxation in a digital-global metaverse without sovereign country boundaries? How much will Web3 play a role in the metaverse economy? Will data become a universal currency, and if so will NFTs be the unit of exchange? How will macroeconomic policy adapt to cover the metaverse? How do you regulate people as businesses? How do you manage an economy with data as a currency?

How will the metaverse economy emerge?

We explored in Chapters 1 and 2 what the metaverse is and how it will evolve, concluding that the metaverse will not be a quick 'Big

Bang' evolution into one consolidated metaverse, but rather will evolve as many separate mini-metaverses and embedded capabilities that will interoperate and converge over time. But what does this mean for the evolution of the metaverse economy?

In Chapter 2 we explored the metaverse landscape and the consumer, industrial, shared and AI metaverses which are emerging and expected to grow significantly. These new metaverse economic sectors are expected to form the foundations of the early metaverse economy and be the key drivers to metaverse economic growth, as outlined in Table 7.1.

TABLE 7.1   Initial metaverse economic sectors

	Description	Economic Model Fit
Industrial metaverse economy	Economic activity associated with metaverse in the industrial sector, including supply chain, manufacturing.	Potential to lower production costs through digital twins, industrial transaction costs, and increase productivity and supply through innovation.
Consumer metaverse economy	Consumer metaverse economic activity.	Lower transaction costs, expand digital supply curve, remove scarcity from digital products, increase global labour supply through removal of some geographic barriers, consolidate global demand.
Shared metaverse economy	Activity in the digital economic area between industrial and consumer metaverse.	Increase supply of content, services to meet metaverse demand creating new employment, businesses and industries contributing to GDP.
AI metaverse economy	Economic activity associated with AI in the metaverse.	Increase the automation boundaries in industry, and the efficiency of resources allocated for consumers. Increasing the ability of business and industries to diversify and personalize digital services. Replacement of human labour by AI robots using metaverse personas and environments can infinitely increase the supply of labour.

We expect the metaverse to continue to emerge in these four sectors, and as embedded metaverse on existing platforms and applications. However, this is only the beginning as the true potential of metaverse economic growth will only emerge when there is more interoperability across virtual and physical world experiences, and convergence gains momentum.

How can the metaverse economy interact with the established economy?

Gartner has predicted that by 2026, 25 per cent of the human population will spend at least one hour a day in the metaverse, which indicates that the metaverse economy will initially grow through user demand and activity. User monetization like advertising, is also expected to grow as the as metaverse economic activity increases.

The embedded metaverse will initially be reflected in the wider GDP components of countries, but as it grows it will become a GDP component of its own. Eventually as the virtual sector grows, the metaverse may have its own GDP do. The traditional GDP is the sum of C (consumption flows) + I (investment) + G (government) + NX (net exports), and in the short term we expect that the metaverse will be embedded in C+I+G+NX in individual countries; however, as the metaverse grows an additional dedicated net metaverse (MX)

FIGURE 7.1 Global GDP with the metaverse

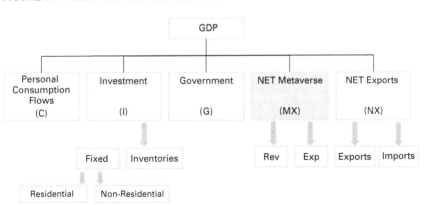

FIGURE 7.2 The 13 components of the metaverse economy

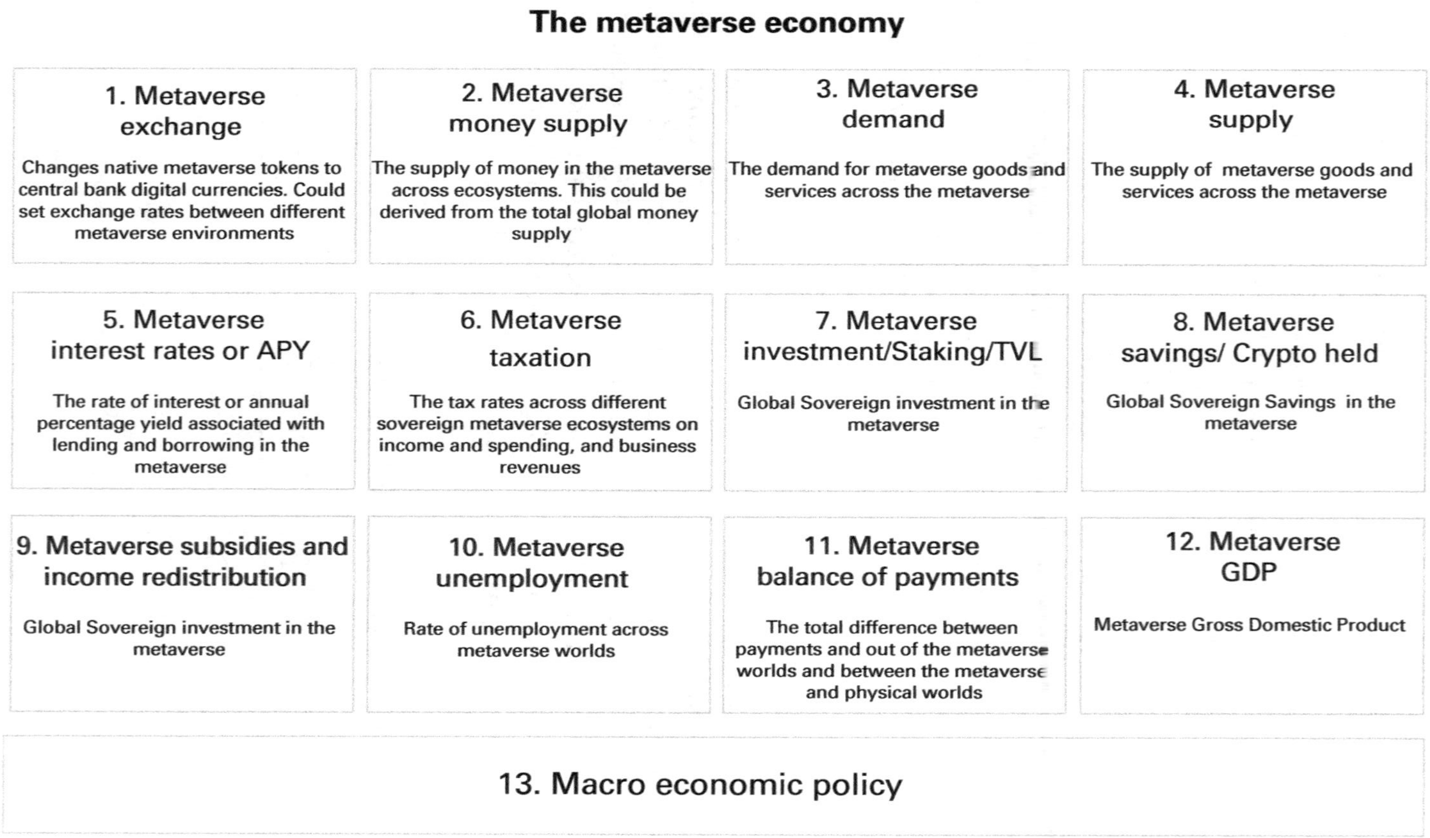

The metaverse economy

1. Metaverse exchange

Changes native metaverse tokens to central bank digital currencies. Could set exchange rates between different metaverse environments

2. Metaverse money supply

The supply of money in the metaverse across ecosystems. This could be derived from the total global money supply

3. Metaverse demand

The demand for metaverse goods and services across the metaverse

4. Metaverse supply

The supply of metaverse goods and services across the metaverse

5. Metaverse interest rates or APY

The rate of interest or annual percentage yield associated with lending and borrowing in the metaverse

6. Metaverse taxation

The tax rates across different sovereign metaverse ecosystems on income and spending, and business revenues

7. Metaverse investment/Staking/TVL

Global Sovereign investment in the metaverse

8. Metaverse savings/ Crypto held

Global Sovereign Savings in the metaverse

9. Metaverse subsidies and income redistribution

Global Sovereign investment in the metaverse

10. Metaverse unemployment

Rate of unemployment across metaverse worlds

11. Metaverse balance of payments

The total difference between payments and out of the metaverse worlds and between the metaverse and physical worlds

12. Metaverse GDP

Metaverse Gross Domestic Product

13. Macro economic policy

component could be added to GDP which is calculated by difference between metaverse revenues minus expenditures C+I+G+MX+NX (see Figure 7.1).

The next stage following C+I+G+MX+NX could be for the metaverse to have its own GDP which would contribute to global GDP.

What are the components of the metaverse economy?

In Figure 7.2 we break down the metaverse economy into 13 component parts which will work together to create, facilitate and manage metaverse economic activity. There will be some overlap with the established physical world economy, but where the size of the metaverse grows to up to 5 per cent of GDP its economic management will impact the wider economy and how these components are managed and incorporated in economic policy will become increasingly important.

FIGURE 7.3 The role of digital exchanges in the metaverse

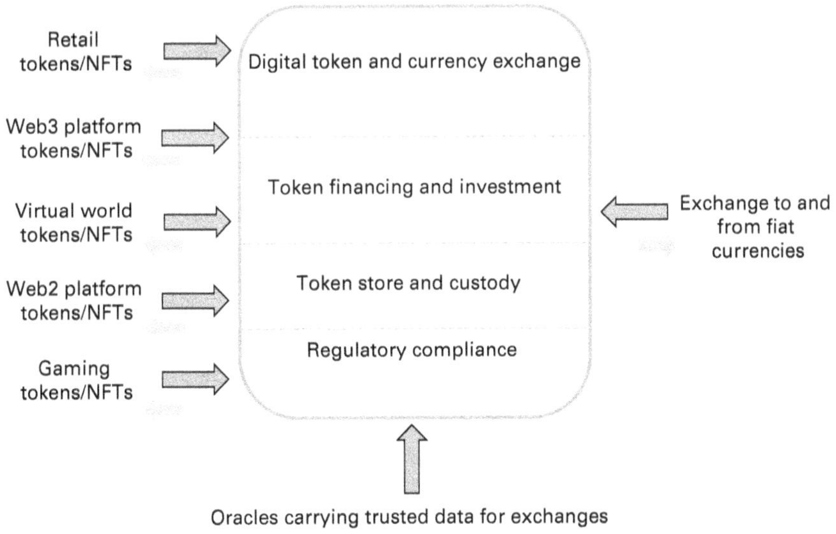

The metaverse economy and exchanges

The metaverse is global and as such there will be many virtual worlds across many countries, platforms and applications; however, rather than operating with national currencies the metaverse could incorporate cryptocurrencies, tokenized asset, central bank digital currencies and tokenized bank deposits for transactions and payments. Tokens, and NFTs in particular, form the basis of solutions for digital ownership and portability across virtual worlds and as a result would be key to enabling and managing economic activity in the metaverse.

In the current real-world economy currency exchanges facilitate the conversion of fiat currencies using market-determined exchange rates. Web3 cryptocurrencies enable users to trade and exchange digital assets using blockchain ledgers, smart contracts and oracles to automate the process. These exchanges can be 'barter' exchanges where tokens are exchanged for other tokens directly, or 'token to fiat' where tokens are exchanged for fiat currency at the market rate; so, what role will digital exchanges play in the metaverse economy?

Digital exchanges facilitate (See Figure 7.3) the inflows and outflows of fund tokens into fiat currencies and banking. This function will be critical to ensure liquidity is able to flow into in virtual world environments for growth, and to provide incentives for digital ownership and adoption in the global banking sector; however, new banking and finance products may be required for developing countries, where Web3 has been making progress.

Direct exchanges between virtual world tokens can also be performed by exchanges, where the requirement is to exchange one token for another without the need to off-ramp into fiat. This could be linked to services, for example where a platform providing virtual training pays for land in a virtual world using its training utility token A, and the virtual landowner pays for training using its virtual land utility token B. This direct exchange from token A to token B and vice versa is called 'digital barter'.

Other functions include store and custody of tokens, implementation of regulations, a library of smart contracts for exchange and finance, and a place to list new tokens as part of business fundraising.

The next generation of exchanges are expected to be split between centralized and decentralized exchanges where smart contracts can, to a large extent, automate management and operations. However, the emergence of AI and agents could take this further and drive more adoption by making the user experience and interactions with exchanges easier.

The metaverse economy, and the role of money supply and cryptocurrencies

In macroeconomics, money supply is the total amount of money circulating within an economy, and has historically included cash, demand deposits and other liquid assets. In economic theory there is a relationship between money supply inflation and economic growth, where typically an increase in money supply can lead to inflation, but can also help increase economic growth, and as a result the management of money supply is a key tool in national and international economic policy.

Government central banks control and manage money supply to maintain economic stability, using interest rates, open market operations and reserve requirements to balance money supply, inflation, economic growth and financial stability. When considering the metaverse do we envisage it having its own central bank, money supply and economic policy, or will the existing economic system be extended to incorporate the metaverse?

In the short term as the metaverse evolves as embedded functionality operating across different ecosystems there should be no change, as the metaverse will not be a 'joined-up' economy. One consideration, however, will be an embedded metaverse in Web3 platforms where cryptocurrencies can function as a medium of exchange and in this context Web3-based metaverse platforms, with their own cryptocurrencies, can effectively create their own money supply. In this scenario the metaverse cryptocurrency effectively acts as the money supply for the metaverse platform and the tokenomics strategy and management can impact prices, growth and economic activity.

The role of tokens, NFTs and cryptocurrencies in the metaverse is the subject of much discussion, and one of the questions that I have often asked is 'if AI were to choose a system of money and a currency for the metaverse would it choose the current fiat system or crypto-currency?'

Cryptocurrencies are digital forms of money which can act as one or all the following functions: medium of exchange, measure of value, digital ownership and store of value, and a standard for future payments. They operate on decentralized blockchain technology where transactions are recorded on a public ledger, ensuring trans-parency and security and secured by cryptography. Users that have digital wallets can send, receive and store cryptocurrencies, all based on decentralized blockchain technology but independently of tradi-tional financial institutions.

In theory, cryptocurrencies can reduce macroeconomic control of money supply in metaverse platforms due to the decentralized nature and lack of a controlling entity like a central bank; however, in prac-tice most cryptocurrencies are traded on major custodial exchanges which are subject to regulation, money supply macroeconomic poli-cies and other tools to control the liquidity of crypto markets. So far, evidence suggests that the overall increases in cryptocurrency values have coincided with periods of loose monetary policy, and falls with significant tightening, and this has generally aligned with the reac-tions of other equities like stocks and shares. However, many challenges to the growth and acceptance of crypto currencies into the mainstream continues, with one of the most significant barriers being the slow progress of regulatory frameworks to adapt.

The real value of tokens could be as a reward for loyalty, currency for utility, a medium of exchange and a store of value in metaverse platforms. In this role economic policies will need to be extended to incorporate 'tokenomics', and the policy goals carried out by smart contracts and AI. Could central bank digital currencies (CBDCs) and retail bank tokenized deposits be the bridge between metaverse tokenized money supply and wider economic policy and tools? See Figure 7.4.

FIGURE 7.4 The metaverse and the token economy

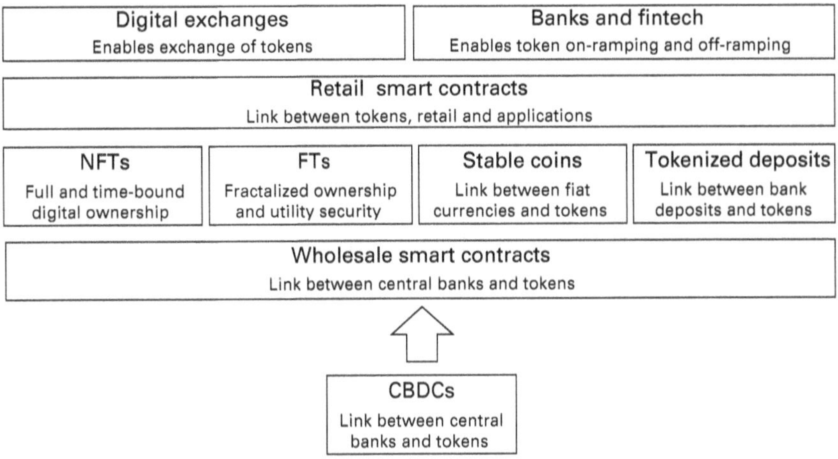

Digital exchanges	Banks and fintech
Enables exchange of tokens	Enables token on-ramping and off-ramping

Retail smart contracts
Link between tokens, retail and applications

NFTs	FTs	Stable coins	Tokenized deposits
Full and time-bound digital ownership	Fractalized ownership and utility security	Link between fiat currencies and tokens	Link between bank deposits and tokens

Wholesale smart contracts
Link between central banks and tokens

CBDCs
Link between central banks and tokens

The role of CBDCs and retail bank tokenized deposits as a bridge between the real-world economy, metaverse economy and Web3

A CBDC is an electronic version of a country's currency issued and regulated by its central bank. It serves as legal tender for transactions, just like physical money. CBDCs are centralized, regulated by the central bank, and backed and managed by monetary policy. Unlike decentralized cryptocurrencies such as Bitcoin, CBDCs are government controlled and designed to enhance payment systems, financial inclusion and monetary policy effectiveness, while maintaining a direct relationship to the nation's official currency and traditional financial system.

On the other hand, tokenized bank deposits are representations of funds in existing bank accounts, which are recorded immutably on blockchain so that they can be used for blockchain token transactions like transaction fees, exchanged for NFTs, or invested in DeFi. The bank liabilities are held by licensed banks and financial institutions. The benefit of tokenized bank deposits over stablecoins which currently are cryptocurrency tokens pegged to a fiat currency is that tokenized deposits use the existing banking network. There is no need for change, and they are centralized, meaning economic policy can be used 'as is'. However, where we have a metaverse that operates across geographic borders would decentralized currencies be a better fit?

If we see CBDCs as the tokenization of central bank national currencies, and tokenized deposits and the transfer of bank deposits into cryptocurrency, they could serve as the link between national currencies and metaverse money, and more importantly enable economic policy at the national level to play a role in managing cryptocurrencies and the metaverse economy.

How important are NFTs to economic activity in the metaverse?

NFTs have gained attention since 2021, but their roots can be traced back to the Coloured Coins concept in early 2010s on the Bitcoin blockchain, which enabled the tokenization of assets. Following these, specific smart contracts were developed for NFTs including on the Ethereum blockchain with the ERC-721 and ERC-1155 smart contracts being widely used; but why could NFTs be important to the metaverse economy?

The answer could lie in the unique ownership and provenance features that NFTs incorporate which can revolutionize digital asset ownership models, create scarcity and pave the way for a new era of digital ownership and monetization in the metaverse. Some NFTs features that play a pivotal role in enhancing digital ownership include:

- **Uniqueness and scarcity:** Each NFT is one of kind, setting it apart from other tokens. This characteristic ensures that each NFT represents a singular entity, be it a digital artwork, a collectable or any other virtual asset. Uniqueness brings scarcity making NFTs a great fit for collectables, art, music and other scarce assets.

- **Ownership verification:** The primary function of an NFT is to provide verifiable proof of ownership. By leveraging the immutability features of blockchain, NFTs offer transparent and auditable records of ownership, which in turn provide trust and authenticity to assets. Individuals can validate their ownership of assets through the public ledger, to establish legitimacy and origin.

- **Metadata:** NFTs incorporate metadata, allowing creators to enrich their digital assets with relevant information. This metadata may include details such as the title, description, image, audio or video associated with the NFT. By incorporating this information NFTs offer a comprehensive and contextual dataset to collectors and buyers, which could also be useful in metaverse finance models like MetaFi.

- **Transferability and interoperability:** NFTs enable automated zero touch transfer of ownership and transferability and ownership revenues are built into the NFT smart contracts, enabling NFTs to be traded on platforms and marketplaces without central control. This transferability could enable digital assets to be quickly and seamlessly transferred across embedded metaverses and virtual worlds, with consistent records of ownership transfer.

NFTs provide records of digital ownership which are stored on blockchains which are important to metaverse economy and associated finance models, products and markets. Digital content, products and services will be created in the metaverse, as well as digital twins of physical assets, and how these are owned, stored, transferred and leveraged will form the basis of metaverse economic activity with NFTs playing a key role, but the real value of the NFTs are their ability to introduce scarcity to digital assets which enables market economics to work.

The metaverse economy demand and supply

In macroeconomics supply refers to the quantity of goods and services producers are willing to provide at varying prices, while demand represents the quantity consumers are willing to purchase at different price levels. The point at which supply and demand meet determines price and quantity in a market.

For the metaverse supply and demand will operate within the established supply and demand we associate where there is a link to physical goods and scarcity of resources. However, for some digital goods, where there is no limit on supply and therefore no scarcity the supply is infinite. A good example of this would be digital land where supply can be increased infinitely to meet demand, and with all things remaining equal this should lower the price. In these cases, there is potential for the metaverse to bring significant increases in supply to markets, lower price and increase the quantity supplied. In the absence of targeted economic policy tools to manage metaverse supply, the impact on markets could be significant (see Figure 7.5).

In this case the metaverse can significantly increase the supply of medical university education. This shifts the supply curve to the right and increases the amount that can be supplied as the price changes (the elasticity of supply). Given this example could the metaverse serve to reduce prices and availability of goods where immersive, digital products can increase supply? If so, can this help to reduce inflation in key markets? What will be the impact on suppliers and profits? Will policies be required to manage this? The indications are that in some markets the metaverse can significantly increase supply and reduce prices. This is potentially a positive thing for consumers, but the use of economic policy may need to be considered to protect suppliers where there are national or strategic factors to consider. On face of it as we transition to more digital goods and services the more that they can be supplied at lower cost could make them available to

FIGURE 7.5 The metaverse impact on supply curves can lower prices

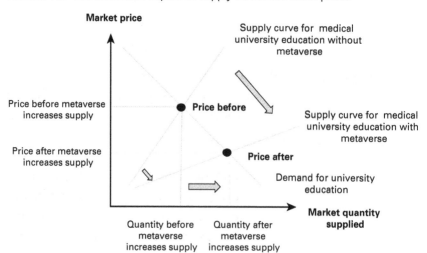

sections of society that have been previously unable to afford them. Could this feature of the metaverse to increase supply and lower costs redefine economics and address poverty?

The metaverse economy wallets, savings, investment and interest rates

Over recent years we have seen many new innovations in finance and investment, including embedded finance, where payments and financing are integrated into the customer journey, and DeFi, where investment and finance raising are completely automated using blockchain and smart contracts, as well as the rise of buy now and pay later. The metaverse has the potential to match person data with investment, finance, data and new levels of automation in ways that can give rise to new products requiring new economic management tools.

As we have discussed some of the key emerging technology applications include self-sovereign digital identity, wallets, tokenization, DePIN, DeFi, fintech and smart contracts, and all of these could provide the foundations for new levels of automation of savings, investment in relation to income and returns including interest rates.

There have been some discussions on the emergence of MetaFi products which combine metadata (which defines the ownership of an asset) and communities and DeFi to drive new levels of finance automation. However, could metaverse communities combined with DeFi models form the ingredients for savings and investment in the metaverse? In this model users in metaverse ecosystems and communities could come together to form liquidity pools (funds in which users contribute assets to provide liquidity for borrowers using Web3 protocols), which automate rewards. MetaFi could provide incentive for users to invest in return for an annual percentage yield (APY), rather a simple interest rate return.

In traditional economics the rate of interest sets borrowing costs or returns on investments, and they are determined by central banks as part of the monetary policy toolset. At the macroeconomic

FIGURE 7.6 MetaFi, smart contracts and new decentralized economic management tools

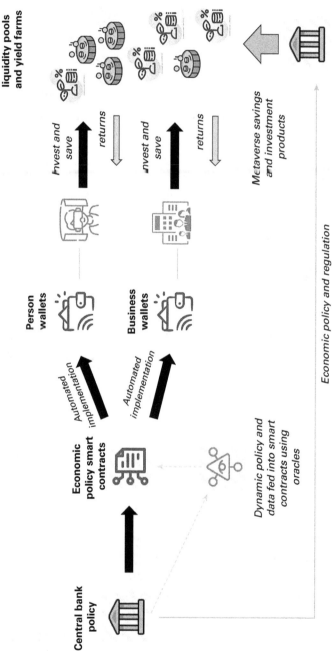

level low interest rates make borrowing cheaper and can increase investment and economic growth, whereas high interest rates have the opposite effect and slow demand and growth, and following years of negative interest rates in real terms we have recently seen interest rates increase across the globe to reduce demand, growth and in turn reduce inflation. If the metaverse investment and savings is based on DeFi liquidity pools and yield farms, then what tools can be used to control growth?

With the DeFi already emerging and gaining traction, as well as the right governance and regulation maybe the central banks need to evolve to encompass decentralized smart contracts where policy and economic management tools are executed through smart contracts and wallets. In this case policy oracles can feed live data and rules into DeFi smart contracts, and the wallets link these automatically to person or business identity, investment amounts and income levels of users.

With economic policy embedded in smart contracts, AI will detect where dynamic data is required in policy and feed this into the economic policy smart contracts using oracles. Digital wallets for people and businesses will be the interface between policy and execution. Where policy aims to slow growth then APY can be increased, and vice versa where growth is desired. Economic policy and governance can also be implemented via regulation of retail financial institutions at the national level.

The social metaverse: economics unemployment, taxation, subsidies, nationalization and government spending

There has been much discussion on the social aspects of the metaverse. Can the metaverse narrow the gap between rich and poor? Can it help us manage the environment? Can it create more social mobility? Can it provide the data for more targeted government subsidies and spending?

The digital identity, wallets and smart contracts outlined in Figure 7.6 could also potentially be used to apply taxation in the metaverse, whether embedded or on dedicated metaverse platforms.

This could be especially effective where metaverse activity crosses international boundaries, and the digital identity can be used to determine where taxation should be paid by an individual or company, with taxation-compliant smart contracts automating the tax payments. The information on income, revenues and location associated with identity could potentially improve the effectiveness of taxation, improve revenues and reduce cost to collect if the right low taxation incentives are applied, but could the same levels of automation be used to redistribute income?

During the Covid pandemic many governments wanted to provide payments and business loans to people who could not work or carry out business. With the current system these governments including the United Kingdom and the US had to do this through banks which added cost and time, whereas using wallets, smart contracts and retail CBDCs these payments could be direct. There is also the potential to build in redistribution of wealth, and even environmental diversion of income, directly into retail and industrial smart contracts in the metaverse; however, the question with this type of automation is how much direct control can be gained at the expense of freedom?

The role of national governments is also challenged by the concept of a global metaverse, especially where investment is required in national infrastructure and security, but users, location and ownership

FIGURE 7.7 Metaverse legal and regulatory flows

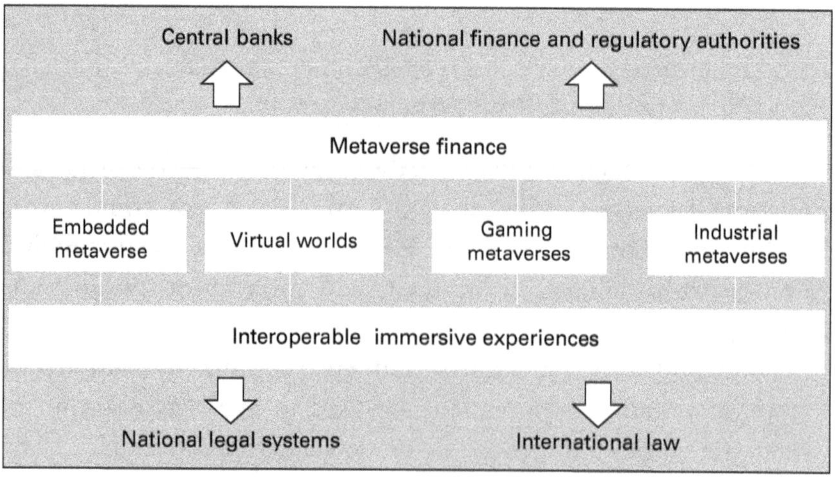

are virtual and across international borders. For example, in many countries schools and education are nationalized, owned and operated by national governments, but if the metaverse were to lead to universities being 90 per cent virtual, and the users 70 per cent outside the nation of ownership, and the teachers were 60 per cent AI robots and 40 per cent human, of which only 15 per cent were from the national country, should this still be state invested and owned?

Another consideration is citizenship and tax status – where today some people who spend the minimum time in any one country can claim non-domicile tax status, there could be similar arrangements for metaverse users and special tax status; again, the combination of digital identity, wallets and location of spending could provide the core tools to manage this.

The metaverse economy and regulation and recourse to legal systems

The metaverse will present new challenges for regulators given its global nature and new legal frameworks (See Figure 7.7) will need to be established to address issues unique to the metaverse, such as ownership and control of virtual assets, virtual harassment and virtual crime. There has been much discussion about regulation of cryptocurrencies, and progress in this area will be important to the Web3 metaverse, but the metaverse will present new challenges in finance, ownership, custody, jurisdiction, trademarks and IP, and given the global reach, questions will also be asked on who can regulate the metaverse.

Are video games showing the way forwards for metaverse regulation video games?

One of the more advanced areas of the metaverse is video games, and many of the issues associated with IP in video games remain unsolved. The metaverse is almost certain to escalate the current problems and introduce new ones.

Video games are considered protected speech in the United States under the First Amendment and therefore cannot be subject to government censorship or regulation based solely on their content.

However, certain regulations do exist, such as the ESRB (Entertainment Software Rating Board) system, which aims to inform consumers about the content of video games and help parents make informed decisions about what games their children play. In Europe and in Asia a similar rating system is used, called PEGI (Pan European Game Information).

The use of real-world objects in games has raised many questions, but is it a cause of alarm for potential IP infringement?

Many games replicate real objects, from vehicles and furniture to electronics and weapons with the aim to increase the realism of the game. These objects often carry IP rights and by using them in the video games, the developers and engineers risk infringing these rights unless they hold an adequate licence or authorization.

There is a plethora of cases before the courts which only show us that the position of the judges fluctuates and changes with time. A breakthrough case from 2020 on this topic was in relation to the use of Humvee tanks in the game *Call of Duty*. The New York district court found that there is no infringement if the use is for artistic purposes and the customers are not misled as to any association to or endorsement by the specific brand. Meanwhile, in the European Union, the use of cars that resemble the popular Ferrari brand in *Grand Theft Auto* has been considered not to be an infringement because the car did not replicate essential features adopted by Ferrari. It was held that the similarity between the cars did not evoke any associations with Ferrari, did not mislead the users nor take any unfair advantage of Ferrari's name and reputation.

While there is a fine line between what constitutes an infringement or not, the common approach that the courts tend to take worldwide is that the use of real objects in video games does not constitute an infringement on the IP rights of the holder as long as it is done for the artistic purpose of making the game more realistic and as long as the users are aware of this.

Why can the metaverse not be treated as art for legal recourse?

For years, video games have been successful due to the creativity of the developers. It would be difficult to mirror the current physical world IP rules which differ based on jurisdiction to the metaverse simply because you cannot amalgamate such a wide range of rights and rules. This would most certainly lead to inconsistency and impact development and creativity.

For this reason, there are strong calls for a metaverse-specific international regulation. The EU is taking the stand and is currently working on a new global governance and regulations which will focus on data, technology and infrastructure while trying to maintain a lawful, open metaverse.

Can video games and end-user licence agreements (EULAs) help with the metaverse?

The end-user licence agreement is the main governing contract for video games. This is key for relations between publishers and players, but also between players. The main two problems EULAs pose are that they are not enforceable against minors, and they may often include unenforceable or inappropriate terms. An example of such a term would be the prohibition of uploading videos from the video game to streaming websites without permission. While the idea behind it is understandable, it is not feasible to monitor all the streaming websites for such content, let alone trace that content back to a specific user and take action against them.

Turning back to the issue on enforceability against minors – minors lack the necessary legal capacity to enter binding contracts. Majority is usually set at the age 18, although it can vary from 16 (e.g. in Iran, Yemen) to 21 (e.g. in UAE, Singapore) across the world. There are certain ways around this, for example such as requiring parental consent. Another issue may be that the minors' presence is difficult to be identified online since most games adopt a 'tick box' approach, asking only for a quick confirmation that they are over 18. This has the undesired effect of escaping the age-restricted content and imposed regulations.

Video game companies are currently trying to overcome these hurdles by providing features such as parental control, stricter community guidelines or better education campaigns to encourage compliance with the terms.

Could non-fungible tokens (NFTs) be the solution to the ownership problem?

NFTs could be a good tool to align ownership in the metaverse. For example, you can buy an asset in a game as an NFT and transfer it to other games or worlds using exchanges. However, NFTs on their own present several IP issues.

One of these is the challenge of determining the true owner behind the NFT. There is a risk that users can claim they own certain NFTs without in fact being the true owner. As a result, it is crucial to ensure that there are proper verification and authentication mechanisms. Additionally, it is also easy to create, sell, replicate and distribute these digital assets, therefore raising even more concerns about people attributing one of the rights of the owners and thus infringing them. For this reason, owners need to ensure that they have a proper licensing system in place and that their digital assets are clearly defined and delimited.

It is important to note that ownership of the NFT does not mean that you also own the underlying asset. This is because the NFT is purely metadata added to a blockchain about an asset.

For creators, protection of NFTs in the metaverse is best done either through copyright or trademarks. Copyright is an automatic right that arises upon the creation of the artwork and is given to creator. Registration is not mandatory, but it can be done by the author to protect their artwork in case of lawsuits with the relevant national authority, e.g. in the US the US Copyright Office. On the other hand, trademarks must be registered to be valid and enforceable.

Metaverse and retail brands protection and opportunities

The metaverse also provides an opportunity for brands to realize more revenue and provide a more immersive experience to their customers. Fashion brands will be able to increase their IP portfolio through digital clothing and even virtual shopping in department stores, while sports organizations and clubs can extend their digital world billboards and acquire more sponsorships. FC Barcelona, Real Madrid and PSG (Paris Saint-Germain) have all filed trademarks to enter the metaverse, intending to offer virtual experiences, wallets and fashionwear.

Brands like Dior, Gucci, Ralph Lauren and Nike are already ahead of the race and have established a good metaverse presence either through virtual shopping experiences or digital fashion lines on *Roblox*. But not all fashion brands have the funds to invest in the metaverse, and in addition to that and the lack of appropriate infrastructure, some think that there is not enough evidence to highlight tangible customer benefits.

Additionally, not everybody is trusting of this innovative technology and the capacity to monetize from it, especially since it is aimed at connecting with the younger Gen Z. For example, Walt Disney halted its metaverse division, joining other big names such as Snapchat in their walk away from the metaverse. Nonetheless, the metaverse is growing and brands are mindful of the changing consumer perspectives and will adapt their metaverse strategies according to their targeted consumers' interests. Whether this will change the future of retail remains to be seen.

The risks that may be associated with digital twins

Digital twins are an important building block of the industrial metaverse. However, they are not a recent invention – they have been around since 2010 when NASA coined the term. But what are they? Simply put, they represent virtual replicas of physical objects or systems. Digital twins have been used for a long time, especially in the automotive business for model development and simulations. Some might even go further and argue that the metaverse is in fact the digital twin of our universe. However, these creations pose a few risks which owners in the metaverse should be aware of.

First, a digital twin carries a large amount of data which takes different shapes and forms, as they draw and integrate statistics and information from sometimes hundreds and thousands of sensors attached to the physical object. This data carries an enormous cybersecurity risk if it is not well protected.

Second, because the digital twin is a dynamic digital version of the real object, it must be updated with real-time data to mimic what is happening to its real counterpart. This attracts a vast amount of data exchange, computer power and, once again, increases the risk of cyber-attacks.

Thirdly, there is a modelling risk. Since the digital twin is based on data of a real model, the data must be correct initially. Owners should have mechanisms in place to ensure that the digital twin is an accurate replica with up-to-date and reliable information.

Finally, determining ownership is a complex challenge. As mentioned, there are vast amounts of data generated from the digital twin because of their connection to the physical object and attributing ownership when there are multiple parties involved may come with risks and disputes.

Everyone can recognize the advantages of digital twins, most notably their efficiency in optimizing existing products and processes at a reduced cost. Their use in the automotive industry has shown incredible benefits, since manufacturers are now able to see exactly what went wrong in the machine through the digital twin and change that specific faulty part rather than waste extensive time to analyse the real machine and sometime even change more pieces than necessary. Will digital twins become an indispensable part of the metaverse? While it is expected that they continue to expand to new areas (e.g. the world's largest twin appears to be a 1:1 replica of the entire country of Singapore), their necessity in the metaverse carries on being explored.

What are the new challenges emerging from generative AI and the metaverse economy

We have all seen the recent developments in AI, especially with the launch of ChatGPT. Generative AI is a new generation of machine learning models, built on large scales of data and special algorithms to generate new and original content. As expected, these new models come with a range of challenges: IP infringement, privacy, misinformation and safety.

Most datasets on which the AI model is trained will be in the public domain or licensed, but this is not the case every time. While the input risk may be mitigated through the creation of special licences, the question remains for the output risk: can the content generated by the AI constitute an infringement as a derivative work based on the dataset used? All depends on the circumstances.

Some of these datasets may include personal information about individuals. When you process information about an individual, you are required not only to provide notice to them, but also have a legal basis for doing so. While there is an exception to the notice requirement under the GDPR (General Data Protection Regulation) rules if the effort required for the notice is disproportionate to the aim, they still need to choose the legal basis for the processing carefully. One option may be legitimate interests. However, in choosing this path, the developers must weight their interests against those of individuals. Another derived challenge brought by privacy is the enforcement of data subject rights. If an individual whose data is part of the dataset requires you to delete their data, this may be impossible without having to completely redo the dataset and retrain the model, which can take weeks of significant computer power.

Another challenge is the potential for bias and misinformation. Datasets inevitably contain the bias of their writers, therefore training AI models on these sets has the undesirable effect of propagating the existing bias. Likewise, the fact that the output resembles the natural language of its creator makes it hard for the reader to spot information that is simply false. The AI does not (at least currently) have its own conscience to differentiate between what is right or wrong and can only produce output based on its training set by the developers. This flows into another challenge: safety. If AI is incapable of determining the good from the bad, it can easily be used for the wrong purposes (e.g. by asking it where to find guns). AI models deployed to the public such as ChatGPT must go through extensive safety evaluation processes, but the question remains about what would happen if a similar model did not in fact go through the same process and end up in the hands of the public.

Lastly, a more controversial issue is that of ownership. Who owns the content generated by the AI? Can AI be listed as a joint author? Now this seems to be a more philosophical rather than legal question. There is no known jurisdiction that accepts AI to be listed as an author and the more obvious answer is that the author of the AI will also be considered the author of what the AI generates. However, AI is still in its incipient stages and perhaps this position is likely to change in the future, allowing more advanced and independent AI to be collaborators.

How will the metaverse and law need to evolve in the future?

The metaverse is a complex concept that is still at its early stages, and as the technology evolves, new concepts will appear. Personal rights of avatars? Rights and liabilities of AI workers? Interoperability of objects? Universal law applications?

Once its shape starts to be defined more clearly, undoubtedly the regulations will follow, but most probably at a slower pace. We expect for legal dimensions of the metaverse to evolve when the metaverse becomes a place for commercial activities and integrations with Web2, Web3 and AI speeds up. However, given the removal of geography in the metaverse, there will have to be an international collective effort for harmonious use.

For now, users, creators, developers and investors are enjoying the blurred lines, testing the limits of this technology which concurrently tests the boundaries of existing laws and of those making them.

08

Communications in the metaverse

In 2021 the United Nations estimated there were still 3 billion people who had not used the internet; however, many of the world's population do own a smartphone.[1] This suggests that despite the focus on AR and MR headsets the key to accessing and experiencing the metaverse will be through the smartphone, and this could present a significant opportunity for companies in mobile and connectivity.

How will telecommunications need to evolve to support communications in the metaverse, e.g. hologram calling? Will communications need to incorporate self-sovereign digital identity? Can the mobile infrastructure evolve to power Web3 consensus? Will the smartphone and AR and MR headsets merge?

The communications industry has in recent times progressed through radio, telephone, television and satellite, with the internet revolutionizing global connectivity and information sharing. Is the metaverse the next evolution of global connectivity?

In this chapter we will explore the relationship between communications and the metaverse, and the impacts of moving from internet communications and mobile, to metaverse communications using metaverse spaces, AR and VR. We will analyse the new requirements on the existing connectivity infrastructure fibre, 5G, and assess if new developments like network slicing and open ran will be enough to support the minimum viable metaverse.

Some of the key questions we will attempt to help readers to answer are What does the metaverse mean for the communications industry? Is the metaverse just a challenge and new point of competition across CSPs, or rather is it a new opportunity to evolve new Metaverse

FIGURE 8.1 The evolution of communications to the metaverse

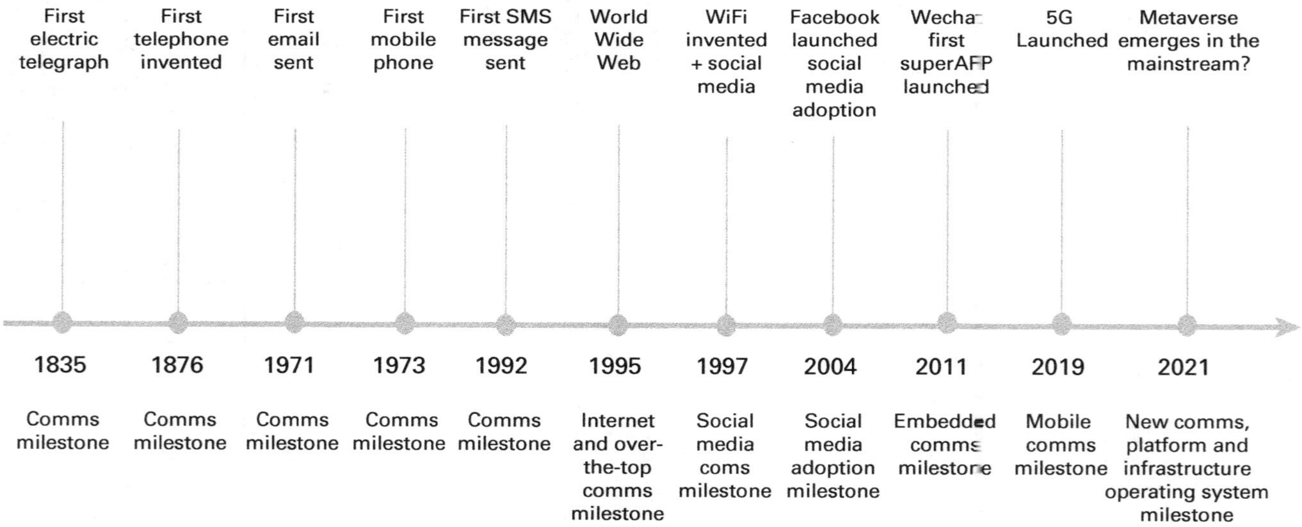

First electric telegraph	First telephone invented	First email sent	First mobile phone	First SMS message sent	World Wide Web	WiFi invented + social media	Facebook launched social media adoption	Wecha first superAFP launched	5G Launched	Metaverse emerges in the mainstream?
1835	1876	1971	1973	1992	1995	1997	2004	2011	2019	2021
Comms milestone	Comms milestone	Comms milestone	Comms milestone	Comms milestone	Internet and over-the-top comms milestone	Social media coms milestone	Social media adoption milestone	Embedded comms milestone	Mobile comms milestone	New comms, platform and infrastructure operating system milestone

Communication Service Providers (MCSPs)? Where are we now on the journey from CSP to MCSP and what are the timelines for change and benefits realization? How can businesses adapt to best utilize MCSPs?

How has the communications industry evolved?

The global communications market was valued at over $1.8 trillion in 2022 and is forecast to exceed $3 trillion by 2030, with enterprise communications the largest growth area. So what are some key milestones in its evolution?

In Figure 8.1 we chart the evolution of communications from telegraph, telephone, mobile, internet, social media and more recent developments in 5G to the emergence of the metaverse. The metaverse could bring about the convergence of communications, social media, Web3 and AI. Therefore, is the metaverse the new communications operating system?

Within the last 30 years, we have seen the emergence of the internet, social media, super applications and games with embedded communications, 5G superfast mobile internet. We've discussed the metaverse as an operating system which includes connectivity at the layer 1 infrastructure level with blockchain and cloud and computer infrastructure potentially incorporated. Could the move to converged infrastructure represent a new opportunity for CSPs and provide them with a key role in the metaverse communications?

What requirements is the metaverse| placing on communications?

XR technologies and solutions that are connected to high performance connectivity networks will be key to the metaverse, but how will these demands for network bandwidth evolve over time?

Today metaverse experiences consume connectivity in the same way as online gaming where reliable, high-speed connectivity is required for consistent gaming experience, with the difference that downloads may cause some spikes in demand. However, as the metaverse evolves it is expected that the following requirements will materialize:

- More content will be streamed, where a file is transferred in real time for viewing. Less will be downloaded which requires local memory. This move to streaming is expected to be driven by the need for smaller, more portable metaverse devices and the result of this will be an increase in demand for consistent high-speed connectivity.

- High bandwidth, low-latency capacity will be required for consistent VR experiences without glitches.

- AR solutions may require higher upload connectivity speeds to transmit data from IoT devices, for graphical placement on physical environments.

- Immersive features combined with graphic, video and video-heavy interactivity is expected to drive new dynamics demanding increased solutions for multiple traffic load, dynamic rate adaptation and latency variation demands.

- More AR and VR devices in addition to smartphones, IoT and other devices will increase the demand for connectivity.

- The metaverse will lead to more being done online with higher fidelity which will increase connectivity demand.

- Interoperability across metaverses and with Web2, Web3 and gaming platforms will drive new dynamics in usage and increase adoption and functions, which is expected to lead to increase in demand, but also different spikes.

Overall, the metaverse is expected to place new demands on communications and connectivity. If the size of the metaverse opportunity is over $1 trillion by 2030 this demand of communications and connectivity is expected to increase quickly. In addition, the metaverse as an operating system is expected to make it easy to incorporate AI and other technologies which should drive demand further, leading to questions on how the connectivity industry is responding.

What are CSPs doing to meet the demands from digital technologies and the metaverse?

In addition to 5G, the telecommunications companies are innovating and introducing improvements to the connectivity infrastructure and performance. Some of these initiatives include:

- Small Cells, which are low-power, short-range cellular base stations that can be placed in densely populated areas to increase network capacity and coverage, especially indoors and in crowded urban areas.
- A distributed antenna system (DAS) which places multiple antennas throughout an area to improve wireless coverage and capacity. The aim of this technology is improving wireless coverage and capacity in large indoor areas like stadiums, arenas, retail parks, shopping malls and conference centres, and could be critical for large MXCs.
- Dynamic spectrum sharing (DSS) enables 4G and 5G networks to share the same spectrum, maximizing efficiency and enabling a smoother transition to 5G without disrupting existing services.
- Carrier aggregation involves using multiple mobile CSP networks simultaneously by combining multiple frequency bands to increase data speed and reduce latency. This enables improved utilization of network resources and optimized capacity.
- Massive multiple-input multiple-output (Massive MIMO) technology uses a larger number of antennas at both the base station and the end-user device to improve network capacity, coverage and overall performance, with the aim to help meet increasing demands associated with densely populated areas and high device density and penetration.
- Network functions virtualization (NFV) is the process of moving functions that run on dedicated hardware to virtual environments to improve and optimize network scalability, flexibility and management.
- Software-defined networking (SDN) separates the network control plane from the data plane, and while NFV is about optimization through moving to virtual environments, SDN aims to achieve this

through new ways of controlling the routing of data packets (small units of data derived from larger messages for the purpose of internet transmission) through central servers.

- Edge computing is the processing of data by devices at the edge to reduce latency and improve response times. This is particularly important for AR and VR metaverse applications that require real-time interactions, and the industrial metaverse links with IoT devices. Edge computing can also play an important role in linking network connectivity with metaverse devices as the edge network can be extended through metaverse devices, potentially creating a network of interconnected wireless radio metaverse devices that communicate directly, creating a mesh of connectivity that does not need a central hub. This would form the basis of a metaverse mesh network and direct connectivity across devices for optimization in virtual environments to supplement central network capabilities.

  o 5G high-speed connectivity at low latency is also a critical enabler at the edge, but this is made even more powerful when mobile connectivity and cryptography at the edge is linked to blockchain as we did with the digital asset broker and data can be secured, signed and transacted, creating a root of trust at the edge. We will discuss this further in this chapter.

- CSPs are exploring the use of low Earth orbit (LEO) satellites to provide global connectivity, especially in remote areas. The most prominent examples include SpaceX's Starlink and OneWeb.

  o Starlink started launching satellites in 2019 and provides internet access to over 60 countries, and is rolling out global mobile phone service, with OneWeb launching similar services in 2023.

  o Satellite coverage has the potential to 'fast track' metaverse accessibility for developing countries without the fixed and mobile infrastructure to support metaverse access at penetration levels required for economic growth; however, the price point will be critical given income levels.

These technologies are helping to increase network capacity, coverage and speed but could the evolution of Rich Communication

Services (RCS) be key to bridging physical connectivity and the metaverse? Could RCS with special messaging and calling, designed and optimized for communication across metaverse users, on metaverse platform, incorporating metaverse devices be the future?

What is the relationship between communications and the metaverse?

The metaverse and communications are closely linked, with connectivity playing a key role in enabling metaverse communication tools, real-time interactions, immersive experiences and collaboration across users within games and virtual worlds. Metaverse users engage through voice, text and video, and avatars for non-verbal expression. Spatial audio in the metaverse creates sounds linked to metaverse environments, and inbuilt tools for content sharing enhances collaboration.

The role of the metaverse so far is as a consumer of connectivity and communications capabilities, but as an operating system this is expected to change with the metaverse acting as a supplier of connectivity and communications that can be bundled with other infrastructure like cloud and blockchain. Could this ability to combine connectivity with blockchain and platforms lead to more innovation in communications in the future?

How will users access the metaverse?

When we look at pictures of the metaverse we often see people with XR headsets, and there has been a lot of focus on these headsets and the way to access metaverse content, but is this going to be enough to drive the critical mass of adoption?

To meet the forecasts that have been attributed to the metaverse opportunity, universal, accessible access to the content at scale will be critical, and the size of the opportunity, which could be as high as 5 per cent of global GDP, indicates that access will need to support a variety of conditions, scenarios and standards in work, home, industry and on-the-go in high numbers.

To meet this demand either billions of new devices will need to be designed, manufactured and sold or an access device with sufficient penetration in the consumer population and business will need to be adapted for access, or a combination of both approaches. The mobile phone currently has over 90 per cent penetration and it can be argued that for the metaverse to scale it will need to be accessible through them. I would expect some development on handsets and accessories to incorporate XR capabilities at a lower cost base, but to enjoy some of the richer feature sets specialists' headsets will be required. Over time we can expect increasing convergence of mobile and headsets to devices that increasingly incorporate both.

Access standards and interoperability will be important as adoption will require mass access across platforms, operating systems and devices. In the future metaverse we expect that the starting point of interactions will be through the metaverse space and wallets which will hold our identity, assets and payment credentials and therefore integration of wallet technologies with access devices will be important when payments are incorporated in experiences.

The embedded metaverse will also allow the metaverse to reach across platforms and ecosystems to accelerate growth, reach and adoption, so how can we start the journey of the embedded metaverse?

The embedded metaverse will require partnerships with established ecosystems like retail, payments, finance, social media, education, as well as business ecosystems like manufacturing and supply chains where immersive metaverse capabilities will be incorporated and accessed as part of their journeys. For example, a retail journey can start normally and then where the customer demands a more online experience before purchase embedded metaverse capabilities would be exposed to the user.

What does communications in the metaverse look like?

We have already set out the increase in connectivity speed and resilience that the metaverse will require from the communications industry, but it could also require convergence of infrastructure beyond connectivity to power the new era of immersive communications. This would include connectivity, blockchain and Web2, Web3, AI, wallets, digital identity, gaming and even payments as communications will be across all of these, with the metaverse in this case acting as the bridge.

In terms of interoperability of communications there is also the use of phone numbers, associated Know Your Customer (KYC) and roaming settlement as tools to accelerate travel between virtual worlds, and communications settlements.

These capabilities of the metaverse to incorporate OTT communications, as well as banking wallets and infrastructure lays the foundations for new types of communications to evolve which will be important to overall metaverse development.

How could the phone number be the digital identity to bridge physical and virtual worlds?

One of the challenges for metaverse growth which we explored in Chapter 2 is ensuring there is a link to a legal entity between virtual and physical activities. This is also one of the barriers to embedded payments in SuperApps, with the need for KYC being a pre-requisite for embedded payments, so what does this mean for the metaverse?

The metaverse will expand the range of activities, ownership and interoperability across the metaverse and with the physical world, and as digital ownership and the associated contracting expands this will need to link back to a physical person or entity. If users could use their phone number as their metaverse identity then this would allow metaverse activity to be traced back to a physical entity, location or jurisdiction, providing a clear recourse to legal processes.

One advantage of this approach is that KYC is already in place for phone numbers, and there are mature authentication processes and even roaming processes for settlement across CSPs. This would allow the metaverse to leverage this infrastructure and accelerate growth and link to established finance and payments.

Can AI change communications?

The potential for AI to enhance communication could be both at the infrastructure and application layers. At the infrastructure level AI can bring intelligence to networks and help optimize utilization, but at the operating system and application layers it can revolutionize communications through things like natural language translation, incorporation of gestures and AI communications assistants.

AI chatbots are already one of the most widely used communication tools for customer service; however, when we add more AI and metaverse immersive technologies their role could be extended beyond online to include more of the roles that human assistants and customer service agents perform now in the real world, providing instant responses 24/7 and allowing human assistants to focus on other more complex roles.

In addition, AI language translation has the potential to break down communication barriers allowing users to communicate in local voice and text and have this translated in real time to the recipient language. This translation capability could also extend beyond language translation to technical translation, where high technical content could be automatically translated to the technical level of the recipient, both capabilities making communications more effective.

AI will be important to personalizing communications in the metaverse, with algorithms tailoring them to the individual user, and helping to predict needs as part of the AI assistant roles. The use of AI in communication is expected to increase in industry to consumer use cases like counselling, GP services and mental health advice as well as education support and tuition and training; in each case the metaverse operating system providing the infrastructure, environment and interaction tools.

What is the relationship between communications, the metaverse and Web3?

Blockchain can play an important role at the infrastructure layer of the metaverse and work with connectivity infrastructure to provide new peer-to-peer communications and messaging to the metaverse. Metaverse messaging is based on peer-to-peer architecture and networks enabling people, organizations and devices to communicate directly with the need for a central intermediary, and this type of solution works on top of blockchains, wallets and cryptography and can even work with decentralized storage solutions. These components also form the foundations for mesh networks, which can potentially enable smartphones and IoT devices to link together and form their own peer-to-peer connectivity networks.

There is another dimension to the role of Web3 which we touched on earlier that is relevant here, which is tokenization and utility tokens forming the basis for new Web3 connectivity payments over blockchain and self-sovereign digital identity which would provide the capabilities for person-centred communications and connectivity solutions.

What is the relationship between IoT, Web3 and the metaverse?

There are forecast to be around 30 billion IoT devices in operation by 2030, in some cases linking to digital twins in the industrial metaverse, but also providing a potential source of data for AI. The Vodafone Pairpoint platform that I co-founded at Vodafone links IoT devices to blockchain and fintech so that they could have an interoperable digital identity, portability of assets and automated and programmable payments, but how is this linked to the metaverse?

When the Pairpoint concept started out we wanted to tokenize IoT assets and transact them using tokens for micro-payments between devices peer to peer. We then worked to build a link from the SIM card to public blockchains so that the cryptography in the SIM could be used to externally sign on these chains so that devices could transact on them. When this root of trust technology was combined with wallets, tokens and fintech it enabled automated device to device transactions, but more importantly it combined Web3 infrastructure with cellular and fintech to power this new IoT economy. This is key to the metaverse as data will be the key currency transacted and this enables IoT devices to transact this in real time providing a key source of data for AI large language models (LLMs), and an ecosystem of digital twins for billions of IoT devices to kick-start adoption.

FIGURE 8.2 The impact of the metaverse on communication

Metaverse connectivity infrastructure, expand to meet demands of metaverse and AI	Embed metaverse products and service and integrate connectivity into the operating system	Differentiate networks by adding features and capabilities in the metaverse operating system e.g. AI	Innovate and implement new ways of communicating and messaging in the metaverse

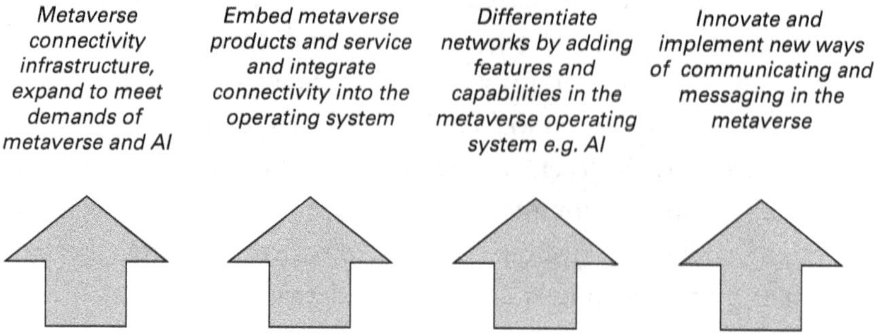

We explored the economy of the metaverse earlier but the combination of the Economy of Things, economy of tokens and the metaverse of economy could be key to power the next level of business and industry.

What are the key impacts of the metaverse on communications?

Communications are evolving to support the new generations of technologies and experiences that are demanding faster and lower latency connectivity, but the metaverse and AI can introduce intelligence, optimization algorithms and drive expansion and innovation in the way we communicate which is closer aligned to platforms, gaming, AI and interoperability across experiences and ecosystems.

In Figure 8.2 we outline four keys impacts of the metaverse on communications. These are driving expansion of the infrastructure, integrating metaverse into the connectivity infrastructure, making metaverse features a differentiator and point of competitive advantage for CSPs, and driving innovation and new ways of communicating.

Note

1 United Nations (2021) ITU: 2.9 billion people still offline, www.un.org/en/delegate/itu-29-billion-people-still-offline (archived at https://perma.cc/9GWN-S96Q)

09

The eight keys to the metaverse

The emergence of the metaverse is just beginning, but as we explored in Chapter 3 the opportunity is significant, but so is the wider potential impact on our lives and the world around us. As we have progressed through significant points in business history one key area of focus has been on improvement of business processes and technological innovations to increase productivity. It can be argued that the metaverse provides us with opportunities to fundamentally increase productivity and, where supply of digital goods and services can be infinitely increased, having the overall impact of lowering price.

The infinite increase in supply of digital goods and services can in some cases extend production at low or even zero marginal costs opening up a new digital supply frontier running in parallel to the physical world. However, as we have discussed in previous chapters the journey to realize the metaverse is just beginning, and the opportunity to reset the productivity boundary has not yet been realized and will require investment and a shift to production and consumption of digital goods as a substitute for physical ones.

In this chapter we explore the following eight keys to metaverse success: 1) adaptation of economic and legal systems, 2) successful use of AI and monetization of the data economy, 3) incorporation of the token economy, 4) use of interoperable digital identity 5) adoption of digital wallets, 6) improvements in connectivity, 7) use of distributed infrastructure, 8) ensuring the right levels cyber security and quantum proofing; see Figure 9.1.

FIGURE 9.1 Eight keys to the metaverse

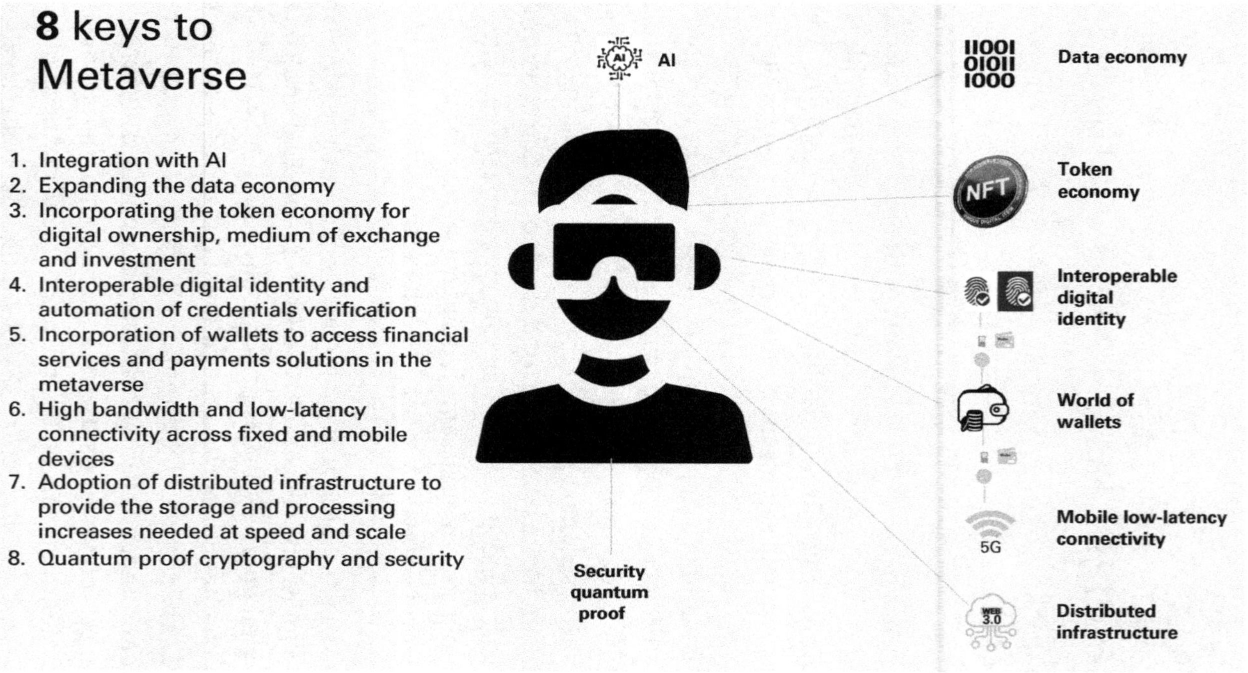

8 keys to
Metaverse

AI

 Data economy

 Token economy

 Interoperable digital identity

 World of wallets

 Mobile low-latency connectivity

5G

WEB 3.0 Distributed infrastructure

Security quantum proof

1. Integration with AI
2. Expanding the data economy
3. Incorporating the token economy for digital ownership, medium of exchange and investment
4. Interoperable digital identity and automation of credentials verification
5. Incorporation of wallets to access financial services and payments solutions in the metaverse
6. High bandwidth and low-latency connectivity across fixed and mobile devices
7. Adoption of distributed infrastructure to provide the storage and processing increases needed at speed and scale
8. Quantum proof cryptography and security

Key 1 – The adaptability of economic and legal systems

The metaverse must work with existing economic policy,
currencies and tools

The ability for governments to apply macroeconomic policy to the metaverse will be critical as citizens increase activity in virtual worlds. It will be important to ensure key factors like inflation, money supply, taxation, unemployment, growth, subsidies and international trade can be managed and aligned with government policies. This leads to questions as to how the metaverse can position itself so that government economic policy, systems and regulations can be quickly and easily adapted.

One approach could be to follow the economic and legal precedents currently applied to Web2 platforms and gaming as the first phase.

The metaverse will run across geographic and national government boundaries and generate new types of cross-border business activities, but the key to adoption is for the metaverse to operate within the existing economic frameworks, categories and reporting, and economic systems. There has been much discussion about the role of Web3 in the metaverse, and while there will be significant Web3 in the metaverse, to gain adoption the metaverse must incorporate mainstream finance and associated macroeconomic governance. The emergence of the metaverse as embedded capabilities within existing platforms and applications makes operation within existing economic frameworks easier; however, new stand-alone metaverse businesses which use new technologies like AI and Web3 are more challenging from a regulatory and compliance perspective.

Taxation management is the process by which governments collect revenue from individuals and businesses based on their income, profits or transactions, to fund public services and infrastructure, and it will be important for metaverse activity to operate within the current national and international systems to gain adoption, although some countries may implement special metaverse taxation incentives to attract metaverse business.

Government subsidies provide funding to industries to promote growth, improve affordability or address market failures. Both taxation and subsidies are essential tools for managing a national economy,

FIGURE 9.2 The keys to quick economic system adoption

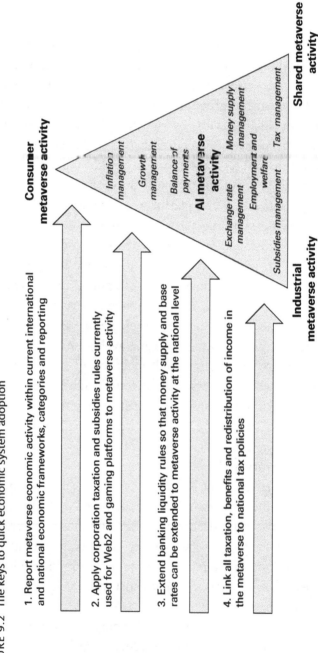

1. Report metaverse economic activity within current international and national economic frameworks, categories and reporting

2. Apply corporation taxation and subsidies rules currently used for Web2 and gaming platforms to metaverse activity

3. Extend banking liquidity rules so that money supply and base rates can be extended to metaverse activity at the national level

4. Link all taxation, benefits and redistribution of income in the metaverse to national tax policies

Consumer metaverse activity

Shared metaverse activity

Industrial metaverse activity

AI metaverse activity

Inflation management

Growth management

Balance of payments

Exchange rate management

Money supply management

Employment and welfare

Subsidies management

Tax management

balancing budgets and influencing economic behaviour, and metaverse subsidies could play a critical role in promoting national industries and businesses in the metaverse, but the metaverse business will need to operate within national government sectors to receive this.

Banking liquidity rules require financial institutions to maintain a portion of their assets as cash or easily convertible assets to ensure solvency and stability. The money supply and base rates, set by central banks, impact the economy. Higher base rates can reduce money supply growth to control inflation. Extending this to the metaverse in the short term would involve creating virtual liquidity rules, digital currencies and virtual central banks to manage the virtual economy's stability and inflation; however, this will take time and in the short term the existing liquidity and money supply systems and policies must extend to metaverse activity. The emergence of embedded metaverse activities should make it easier for incorporation of existing money supply and liquidity rules but this will require incentives for existing banking lending and finance to be dominant in the metaverse.

Personal taxation places taxes on the incomes of people, assets or transactions, while redistribution of income involves transferring wealth from high-income individuals to low-income ones through progressive taxation and social welfare programmes.

In the metaverse these tools could provide mechanisms for governments to implement policies for social equity, fund new metaverse public services, and apply taxation and redistribution systems. However, for this to happen governments must be able to apply taxation and spending in the metaverse in line with what it does in the physical world. This will be key to achieving government funding and wider participation in the metaverse.

Existing legal, regulatory systems must apply to the metaverse

The metaverse will present many new regulatory and legal challenges, including jurisdiction, IP and trademarking; however, developing new regulation, laws and legal precedence will take time and sizeable investment in the metaverse and will require some legal certainties for management of risk. Some of the questions will be how can disputes in the metaverse be settled. Will there be special courts in the metaverse? How can my IP and trademarks be protected given the platforms in the metaverse can duplicate land and other services? How can privacy be managed? How can regulations be implemented and managed when the metaverse goes across international boundaries?

For the metaverse to gain adoption investment is needed, and for investment legal and regulatory certainty will be required, meaning that in the short term at least the current legal and regulatory systems must work for the metaverse also. So, could the regulations and laws that relate to the internet work for the metaverse?

For example, the law that applies to the internet is largely determined by using the jurisdiction of where the website is directed to, and other factors like physical location, server location, citizenship or residency, international treaties, data protection laws, as well as legal principles and international agreements. However, even with the maturity of the internet some complexities arise due to its global nature, with countries able to assert authority over activities within their borders, or involving their citizens, where established international legal principles and international organizations are required to resolve disputes. For the metaverse to accelerate adoption following the internet regulatory and legal approach could be the logical route forward, but there could still be challenges.

In the metaverse can you register a trademark? Can you direct activity in the metaverse to a place? These are some of the metaverse-specific challenges to directly translating internet regulation and laws to the metaverse and could even pose problems where the metaverse is embedded.

NFTs, for example, can be considered property under existing laws; however, there are challenges related to legal jurisdiction due to the anonymity associated with the underlying blockchain platforms. This indicates that adoption may initially be dependent on Web2 platforms, and the establishment of regulatory and legal sandboxes to test the more complex challenges of regulating NFTs and the metaverse in general.

However, there has been positive developments in the United Kingdom where it has been determined that no new laws are needed to legalize smart contracts may indicate the immediate way forwards.

In addition, there are no specific laws or regulations in place for smart contracts. However, contracts executed on a blockchain network are subject to the existing laws that are applicable to traditional contracts, such as contract law, fraud law and property law. As smart contract technology advances, like the metaverse there may be a need for additional regulations and laws to provide clarity and certainty for businesses and consumers using this technology, but these types of developments indicate that there is a way forward for the metaverse.

Key 2 – AI and the data economy

Is AI and the data economy key to the metaverse?

We have previously discussed the role of data in Chapter 2 and explored the relationships between the metaverse and AI throughout this book. It is clear that the data economy will provide the incentives and machinery for the exchange of data across people, businesses and machines in the metaverse, but also that AI will provide the intelligence and insights which are both key to the metaverse as the new web browser and interaction point with digital content, applications and services and a provider of the insights needed for personalization. The relationship with the metaverse and AI is two-way, however, with the metaverse providing the environment for 'AI on earth' and as well as the intelligence. AI will also provide a new digital workforce of AI robots that will resource much of the new activity in the metaverse, with the relationship between AI and the data economy being a critical success factor to metaverse success.

AI can be described as technology which makes machines process information, make decisions and think like humans and perform tasks that would normally require human intelligence. AI algorithms are rules or instructions for the analysis and interpretation of data which is used to derive output intelligence from data. These algorithms enable outputs from data that would typically require human intelligence, but given the scalability of AI, once the learning is validated, AI has the potential to scale intelligence to areas beyond humans including the IoT and the metaverse. AI algorithms also play

FIGURE 9.3 The keys of AI and the data economy

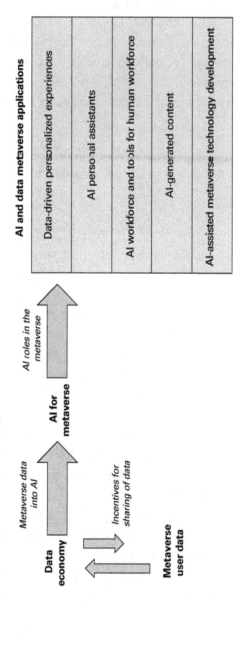

AI and data metaverse applications

Data-driven personalized experiences

AI personal assistants

AI workforce and tools for human workforce

AI-generated content

AI-assisted metaverse technology development

AI roles in the metaverse

AI for metaverse

Metaverse data into AI

Data economy

Incentives for sharing of data

Metaverse user data

a significant role in personalization, generating and populating virtual environments, providing the intelligence for metaverse and AI assistants and workers where realistic behaviour could be simulated and forecast for context-aware experiences. In this context, AI can turn the data generated in the metaverse into insights, and AI robots can also be a key part of the metaverse workforce.

The main types of AI are reactive machines, limited memory machines, theory of mind, and self-awareness. Generative AI is a type of 'limited memory AI', which means that it is trained on a set of data and makes its predictions based on the AI algorithm and LLM. AI's inception dates to back the mid-20th century. In 1956, John McCarthy coined the term 'artificial intelligence' during a Dartmouth College workshop. Early AI pioneers aimed to create machines that could mimic human thought processes. The field evolved with the development of algorithms and computational power. Key milestones include the first chess-playing program in the 1950s and the emergence of machine learning and neural networks in the 20th century, paving the way for modern AI advancements.

AI has the potential to play a significant role in differentiating the metaverse from the traditional internet experience. While the internet primarily serves as a means for information exchange and communication, the metaverse aims to create immersive and interactive virtual environments where users can engage with each other across virtual worlds and embedded metaverse experiences in more dynamic ways, in these cases AI enables the metaverse to provide more intelligent, responsive and lifelike experiences. The metaverse as an operating system is expected to grow with the development of AI through reactive machines, limited memory through to future self-awareness. The current capabilities already can provide personalization, insights, intelligence, tools and even a workforce of AI robots to resource metaverse platforms and applications. However, AI is only as good as the data that feeds into it and for AI to be effective the metaverse must deliver data, which makes the data economy key (see Figure 9.3).

In the context of AI and the data economy the combination of the data economy and AI can provide the metaverse with the dynamic insight and resources required to drive and resource metaverse platforms, content and applications. When linked to the transparency, trust and smart contract capabilities that Web3 can provide, there is also the potential for new levels of automation and monetization. The potential applications of the AI and data economy that differentiate the metaverse from the current internet include:

- Generation and management of intelligent avatars: Users can create virtual representations of themselves in the form of digital avatars. AI algorithms fed with user data can enhance these avatars with intelligent behaviours, natural language understanding and even limited autonomous decision making. This allows for more realistic interactions within the virtual world.

- AI-powered non-player characters (NPCs) can provide the metaverse with virtual characters for users to interact with, and can be extended to virtual workforces, including metaverse retail stores and virtual showrooms staffed by dedicated NPCs. With AI these NPCs can demonstrate realistic behaviours, adapt to user interactions and even engage in dynamic dialogue enhancing the sense of immersion and helping to enhance the experience. However, this could also be viewed as the metaverse providing the environments and interaction points for AI to expand and bring about change, which raises questions on policy requirements on the boundaries for use.

- AI-generated intelligent environments are virtual environments which are dynamic and responsive, with the ability to simulate real-world conditions like weather, environments and other physical attributes. They can also modify these virtual environments, landscapes and objects in real time to support more dynamic and interactive experiences for users.

- AI-generated content can assist in creating and curating content within the metaverse. It can automate the creation of virtual objects, environments and assets, reducing demands on people and providing tools for them to increase productivity in this area and focus on value-added areas, which in some cases would be beyond the scope of AI. These AI algorithms can also analyse, categorize and output user-generated content contextually, making it easier to support dynamics relevant to high-quality metaverse experiences.

AI and the data economy has the potential to become the fuel for metaverse content. AI could become tool for development of metaverse technology, and the new digital labour force to resource the metaverse, ultimately enabling the metaverse to evolve beyond the static and passive nature of the traditional internet, to provide a more immersive, interactive and personalized virtual experiences. This will be key to its success. However, the ability to integrate AI into applications will, to an extent, depend on the evolution of the metaverse as an operating system which allows developers to easily incorporate AI capabilities. This will require incentives and common standards for data, as well as ecosystem to scale, and must be considered within the critical success factors. So, is generative AI based on limited memory AI the key to what we have now, and could open AI be the initial step?

ChatGPT is an advanced language model developed by OpenAI, specifically designed for interactive conversations. It is based on the GPT-3 architecture but fine-tuned for chat-based applications. GPT-3 is already performing task-like text contextual information reporting, text completion, translation, summarization, creative writing, and demonstrating differing linguistic styles for different prompts and associated parameters. Although Open AI is not fully open-source given its already widespread use, it is already being used to enable the initial metaverse AI robots. And it has the potential to become more powerful when metaverse user data is incorporated. While GPT-3 is a powerful general-purpose language model, GPT-4 represents the next iteration.

The emergence of GPT-4 is an advanced language model by OpenAI, building on GPT-3.5. It now provides enhanced natural language processing capabilities, improved context understanding and increased accuracy, enabling more sophisticated and human-like interactions, with the potential to improve metaverse experience and the performance of the AI robots; however, maybe the biggest step could be with GPT-5 which could extend interactions to voice and enable more dynamic metaverse content creation.

GPT-5, the next iteration of OpenAI's language model, is expected to bring further advancements in natural language processing. With even larger parameter sizes and improved contextual understanding, it has the potential to enhance automation in various fields. Direct benefits for metaverse applications may include improvements in AI robot performance, automated content-generation, improved language translation and increased performance in data analysis tasks. In the future OpenAI has the potential to incorporate voice, rule-based and thought prompts into its language models, including various versions of GPT. Voice prompts would enable users to interact with the models through spoken commands and receive spoken responses, enhancing natural and immersive conversational experiences. Rule-based prompts could allow users to define specific guidelines or constraints for generating responses, ensuring adherence to specific rules or requirements. Thought prompts have the potential to provide deeper context by allowing users to communicate their thoughts or intentions, enabling more nuanced and personalized interactions. The current GPT-3 and GPT-4 provide a good start, but are there legal questions about the application of generative AI in the metaverse?

Could the legal position on generative AI be a barrier to metaverse adoption?

Generative AI presents several potential IP issues around ownership of content, copyright infringement, derivative work and recognition of base content creators, patents and trade secrets, and attribution of rights following collaborations using generative AI tooling, which could indicate that Web3 and blockchain could be key to provide the trust, transparency and automation required for more widespread and dynamic use in the metaverse going forwards.

- Who owns content, the original creator or generative AI? When generative AI algorithms create new content, such as artwork, music or written text, there are potential issues around determining whether the original creator or the generative AI holds the IP rights to the generated output. This also raises further issues on the extent to which AI-generated content can be protected, who has the authority to use it, how monetization of content should be divided and how. More certainty in this area will be key to the adoption and wider use of generative AI in the metaverse.

- Do generative AI models infringe copyright of the data used where that data includes copyrighted materials? There is a risk in these cases that AI-generated content may inadvertently infringe copyrighted work, which could be more probable where the AI models are trained on a large dataset containing copyrighted content without proper permissions or licences. Obviously, it will help the metaverse to have more data used and even real-time data, but the risks and potential legal challenges could delay this and present new steps to clear the data. Web3 self-sovereign digital identity and consent trustee solutions, which we discuss later in this chapter, could hold the keys to automation of consent.

- Do derivative works created from generative AI implicate the original creators copyright? Generative AI models often generate content that resembles or builds upon existing works, potentially resulting in derivative works. The creation of derivative works can implicate the original creator's copyright and may require permission or licensing. It can be challenging to determine the extent of transformation and originality in AI-generated content, leading to potential copyright disputes, but again Web3 identity and smart contracts solutions may hold the key here.

- Where generative AI use results in plagiarism how are issues on attribution, recognition resolved? Generative AI can produce content that closely resembles the style or characteristics of specific artists, writers or musicians. In such cases, issues may arise regarding proper attribution and recognition of the original creators. AI-generated content may also be used for plagiarism, as it can mimic existing works without acknowledging the source or obtaining proper authorization. Web3 could hold the key where solutions like turning content and style into a pay-per-use credential could be considered.

- What happens with rights and ownership when people collaborate with AI? Generative AI combined with metaverse environments has the potential to facilitate creative collaborations between human creators and AI algorithms. However, determining the rights and ownership of jointly created works can be complex.

Agreements and legal frameworks will need to be established to address issues of joint authorship, attribution and the respective contributions of human creators and AI systems, but again Web3 could be used to immutably log and secure collaboration activities and milestones providing the provenance for allocation of ownership.

· What are the implications if AI algorithms and processes are considered inventions and subject to patent protection? Generative AI may raise challenges in patent law and trade secret protection as the models, algorithms and processes used may be treated as inventions and subject to patent protection complicating use of generative AI, and the associated returns on investment, which may limit progress.

Addressing these IP problems associated with generative AI requires a thoughtful and balanced approach, and we are just at the beginning of the journey and legal frameworks, regulations and industry best practices need to evolve to provide guidance on digital identity, licensing, attribution and the protection of both human and AI-generated creative works. This introduces risk to investment which could delay development and limit AI use in the metaverse. Open-sourced AI, Web3 blockchain, decentralized identity and data credentialing solutions could hold the key in the future, but in the short-term generative AI in the metaverse is key to success. However, it will need to be implemented with care.

Data economy – incentives for user data

User data remains critical to overall platform development and the wider metaverse economy, but customer data is key to personalization of experiences, and will be critical to commerce in the metaverse economy.

The metaverse has the potential to build on the customer datasets that are collected in Web2 and extend to these datasets to include biological data such as fingerprint and face recognition since these are likely to be standard for the metaverse authentication. For example, tracking of bodily movement data such as eye position will be part of the AR and VR interaction with customers.

FIGURE 9.4 Customer data incentive models

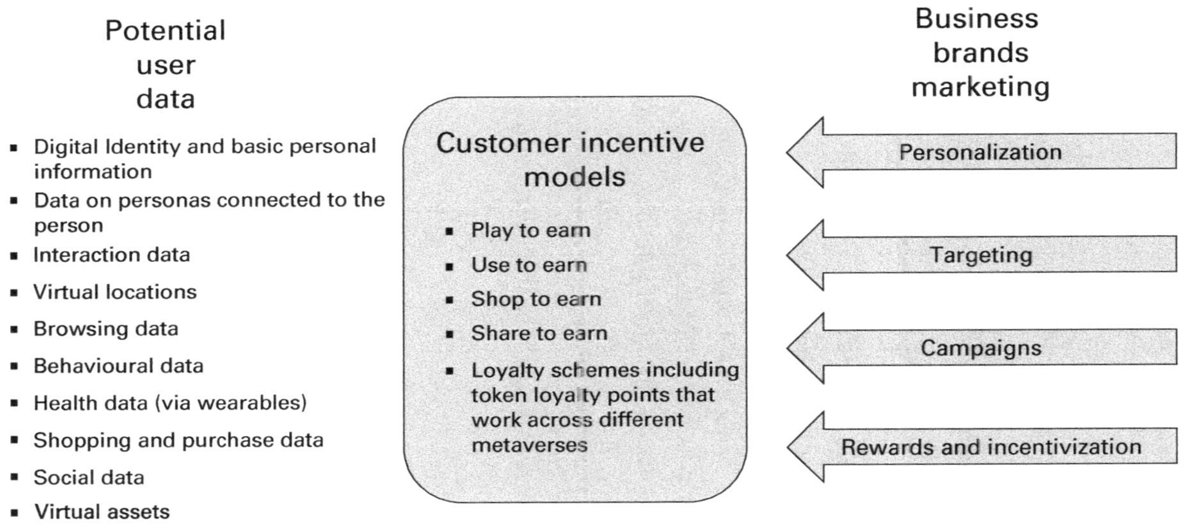

Potential user data

- Digital Identity and basic personal information
- Data on personas connected to the person
- Interaction data
- Virtual locations
- Browsing data
- Behavioural data
- Health data (via wearables)
- Shopping and purchase data
- Social data
- Virtual assets

Customer incentive models

- Play to earn
- Use to earn
- Shop to earn
- Share to earn
- Loyalty schemes including token loyalty points that work across different metaverses

Business brands marketing

Personalization

Targeting

Campaigns

Rewards and incentivization

Given the close interaction with the customer and metaverse applications the user and customer data could even include biometrically inferred data (BID), which come from inferred data and information gained from physical, behavioural, psychological and other non-verbal interactions, which with AI could lead to new more effective way to personalize content, experiences, goods and services as well as provide richer customer datasets into AI large language models (LLMs).

In the data economy the value of data is determined by the level of insights they provide to brands and marketing companies and although this has improved the metaverse offers more scope for personalization and will require better data to meet demands for personalization. In addition to BID and more personal interaction data there is some discussion that the immersive experience of the metaverse could increase dwell time which could in turn increase the probability of a user becoming a customer (see Figure 9.4).

We expect a richer set of customer data points to be available in the metaverse due to the closer interaction, but also from the increased ability to merge data from existing data sources. For example, wearables and eyesight could provide the ability to enrich and augment basic customer data with health, behaviour, performance and reaction time data.

For the data in the metaverse to flow, it will need to flow across the different platforms and ecosystems, and the SSI approach function in the context of incentivization models, as outlined in Figure 9.2, could help to achieve the required interoperability.

This approach would enable consumers to move digital assets, avatars and their data between platforms and ecosystems across the wider metaverse. Brands will need models to either engage with data aggregators or engage personally with metaverse users using the incentive models for data sharing, ensuring that within the incentivization models, automated consent is built in. Web3 smart contracts within the SSI solutions could be effective for this.

Data is a critical component of the metaverse, driving personalization, immersive experiences, social interactions, AI advancements and the virtual economy. By leveraging data effectively and responsibly, the metaverse can evolve into a dynamic and vibrant digital world that caters to the unique needs and requirements of users, but also provide users and stakeholders with new opportunities for monetization that includes users and customers at the centre of the monetization models. This should provide the incentive for more data to be collected, which is richer and higher quality than the current position. With AI the potential of this to drive better products, goods, services, content and experiences is unparalleled.

Key 3 – The token economy

Is the development of tokenization and the token economy key to metaverse success?

Security and banking tokenization is the process of substituting a sensitive data element like a banking card with a non-sensitive token equivalent with no intrinsic value; however, in Web3 tokenization is the process of converting or representing a digital or real-world asset as digital tokens that can be represented on a blockchain, transferred and exchanged. We discussed tokenization in Chapter 7 and outlined the components that bring the metaverse and token economy together in Figure 7.4, and now we explore the importance of tokenization as a key to the metaverse in this section.

Tokenization is now evolving and within the context of Web3 it is having an impact on how people, businesses and intuitions invest in and store assets therefore providing a tool to drive the conversion of physical assets into tokens digital assets, but also as these tokens can be programmed the technology also has the potential to change the way people, businesses and institutions interact with digital assets and the underlying liquidity and investment options. For the metaverse tokenization can translate physical assets into a form that can be represented digitally in virtual worlds, and for the physical world, tokenization can represent digital assets and incorporate them in physical experiences, financial and ownership processes.

The token economy is growing but the future potential opportunity is significant with reports by consulting firms BCG and ADDX

FIGURE 9.5 The asset tokenization model

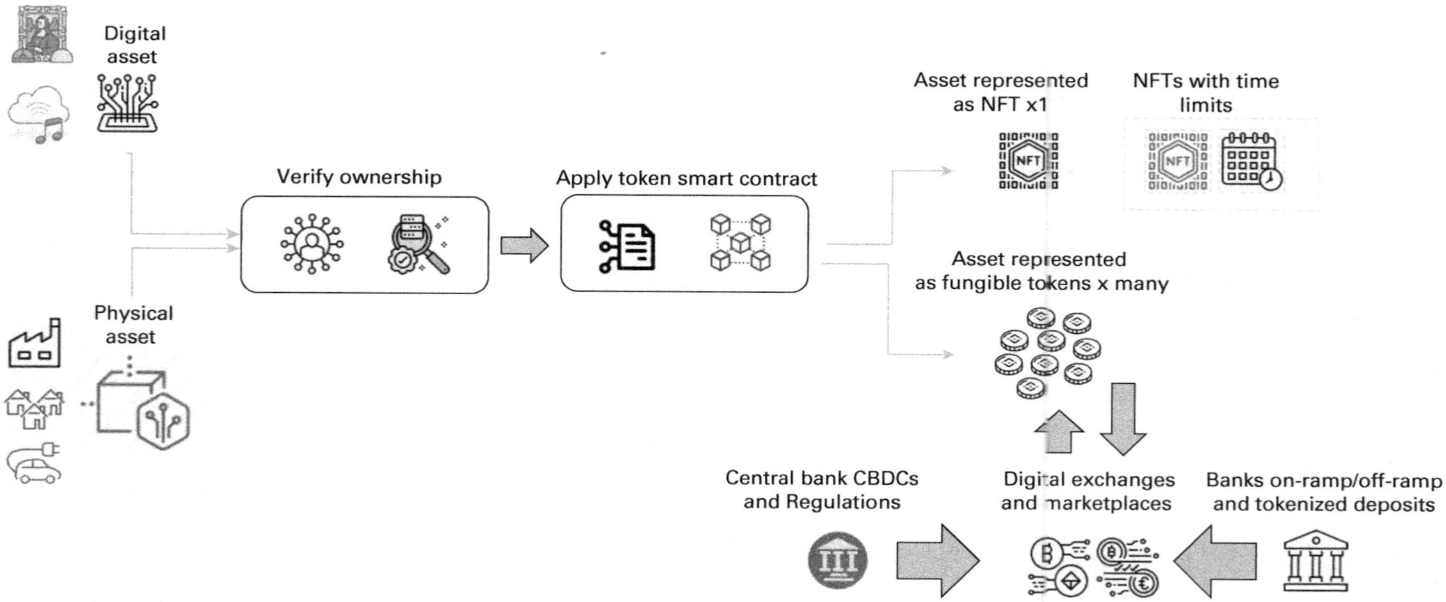

forecasting that asset tokenization could expand into a $16.1 trillion business opportunity by 2030.[1] This will undoubtedly include tokenization of assets in the metaverse, but how does tokenization work?

The first step to tokenization is to verify the ownership of the asset, and once this is completed then one of the many smart contracts for tokenization can be used. Typically, public blockchains and the Ethereum or equivalent ERC20 smart contracts is used for fungible tokens, ERC721 and ERC1155 for NFTs, and ERC4907 for time-bound NFTs. Once the tokens are generated, they are issued on an exchange and can be stored in a wallet, allowing the tokenized asset to be stored, transferred permanently or temporarily. In this case central banks provide regulation and potential interface with CBDCs, and commercial banks provide on-ramp and off-ramp facilities and potentially bridges to deposits with tokenized deposits. The tokenization model provides the metaverse with capabilities to tokenize assets, trade, transfer and transact and move them across virtual worlds, and in the physical world. In some cases, the token acts as the gate or bridge between both. This link is key to the success of metaverse see Figure 9.5.

Recently we have seen the asset tokenization concept extend to assets like patents, ideas and in-game assets all of which could provide a monetary structure for investment in the metaverse and extend the types of assets that can be monetized to include shared metaverse outputs like content, IP and even innovative creation. Could tokenization be key to financing the metaverse?

What is the role of blockchain in tokenization?

Blockchain provides secure, transparent, immutable and intelligent ledger capabilities for creating and securely storing, managing and exchanging digital tokens. Through smart contracts, blockchain enables the creation of tokens that represent ownership, assets or rights. These tokens can be easily transferred, traded and verified, reducing the need for intermediaries.

Blockchain can be described as the trust layer of the metaverse, enabling peer-to-peer transactions, smart contracts and tokenization including NFTs. While it is possible to have a metaverse without blockchain, there are some metaverse platforms where blockchain already acts as the governance and security layer providing trust and traceability in transactions, identity and events, and with smart contracts and tokens also providing the automation, identity and asset portability. So, what is blockchain and how does it work?

A blockchain is a decentralized and transparent digital ledger that records transactions across multiple computers. It works by creating a chain of blocks, where each block contains a list of transactions. Each block is linked to the previous one using cryptographic hashes, forming an immutable and tamper-resistant record. Consensus algorithms are employed to ensure agreement among network participants, and the distributed nature of blockchain eliminates the need for a central authority. Blockchain and the proof of work (PoW) consensus has historically been associated with the first major blockchain layer 1 platform Bitcoin, which launched in 2009 and forms the basis of secure and transparent peer-to-peer transactions associated with the Bitcoin cryptocurrency.

Bitcoin introduced the concept of Turing completeness in layer 1 blockchain, which emerged and introduced the use of conditional statements and loops enabling the blockchain to incorporate the programming of smart contracts and programming capabilities to support application development. Some of the major layer 1 blockchains that emerged over this period include Ethereum, Cardano and EOS, and following this new public layer 1, blockchains have emerged with improvements in security, performance and reduced environmental impacts, and they now form the foundations of tokenization solutions, but will this still be the case in the metaverse?

There has been much discussion about the role of blockchain and Web3 in the metaverse, and the extent to which blockchain could be converged into the metaverse operating system. For example, will the metaverse incorporate its own blockchain, and develop a specific metaverse protocol and consensus, or will it rely on Web3 public blockchains? One advantage of the metaverse developing its own blockchain would be its features could be optimized for the metaverse, and it could be designed for specific metaverse tokenization and associated finance and banking products. At the same time, it could have closer incorporation of Web2 and traditional banking and finance, which could drive choice and adoption for metaverse users.

Key features of blockchain and Web3 for the metaverse includes:

- Transition from centralized entities and intermediaries that control data and user interactions to blockchain technology and decentralized networks where distribution control and decision making is across users and participants.

- Trust based on tamper-proof and decentralized blockchain infrastructure for recording and verifying data, creating a foundation for Web3 applications.

- Smart contracts with the terms of the agreements written directly in code to enable automation and programmability of transactions, removing the need for intermediaries, and enabling decentralized applications to operate autonomously.

- Interoperability between different blockchain networks and protocols for seamless communication and data exchange between applications, blockchains, platforms and decentralized services.

- Self-sovereign user control over personal data and privacy to enable individual ownership and sovereignty over digital identities and data.

- Tokenization and use of tokens and cryptocurrencies as a means of value store, ownership, exchange, transfer, incentivization and governance.

Blockchain and Web3 represents a shift towards a more open, inclusive and user-centric metaverse where individuals have greater control over their presence and interactions with tokenization acting as the currency and financial system, and these functions of tokens being key to the development of the metaverse.

Key 4 – Interoperable digital identity

Is interoperable digital identity the key to unlocking the metaverse?

Imagine a world where you can travel without a physical passport, shop without physical contact or payment, bank without showing identification or physical banking, apply for finance without completing forms and providing information, use online services without passwords and where you can have different personas for different platforms, but link them to your legal identity and manage them accordingly. This world we describe could be made possible with digital identity and it could be the key to unlocking the potential and growth of the metaverse. But how does digital identity work and what is its role in the metaverse?

Identity is a mathematical term which belongs to the scientific theory of social mathematics and refers to the algebraic concept of equality among citizens in terms of legal rights and obligations. The concept of identity has evolved and now forms the foundations and keys to individuals and their interactions with people, business, governments, platforms and machines. Identity plays an important role in empowering individuals to exercise their rights and responsibilities fairly and equitably, and is important for social, economic and digital inclusion as it provides access to basic human rights such as healthcare, pensions, social benefits and the ability to exercise our right to vote, and for the metaverse this could be extended to include the right to work and socialize. To be able to access these rights, the ability to prove your identity is key. Historically, official documents such as passports, identity cards, utility bills and certificates have been used as a proof of your name, and your photo on these documents and signature for verification. Along the application and internet journey the evolution of digital identity has undergone significant milestones, including:

- The use of usernames and passwords as basic login credentials to proof identity and access applications, platforms and services; however, security for this method has become more limited as cybersecurity attacks have developed in sophistication and grown in number.

- Multifactor authentication (MFA) was later introduced an extra layer of security to usernames and passwords, requiring users to provide additional factors of verification to enhance protection against unauthorized access and attacks.

- Biometric authentication solutions such as fingerprints, voice and facial recognition added improved security and user convenience moving away from signatures to biometric confirmation as a means of authentication, which can be included in MFA solutions.

• Social media profiles which verify the identity of the user are sometimes used on social media platforms as part of their identity solutions to facilitate social interactions and networking; however, to contract and engage in some other activities including finance KYC is required, which limits this as a means of identity.

• Utility, banking and credit score profiles which incorporate KYC and financial information are often used in application, payment and onboarding experiences and provide another layer of identity information. However, they often require manual proof and verification steps. Web3 decentralized identity solutions may provide direction on alternative possibilities.

• Decentralized identity which incorporates decentralized identifiers or credentials (DIDs) based on self-sovereign identity (SSI) empowered users with control over their digital identities, enhancing privacy. However, they can also automate verification with new Web3 tools like smart contracts and zero knowledge proofs, potentially expanding the number and range of identity items that can be verified automatically. This will be key to making the metaverse work.

• Federated identity: Federated identity systems enable users to use a single set of credentials across multiple services, simplifying access management, which could help with embedded metaverse where experiences cross applications, platforms and virtual world experiences.

Benefits of these identity evolution milestones include increased security, reduced fraud, enhanced user convenience, greater privacy control and streamlined access to online services, ultimately improving the user experience in both society and business, but ultimately automation and interoperability are key to the metaverse and these enablers centre around decentralized and federated identity. Traditionally, identity was determined by personal attributes such as name and family and verified by paper documents like certifications and branded correspondence in conjunction with written signatures. Indeed, some of this legacy still exists today in many

FIGURE 9.6 Metaverse wallets as the gateway between traditional finance and Web3 finance

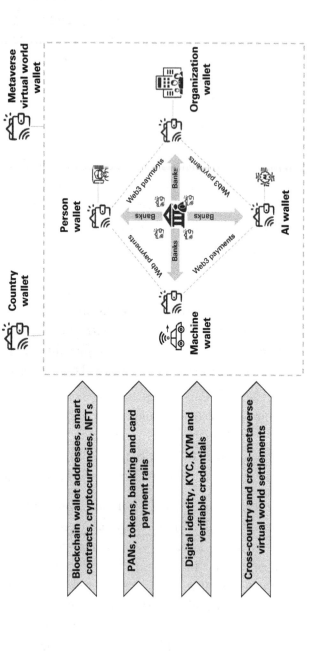

customer experiences and processes including KYC, but this is clearly not fit for purpose in the metaverse where individuals and business can be part of many platforms, have many personas, across multiple geographies and jurisdictions. This may require real-time authentication.

The metaverse is redefining how people connect and interact in virtual worlds where we can choose our digital avatars and personas, which can be different across applications, platforms and environments, but some interactions will still require some proof of identity attributes, for example location, age, qualification, address. To maximize growth and adoption proofs of identity will need to be interoperable to enable experiences across embedded metaverses and virtual worlds.

Key 5 – The world of wallets

Is the world of wallets key to the metaverse?

Digital wallets also known as e-wallets or mobile wallets are applications which run on connected devices or a blockchain address and store or link to payments, financial and other identity information credentials to enable users to make electronic transactions online, at physical locations and across platforms without the use of physical credentials or documents.

There are currently over 3 billion digital wallet users providing access to financial services, and as the metaverse grows to incorporate more financial services what will be the role of digital wallets? Why will digital wallets be key to metaverse success?

The metaverse will bring more people, businesses, machines and AI together in the context of digital user experiences, but it will also increase demands for embedded financial services. Metaverse wallets which hold private keys and identity credentials could hold the answers to incorporating embedded financial services and they act as a gateway between virtual worlds and traditional financial and Web3 financial services as outlined in Figure 9.6.

Mainstream digital wallets provide different services and come in different forms, for example personal wallets can be e-money wallets, which serve as web applications for online payments. Mobile wallets can serve as online or offline wallets on mobile devices for point-of-sale payments using contactless near field communications (NFC). Web3 crypto wallets provide addresses and store the keys for users to access their cryptocurrencies, manage transactions and interact with exchanges, while also acting as a payment mechanism for other decentralized financial products.

However, wallets are not limited to people, IoT wallets (one of which I have personally been involved in developing for the Vodafone DAB platform) are linked to IoT devices, while organization wallets extend wallet functionality to businesses. As AI robots increase in use online and in the metaverse, I expect AI wallets to emerge to provide transaction and payments capabilities.

Country wallets could operate at the national level across person, organization, IoT and AI wallets and could used for aggregated settlements and to represented national balance of transactions with other countries. This could also be extended to incorporate settlements across virtual metaverse worlds in a similar way to a national balance of payments today.

Web3 cryptocurrency wallets addresses could hold the key to the metaverse wallet and linking them to embedded metaverses and virtual worlds. Cryptocurrency wallets store private keys, allowing users to access their funds on blockchains, and within this solution. addresses are public identifiers that recipients share to receive funds, generated from the wallet's public key. Where these identifiers are linked to metaverse addresses, then this could potentially transform the metaverse into a system of peer-to-peer payment rails, with wallets facilitating settlements. However, to really scale, incentivize and manage liquidity traditional finance will need to be incorporated.

One of the most exciting developments in Web3 has been account abstraction and smart contract wallets which enable users to operate outside of the Externally Owned Accounts (EOAs) associated with a wallet addresses on blockchain to incorporate new account management and wallet structures which are interoperable and include better user experience in line with fintech standards, as the need for detailed blockchain processes are removed.

Account abstraction and smart contract wallets combined with fintech accounts could be the bridge to create a 'world of wallets' which incorporates over 4 million digital wallets, with Web3 wallets, tokens and peer-to-peer transaction capabilities for use in metaverse virtual worlds.

Key 6 – Fast low-latency connectivity

In Chapter 8, we explored metaverse communications with low-latency connectivity key to those communications and the immersive features. Connectivity has been evolving with high bandwidth fibre and 5G. These demands will increase with the metaverse as the demands move from simply connecting voice and data, to supporting immersive applications and the communications between them. The current demands for metaverse connectivity are largely on-premises, but as the applications expand there will be more mobile demands, which will be particularly apparent in the industrial metaverse where billions of IoT devices will transfer data between the physical and virtual worlds as digital twins. To meet these demands connectivity is expected to evolve further with much discussion about 5.5G and mesh network technology. Like cloud connectivity, it will be the fuel of the metaverse providing the means for actors in the metaverse to communicate and experience.

We will also need 5G or 6G connectivity to reduce latency between multiple devices and the cloud to send all this data to one IP address without needing to synchronize across servers. As the metaverse evolves we will need advanced analytics to react in real time and blockchain to record and create trusted transactions to support the demands of new experiences and applications, but what about mobile networks and IoT?

VR and MR technologies connected to high-performance networks will be one of the cornerstones and key enablers of metaverse use cases, making 5G crucial to ensuring that this new immersive internet can be experienced anywhere and everywhere. But can 5G deliver on the high-performance demands of the future metaverse?

The metaverse will demand fast low-latency connectivity everywhere, and the mobile network infrastructure has been evolving to support this including the recent roll out of 5G, OPEN Random-Access Network (OPEN RAN). In addition, IoT is growing with digital twin applications increasing significantly.

Most of today's metaverse experiences place similar demands on the network as online gaming. Reliable, high-speed connections are required for seamless gameplay, while occasional downloads of virtual assets require networks that can cope with regular traffic spikes.

As we discussed in the communicating in the metaverse section, CSPs will want more of the value chain in the metaverse. Some of the areas where they are expected to play a role beyond connectivity include digital identity, wallets and payments. An example would be the Vodafone Pairpoint platform which goes beyond connectivity to provide these services, connecting cellular with Web3 and AI for IoT.

Key 7 – Distributed infrastructure

Distributed infrastructure refers to infrastructure which is interconnected with servers and resources spread across multiple locations, designed to enhance scalability, redundancy and reliability in computing and data management systems which is critical to the operations and growth of embedded metaverse and virtual worlds.

Cloud computing functions as the data and storage layer for the data that will be generated and stored in the metaverse. There are many Web3 protocols that work with distributed storage platforms like the Interplanetary File System (IPFS)and there are now distributed cloud solutions emerging as well. Given the importance of data and storage, the cloud will have to be across all metaverse activities.

As the metaverse is expected to generate significant amounts of data from its new role as the new web browser and user interactions with content. Cloud data processing, storage and management will be important to support metaverse growth and expansion and ensure smooth experiences, and to maintain persistence and consistency across platforms, and records for cross-platform interoperability.

The metaverse may also need to incorporate real-world data sources, such as weather conditions, traffic information, social media feeds and others to create dynamic, contextual and real-time experiences. Processing and rendering this real-world data in real time will be an important enabler and key to the layer 1 technology infrastructure of the metaverse.

The metaverse involves the creation of virtual environments, ranging from entire virtual worlds to individual spaces or rooms. These environments can be generated through a combination of computer-generated graphics, 3D modelling and procedural generation techniques.

Rendering is the process of generating the visual and audio components of a virtual environment. It often involves creating and displaying 3D objects, textures, lighting effects, animations and soundscapes to provide users with an immersive experience. Rendering is normally performed on high-performance virtual machines in the cloud or on local devices, depending on the specific metaverse implementation. Real-time rendering engines are increasingly becoming widely used beyond video games. This includes the high specification Unreal Engine by Epic Games which is used by game studios, wider entertainment and the metaverse applications.

Processing and rendering play crucial roles in the architecture of the metaverse. Processing involves the computational power needed to handle complex interactions, simulations and calculations within the virtual world. This includes tasks like physics simulations, collision detection, AI algorithms and more. Rendering, on the other hand, focuses on generating realistic graphics and visual effects to create immersive experiences for users. Both processing and rendering contribute to the overall performance, interactivity and visual fidelity of the metaverse.

FIGURE 9.7 Decentralized rendering model

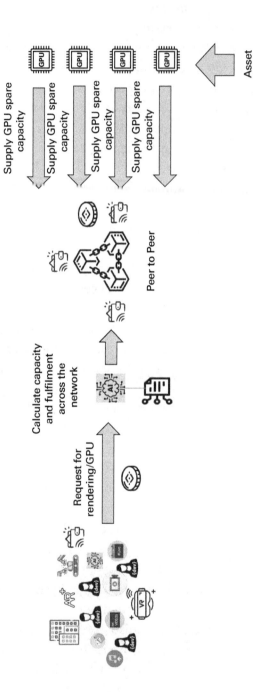

One of the best examples of the new rendering in use includes in-game cinematics that are rendered in real time in same game engine as gameplay activity and provide better results than pre-rendered content. This real-time rendering capability will be key to the evolution of the metaverse and a key enabler for businesses in this area; however, can Web3 be part of the solution?

We expect the Web2 platforms, film making, AI and metaverse to increase the demands on processing and rendering in the coming years. The Render Network is a decentralized rendering platform that connects those who require processing and rendering to providers with excess computing power and distributes the demand using blockchain. This enables peer-to-peer transactions using the native RNDR token for payments, incentivizing providers to offer excess computing power to others see Figure 9.7.

This decentralized approach unlocks spare processing and rendering capacity in near real time. Web3 could potentially help with investment too, where graphic processing units (GPUs) could be tokenized as assets, allowing more people and companies invest in the tokens for returns. This would require some clarity on the regulations on security vs utility but the concept of tokenizing GPU for investment could help to increase investment and supply, and be critical to laying the computer infrastructure required for the metaverse to grow.

Key 8 – Security and quantum proofing

Security in the metaverse encompasses several facets. Identity verification ensures participants are legitimate and protects against impersonation. Data encryption is key to safeguarding sensitive information while authentication enablers like biometrics or blockchain-based IDs enhance user privacy and security, but there is also more risk if security is breached, and more incentive for bad actors as there is more they can do with the identity. One of the key threats include quantum computing which has the power to break some of the key cryptographies used in Web3.

FIGURE 9.8 Metaverse cybersecurity threats

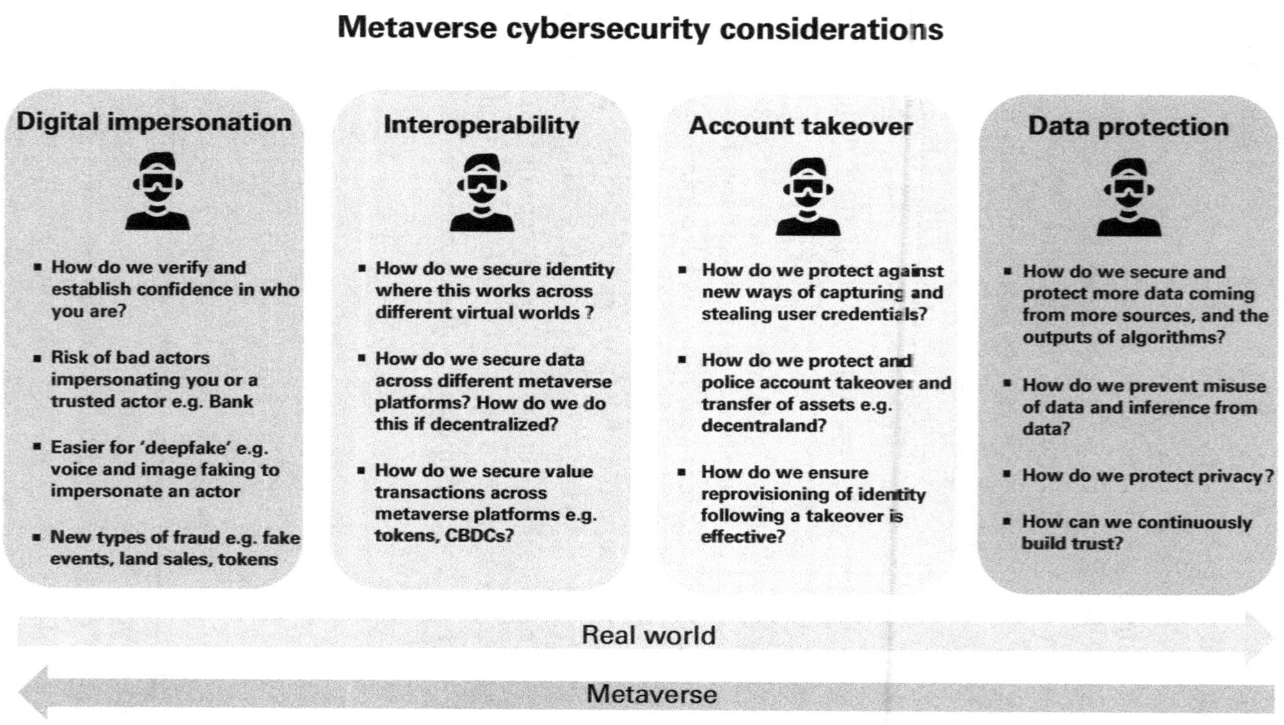

Metaverse cybersecurity considerations

Digital impersonation

- How do we verify and establish confidence in who you are?

- Risk of bad actors impersonating you or a trusted actor e.g. Bank

- Easier for 'deepfake' e.g. voice and image faking to impersonate an actor

- New types of fraud e.g. fake events, land sales, tokens

Interoperability

- How do we secure identity where this works across different virtual worlds ?

- How do we secure data across different metaverse platforms? How do we do this if decentralized?

- How do we secure value transactions across metaverse platforms e.g. tokens, CBDCs?

Account takeover

- How do we protect against new ways of capturing and stealing user credentials?

- How do we protect and police account takeover and transfer of assets e.g. decentraland?

- How do we ensure reprovisioning of identity following a takeover is effective?

Data protection

- How do we secure and protect more data coming from more sources, and the outputs of algorithms?

- How do we prevent misuse of data and inference from data?

- How do we protect privacy?

- How can we continuously build trust?

Real world

Metaverse

FIGURE 9.9 Metaverse security considerations

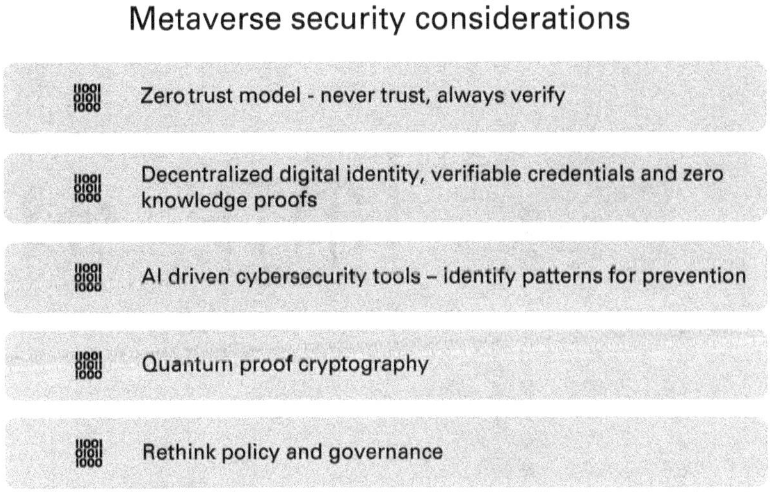

Metaverse security considerations

▦	Zero trust model - never trust, always verify

▦	Decentralized digital identity, verifiable credentials and zero knowledge proofs

▦	AI driven cybersecurity tools – identify patterns for prevention

▦	Quantum proof cryptography

▦	Rethink policy and governance

Securing the metaverse is therefore critical to provide trust, prevent cyber-attacks and safeguards digital assets. It is also important for user adoption to ensure that data and interactions are protected. This security, trust and safety create an environment that will help to transition commerce, social interactions to the metaverse.

However, securing the metaverse is not without complexities, as the metaverse includes a combination of advanced technologies like AR, VR, AI and Web3 which add to the demands on security solutions. For example, metaverse gaming, retail, land, workplaces and collaboration add to the cybersecurity threats and vulnerabilities. Particular threats emerge from data impersonation and interoperability across embedded metaverses and virtual worlds (see Figures 9.8 and 9.9).

As the metaverse becomes the user interaction point with applications, content and services, malicious users could monitor and collect information on the behaviours and biometrics of others in real time increasing the risk of impersonation. Providing security to users' cybersecurity and privacy should provide solutions to ensure that users, platforms, systems, applications and data are protected from these diverse threats and vulnerabilities. The specific attack points are at the edge, platform, data and blockchain layers, as outlined in Figure 9.10.

FIGURE 9.10 Cyber threats attack points

Metaverse and cybersecurity attack points

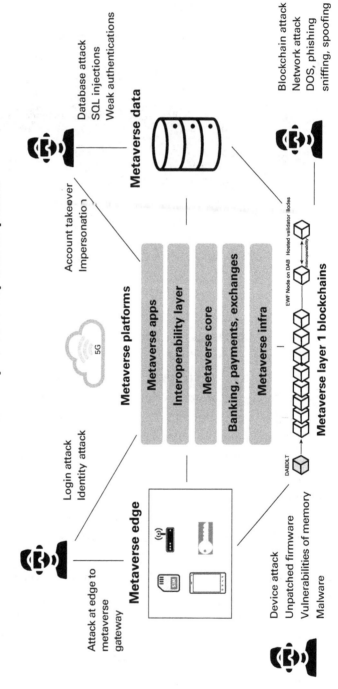

Attacks at the edge target the device(s) used to access the metaverse and the transport of the data from device to cloud. The risk is increased where the VR/AR headsets, head-mounted display and IoT devices can be used for authentication and access control, as hijacking the device could then bypass other authentication and give a bad actor access, therefore linking to biometrics and other factors of authentication would need to be dynamically incorporated in a way that could preserve seamless experiences which could present new challenges.

In addition, information on users' digital identities and the associated content stored in embedded metaverses and virtual worlds can be duplicated increasing the risk of fraud. For example, a metaverse users' information such as image, voice and video records could be hacked and used to duplicate a user's identity, and therefore it is difficult to direct and target security measures, as information is shared dynamically and in real time rather than at specific times and conditions. In addition, the current internet security solutions like user access management have limited capabilities to protect virtual environments due to interoperability, real-time data sharing and dynamic generation of personal data, which suggests that Web3 security, identity, smart contracts and cryptography have some of the solutions.

Personal data could be of particular concern as we expect users in the metaverse to generate far more personal data, which could also include more sensitive data, for example where AI assistants are linked to users and always listening when headsets are on, and if this is then combined with cameras that support gesture and even eye tracking this will generate high volumes of more sensitive data and present new challenges. Some of the solutions being discussed include having no avatars in some interactions. If there is an avatar, the solution would be to implement measures to prevent duplication, including establishing new privacy frameworks, strategies and policies for metaverse platforms, suppliers, users and software developers. On the data side, establishing ethical guidelines for data collection, usage and monetization to protect user rights and prevent exploitation as well as implementing regulatory frameworks and industry standards that address privacy, data security and accountability in the metaverse ecosystem could be key.

The security of the embedded metaverse platforms include may of the traditional platform threats including malware, unpatched software from hackers, but there are also some new threats to people and the physical world including AR and VR headsets being used to harm the eyesight of users, and digital twins being used by bad actors to target physical installations. These threats mean that new metaverse security by design should be implemented to ensure the sensitive areas of the metaverse security and privacy are covered at the architecture and development stages.

Securing the metaverse is not only key to metaverse adoption and the management of the new risks and threats that it brings, but it could also be key to success, a differentiator and a feature that will incentivize adoption from the existing solutions. For example, quantum proof cryptography and security could be built into the metaverse by design, as well as solutions like automated self-sovereign digital identity with verifiable credentials and zero knowledge proofs. What is certain is that the metaverse is emerging and is presenting a bigger prize for bad actors and with it come new security challenges. How to protect people, businesses, machines and AI in this new world will require new approaches and solutions, but because the metaverse is new it also affords the luxury of building these new solutions in at the beginning, rather than having to retro fit them, but one thing for sure is that securing the metaverse is key to success.

Note

1 ADDX (2022) BCG, ADDX report: Asset tokenization to grow 50x into $16 trillion opportunity by 2030, addx.co/insights/bcg-addx-report-asset-tokenization-to-grow-50x-into-us-16-trillion-opportunity-by-2030/ (archived at https://perma.cc/22QG-3H82)

APPENDIX

FIGURE A1 The eight layers of the metaverse

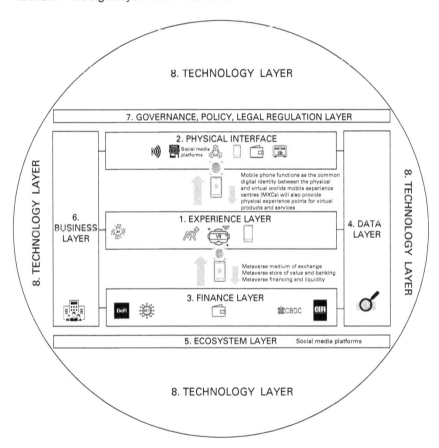

FIGURE A2 The metaverse operating system acting as the developer marketplace of marketplaces

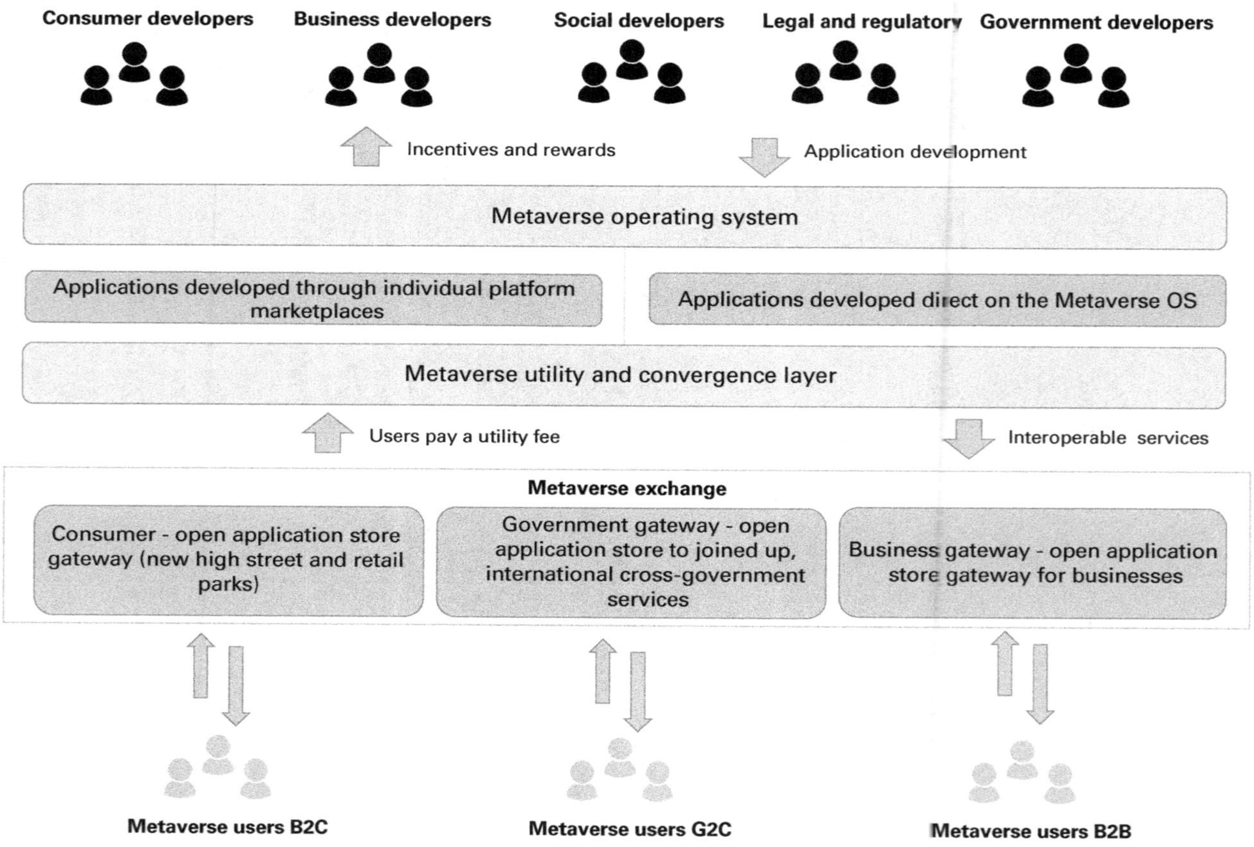

Consumer developers **Business developers** **Social developers** **Legal and regulatory** **Government developers**

← Incentives and rewards

Application development →

← Users pay a utility fee

Interoperable services →

Metaverse operating system

Applications developed through individual platform marketplaces

Applications developed direct on the Metaverse OS

Metaverse utility and convergence layer

Metaverse exchange

Consumer - open application store gateway (new high street and retail parks)

Government gateway - open application store to joined up, international cross-government services

Business gateway - open application store gateway for businesses

Metaverse users B2C

Metaverse users G2C

Metaverse users B2B

FIGURE A3 The metaverse landscape

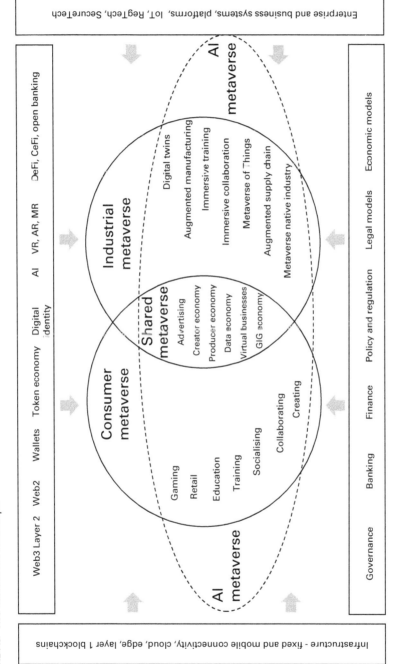

INDEX

NB: page numbers in *italic* indicate figures or tables

Looking for another book?

Explore our award-winning
books from globul business
experts in Business Strategy

Scan the code to browse

www.koganpage.com/business-
strategy

More books from Kogan Page

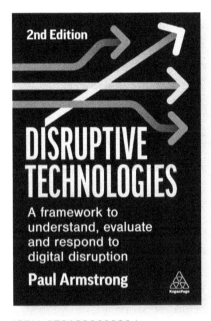

ISBN: 9781398609204

ISBN: 9781398609044

ISBN: 9781398615700

ISBN: 9781398610538

www.koganpage.com

Printed in the USA
CPSIA information can be obtained
at www.ICGtesting.com
JSHW061905230524
63642JS00004B/17

9 781398 613089